Primed for
Violence

Primed for
Violence

Murder, Antisemitism,
and Democratic Politics
in Interwar Poland

Paul Brykczynski

THE UNIVERSITY OF WISCONSIN PRESS

Publication of this volume has been made possible, in part, through support
from the Andrew W. Mellon Foundation.

The University of Wisconsin Press
1930 Monroe Street, 3rd Floor
Madison, Wisconsin 53711-2059
uwpress.wisc.edu

3 Henrietta Street, Covent Garden
London WC2E 8LU, United Kingdom
eurospanbookstore.com

Printed in the United States of America
This book may be available in a digital edition

Library of Congress Cataloging-in-Publication Data
Names: Brykczynski, Paul, author.
Title: Primed for violence : murder, antisemitism, and democratic politics in
interwar Poland / Paul Brykczynski.
Description: Madison, Wisconsin : The University of Wisconsin Press, [2016] |
©2016 | Includes bibliographical references and index.
Identifiers: LCCN 2015036809 | ISBN 9780299307004 (cloth : alk. paper)
Subjects: LCSH: Narutowicz, Gabriel, 1865–1922—Assassination. | Antisemitism—
Poland—History—20th century. | Jews—Poland—Politics and government—
20th century. | Nationalism—Poland—History—20th century. | Political
persecution—Poland—History—20th century. | Poland—Politics and
government—1918–1945. | Poland—Ethnic relations.
Classification: LCC DS146.P6 B79 2016 | DDC 305.892/4043809042—dc23
LC record available at http://lccn.loc.gov/2015036809

ISBN 9780299307042 (pbk. : alk. paper)

In memory of my grandfather
ANDRZEJ PIECZYŃSKI,

who never talked about patriotism but whose life bore witness
to its most beautiful traditions, and who taught me both to love
the history of Poland and to think about it critically.

While assassination has generally failed to *direct* political change into predetermined channels, it has repeatedly demonstrated the capacity for affecting, often in the most drastic fashion, situations which, in the absence of lethal violence, might conceivably have developed very differently. Some of these interventions have seemed so fortuitous, so unrelated to rational grievances or purposes, as to deserve nothing better than inclusion among pure accidents of history, comparable to natural disasters, human illness and death by misadventure, chronological coincidence, and the like. On other occasions personalized violence has struck in the midst of an atmosphere so charged with hatred and foreboding that some such flash of deadly energy seemed then, and still seems in retrospect, all but inevitable.

—Franklin L. Ford, *Political Murder: From Tyrannicide to Terrorism*

The President of Poland was murdered as a Jewish President. [Nationalist] demagogues reduced the question of the first President of the Republic of Poland to the Jewish denominator. The same hand that went unpunished after it was raised against the life or health of a Jewish Polish citizen . . . was raised against the President of the Republic.

—Jewish Circle Deputy Ignacy Schiper in a speech to the Polish Sejm

Contents

Illustrations

Preface

In any project of this magnitude, there are innumerable people to thank. While the list will never be comprehensive, I will nevertheless do my best to acknowledge at least some of those who helped to make this book possible.

Most important, there will never be a way to adequately thank my wife and best friend, Andrea, for standing by me 150 percent through this long and often difficult journey. Both life and academia have their share of ups and downs. Without Andrea, I would not have made it through the latter. Her faith in my work and in the path I had chosen never wavered, even when mine occasionally did.

An enormous thank you must also go to my parents, Mikołaj and Ewa Brykczyński, who raised me in an environment in which books were read, ideas were discussed, and intellectual curiosity was valued and encouraged. Their support was especially critical in the final stages of this project, when I struggled to cope with the competing demands of being a dad (always the most important), working in the private sector, and finishing this book. Without their help, I would not have completed this project.

The research for this book was guided by Robert Blobaum, Ronald Grigor Suny, Geneviève Zubrzycki, and, especially, Brian Porter-Szűcs, who helped shape not only this project but also my approach to the study of history. As the project progressed, the content benefitted from the constructive criticism offered by many friends and colleagues who took time out of their busy schedules to read the manuscript. I must especially thank the following: Jordana de Bloeme, Matti Friedman, Zeev Friedman, Kamil Kijek, Adam Korzuchowski, Petet Kracht, Grzegorz Krzywiec, John Merriman, Michael Newmark, Eva Plach, Meghann Pytka, Scott Ury, Marek Wierzbicki, and Piotr Wróbel. Wilhelm Dichter not only read the manuscript in its entirety and offered invaluable feedback but also invited me to stay at his home in Tewksbury, Massachusetts, where, along with his wife, Olga, he created an environment in which I was able to escape the distractions of daily life and complete this book. I would also like to thank Clifford Orwin; although he was not directly involved in this project, I cannot overemphasize the life-long intellectual debt I owe him for teaching me how to read critically.

A very special mention must be made of my late uncle Marek Pieczyński, the very first person to hear about and voice support for my idea to write about the murder of Gabriel Narutowicz. A true embodiment of the Central European intellectual, Marek generously shared both his personal experience from the interwar years and his extraordinary knowledge of history, of literature, and of the human soul. He was the first one to introduce me to many books, such as those of Stanisław Brzozowski and Bernard Singer, which would play a critical role in this project. This work would not have been what it is without him, and I can only hope that he would have recognized some of his intellectual and spiritual influence in its pages.

The research for this work would not have been possible without the support of numerous members of my family and friends in Poland. In particular, I have to thank Jerzy Brykczyński, Małgorzata Brykczyńska, Adam Pieczyński, Justyna Pochanke, and the Krawczyk clan, as well as my grandmother Zofia Pieczyńska, who generously and unconditionally opened their homes to me during extended research trips to Warsaw. Katarzyna Raczkowska, of the Warsaw National Library, singlehandedly introduced me to the Polish library and archive systems. My sister, Małgorzata Popiołek, a PhD student in art history at the Technische Universität Berlin, was extraordinarily helpful with many aspects of the research for this book.

I must also thank my editor at the University of Wisconsin Press, Gwen Walker, who believed in this project from day one and consistently offered her support, understanding, and patience. Finally, this work would not have been possible without the support of the University of Michigan and the Social Sciences and Humanities Research Council of Canada, which generously provided the funding for my research and graduate studies.

Pronunciation Guide

Polish is a notoriously difficult language and pronunciation often poses a barrier for English speakers attempting to learn more about Polish history. The chart below is provided to help readers get a better handle on the correct pronunciation of Polish terms, names, and places that appear in the book.

a	*a* is in "father"		o	*o* as in "go"
ą	nasalized *a*		ó	*oo* as in "boot"
c	*ts*		rz	*zh*
ć	*ch*		ś	*sh*
cz	*ch*		sz	*sh*
ę	nasalized *e*		u	*oo* as in "boot"
i	*i* as in "ski" or *ee* as in "beet"		w	*v*
j	*y* as in "yet"		y	*i* as in "it"
ł	*w*		ż	*zh*
ń	*n* as in "onion"		ź	*zh*

Abbreviations

ChJN	Chrześcijański Związek Jedności Narodowej (Christian Coalition of National Unity)
Endek/ND	Nardowa Demokracja (National Democrat)
NPR	Narodowa Partia Robotnicza (National Labor Party)
POW	Polska Organizacja Wojskowa (Polish Military Organization)
PPS	Polska Partia Socjalistyczna (Polish Socialist Party)
PSL	Polskie Stronnictwo Ludowe "Piast" (Polish Peasants' Party "Piast")
UNP	Unia Narodowo-Państwowa (National Civic Union)
ZPK	Związek Państwowy na Kresach (Civic Union of the Borderlands)

Primed for
Violence

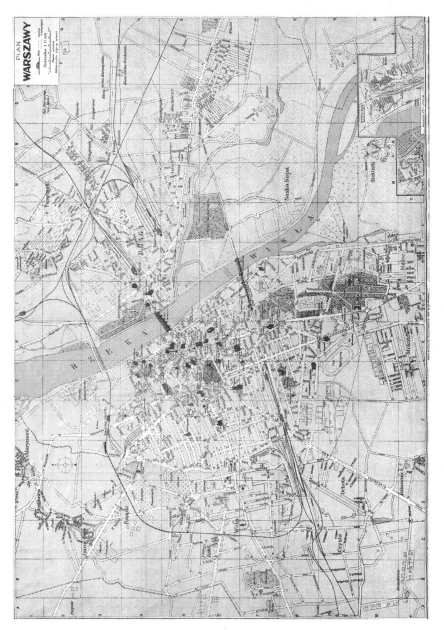

Warsaw in the interwar period. (Mazowiecka Biblioteka Cyfrowa)

Introduction

On December 9, 1922, the Republic of Poland elected its very first president. After five rounds of voting, the choice of the National Assembly fell upon Gabriel Narutowicz. To an outside observer, the president-elect, a Swiss-educated civil engineer, would not have appeared as an overly controversial choice. He was reputed to be a moderate liberal and a friend of the popular and charismatic Marshal Józef Piłsudski, the man credited by many Poles with securing their country's independence four years prior. However, among the broad coalition that gave the president its support in the National Assembly was the National Minorities' Bloc, a loose alliance of Jewish, Ukrainian, Belarusian, and German parties. The support given to the president by "the Jews" triggered an angry and violent response from the nationalist right, known in Poland as the National Democrats (Endeks or NDs). Within hours of the election, Warsaw exploded into violent antisemitic riots, which convulsed the capital for days, shook the very foundations of Polish democracy, and forced the government to impose martial law. On December 16, just seven days after the election, the first president of the Republic of Poland was murdered by Eligiusz Niewiadomski, a well-known painter who believed that by murdering the president he was saving Poland from being subjected to Jewish domination.

There is no doubt that the riots and the murder of the president represented a serious crisis in the constitutional order of the Republic of Poland. Yet, somewhat surprisingly, Polish democracy appeared to emerge from the crisis unscathed.[1] Street protests subsided, as politicians and journalists of all political stripes called for calm.

Eight days after the murder, a new president, Stanisław Wojciechowski, was elected by the National Assembly with the very same combination of votes as Narutowicz's. Even though it was again the votes of the Bloc of National Minorities

3

that helped tip the balance, this time in Wojciechowski's favor, there were no further protests from the right. It may have appeared that a new mood of reflection,
and perhaps even repentance, had seized the nation. Within two weeks the murderer was tried, sentenced to death, and duly executed. Polish democracy continued to teeter on for another four years without experiencing a comparable crisis.

Therefore, at first glance, the historical significance of the election and murder
of Narutowicz appears to have been limited. Historians have treated them as
minor episodes. The most popular English-language history of Poland, Norman
Davies's *God's Playground*, barely mentions Narutowicz or the assassination.
"The assassination in December 1922 of the first constitutional President, Gabriel
Narutowicz (1865–1922)," Davies writes in his sole reference to the president,
"was followed by a series of notorious political murders, including that of the
Soviet ambassador, Voykov, in 1927."[2] Specialist works on interwar Polish history
usually depict the murder as an important episode in the ongoing conflict
between the National Democrats and the followers of Marshal Piłsudski, but do
not ascribe it causative power or deeper significance.[3] The historiography by and
large follows contemporary accounts, which portrayed the murderer as a "fanatic,"
and assumes that the assassination's primary effect was to temporarily embarrass
the National Democratic movement.[4] To date, no scholarly study of these events
has been undertaken.[5]

This book takes a different view of the Narutowicz assassination, as it tells the
story of the elections, riots, and murder, collectively known as the "December
Events," their causes, and their short- and long-term significance. My approach is
informed by political scientists', sociologists', and historians' (renewed) interest
in the importance of crises and contingent events for understanding political and
discursive change. Political scientists have paid close attention to "the dynamic
processes of crisis, breakdown, and reequilibration of existing regimes" since
Juan J. Linz and Alfred C. Stepan's landmark study of regime transitions.[6] Perhaps
less intuitively, the case for the importance of contingent events in explaining
change in established cultural and discursive patterns has been made by William H. Sewell.[7] Recently, Scott Ury has demonstrated an important, and deeply
troubling, relationship between the dynamics of electoral politics in Russian-
ruled Poland, on the one hand, and radicalization and dissemination of political
antisemitism among the masses, on the other. My approach complements Ury's,
but places more weight on the role of contingent variables in structuring the
discourse of the nation during electoral contests.[8] Political assassinations, too,
are contingent events that provide political communities with opportunities for
reflection and the reevaluation of political and cultural values.[9]

The December Events can help us better understand not only the anatomy of constitutional crises but also, more controversially, the discursive transformation of Polish nationalism and the acute intensification of antisemitism in the interwar period. Specifically, the series of contingent events that brought the little-known Gabriel Narutowicz to the presidency with the aid of the national minority parties triggered the most explicit and sustained press debate regarding the imagined community of the Polish nation, and the place of the Jews in that community, ever to take place in the interwar period. This discussion led the right to explicitly formulate what immediately became known as the "Doctrine of the Polish Majority," which stated that only "ethnic Poles" had the right to rule Poland. In return, the left put forth a forceful counternarrative of nationhood that emphasized citizenship and culture at the expense of ethnicity.

Intuitively, we might expect that the violence perpetrated by the champions of antisemitic nationalism, which culminated in the president's murder, would provide the right with a moment of reflection and discredit antisemitism in the eyes of many Poles. In fact the very opposite happened. The left, bullied by violence, retreated from its earlier defense of the national minorities. While examples of candid, robust, and sophisticated attempts to defend the civic idea of the Polish nation can be found in left-wing rhetoric immediately prior to the presidential elections, after the election and murder of Narutowicz the left for all practical purposes ceased to publicly challenge the nationalist claim that only ethnic Poles had the right to rule Poland.

In most ways, this is not a happy story. But it is an important one, which allows us to get a better view of some of the most critical issues—many of which still resonate today—faced by Poles and Europeans in the tumultuous period between the First and the Second World Wars. This story is about nationalism and the struggle, as some contemporaries put it, for the "soul of the Polish nation." It is a story about the role of antisemitism in Polish history and politics, and the challenges faced by those who sought to resist it. It is also a story about the rise of the radical right and the breakdown of democracy, in which Poland was just one of the many theaters of a transnational European-wide conflict, and about the power of hateful rhetoric and violent action to transform political culture.

Nationalism and Antisemitism

The root causes of the murder of Narutowicz must be seen in the context of the struggle between the partisans of civic and ethnic nationalisms in Poland.[10] The traditional nineteenth-century Polish national movement, which evolved during the 123-year-long period when Poland was partitioned between Russia, Prussia, and Austria, was civic—it was deeply linked with romanticism and framed by the historical memory of the Polish-Lithuanian Commonwealth rather than by notions of race, ethnicity, or blood.[11] This doctrine was challenged fairly late (roughly between the 1870s and the 1910s) by the National Democrats, led in both the political and ideological realms by Roman Dmowski, who is generally credited with formulating and popularizing the doctrine of ethnic Polish nationalism.[12] Influenced by Social Darwinism, the National Democrats saw the social world as an endless struggle of national organisms in which only the fittest survived. If the Poles wanted to survive, the National Democrats believed that Poland had to give up the quaint romantic nationalism of the nineteenth century and embrace discipline, social cohesion, and what they called "national egoism," which stressed the welfare of their own nation over universal humanitarian principles. By 1905 it was the Jews, rather than the more obvious occupiers and political oppressors such as the Russians or Germans, who were defined as the Poles' chief competitors in the struggle for survival and who became the main focus of National Democrats' hatred.[13]

The Jewish community in interwar Poland, numbering some 3 million people or about 10 percent of the population, was the world's second-largest Jewish community in absolute terms and the largest per capita. By comparison, interwar Germany was inhabited by some 500,000 Jews, who made up less than 1 percent of that country's population. Poland's Jewish community was largely Yiddish speaking and unacculturated, and played a disproportionate role in commerce, finance, and the related professions.[14] It was also disproportionally urban. In many regions, the Jews de facto constituted the entire middle class. It can certainly be argued that this state of affairs could lead to interethnic tensions and competition between Poles and Jews.[15] Yet such explanations should not be taken too far—antisemitism usually tells us more about the imagination of the antisemites than it does about any "objective" relations between Jews and non-Jews. Thus, in Poland, antisemitism was traditionally strongest in the west of the country, where there were very few Jews and where the occupational imbalances between Jews and non-Jews were much less pronounced. As we shall see, the antisemitism championed by the National Democrats transcended any rational economic demands or issues and very quickly devolved into a chimeric hatred aimed at freeing Poland from supposed "rule by the Jews."[16]

Nor did the National Democrats' high visibility mean that they alone represented the Polish national movement or that they spoke for all Poles. A very different strain of patriotism and thinking about the nation was embodied by the larger-than-life figure of Marshal Józef Piłsudski. Piłsudski had been raised in and subscribed to a tradition of romantic patriotism, which emphasized continuity with the traditions of the Polish-Lithuanian Commonwealth. He was a self-described "Lithuanian," who had gone out of his way to reach out to Lithuanians, Belarusians, and Jews of the multiethnic Borderlands (*Kresny*) region from which he hailed, in order to win their approval for his plans to recreate the Commonwealth as a modern, democratic federation.[17] Although Piłsudski began his political career as a socialist and was a long-time leader of the Polish Socialist Party (Polska Partia Socjalistyczna , or PPS), he eventually moved away from socialism and dedicated himself to the creation of a nonpartisan military structure designed to challenge the partitioning powers (and especially Russia). While the National Democrats worked for cooperation with tsarist Russia, the PPS and the followers of Piłsudski (Piłsudczycy or Piłsudskiites) consistently made up the vanguard of the Polish struggle for independence.[18] The nationalism of Piłsudski and his followers has often been romanticized, and to be sure, they were not quite the champions of multiculturalism they are sometimes made out to be.[19] Nonetheless, on the eve of Polish independence, the "Patriotic Left"—a broad coalition of socialists, peasant radicals, and liberals grouped around the charismatic Marshal—championed a more inclusive, liberal, and civic idea of Poland.[20]

The reason why the conflict between the Piłsudskiites and the National Democrats continues to captivate historians and journalists today is that it transcends tactical differences, economic programs, and even the question of the proper relationship between the nation and the state.[21] As Poles entered the world of modern politics in the late nineteenth and early twentieth centuries, they necessarily became drawn into new modes of talking, thinking, and feeling about "Poland" and, thereby, in "being Poles." At its core, to paraphrase Benedict R. Anderson, the conflict between the followers of Dmowski and Piłsudski revolved around different ways of *imagining the imagined community*.[22] It could even be said that at the most fundamental level, the disagreement between the NDs and the followers of Piłsudski boiled down to identifying with different imagined communities. The fact that both the imagined communities in question had the same name and many common features should not blind us to the fact that the Poland that the National Democrats fought for was very different from the one that prompted the Piłsudskiites to put their lives on the line.[23]

The conflict between the NDs and the followers of Piłsudski was long-standing and bitter, and involved not only fundamentally different readings of Polish history and identity but also profound disagreements over strategy and tactics. When the 1905 Revolution broke out in Russia, Piłsudski and the PPS saw the chance to overthrow the tsarist regime and wholeheartedly joined the fray. The

Marshal Józef Piłsudski, a former socialist, revolutionary, and freedom fighter, was the first ruler of modern Poland. He was a self-described "Lithuanian" and embodied the civic idea of Polishness, which welcomed all who chose to join the Polish nation regardless of their ethnicity or religion. (Narodowe Archiwum Cyfrowe)

Roman Dmowski, the founder of the National Democratic movement and originator of the doctrine of national egoism, led the Polish delegation at Versailles but was never able to assume power in the country. He believed that the Poles were locked in an endless struggle for survival against other ethnic groups, especially Jews and Germans. (Narodowe Archiwum Cyfrowe)

NDs, on the other hand, saw chaos, anarchy, and a needless waste of Polish blood. When Piłsudski traveled to Tokyo to seek Japanese arms and ammunition for Polish revolutionaries, Dmowski followed him in order to foil his attempt and tried to persuade the Japanese that the Polish Revolution was doomed. On the ground in Poland, NDs sought to restore order and sometimes cooperated with the tsarist police in breaking socialist strikes. Hundreds of Poles from both camps were killed in fratricidal battles between the two groups. While both the NDs and the PPS emerged from the 1905 Revolution with new mass followings, equally important was the legacy of bad blood, which the revolution and its aftermath left between them.[24]

When the revolution failed, the PPS went underground and Piłsudski eventually withdrew from the party (though he continued to maintain a close relationship with it) in order to build nonpartisan Polish military units in Austrian Galicia. The NDs, on the other hand, continued their policy of loyalism to tsarist Russia, which eventually won Dmowski a seat in the Russian Duma. However, because the Duma elections were based on a skewed Russian electoral franchise, they pitted Polish and Jewish electors in a zero-sum game for Warsaw's single mandate and acted to further reinforce the NDs' obsession with the Jewish question. Then after Dmowski's failure to win a seat in 1912, the National Democrats organized a massive economic boycott of Jewish-owned shops in Warsaw, which did much to poison relations between Poles and Jews in Poland's largest city.[25]

On the eve of World War I, the NDs and followers of Piłsudski found themselves on opposite sides of the front lines. Dmowski believed that military effort on the Poles' part was futile and expanded his energy on lobbying the Triple Entente (including Russia) for the Polish cause. Piłsudski, in turn, believed that Poles could win independence only through their own efforts and to this end led his Legions into war against Russia at the side of the Central Powers. These debates about so-called orientation (*orientacja*) were extremely bitter since they involved, literally, matters of life-and-death. Understandably, soldiers fighting in Piłsudski's Legions against the Russians viewed the National Democratic leadership's Russophilism as treason to the national cause. On the other hand, the NDs, who strove to gain Allied recognition for Polish aspirations, viewed Piłsudski's involvement on the Austrian side as a politically counterproductive and deeply tragic waste of young lives.[26]

To make matters even more complicated, both sides could arguably be credited with having done more to secure Polish independence. While Piłsudski arranged the transfer of power from the German command in November 1918 and de facto created the government and army from scratch, the National Democrats could argue that their efforts in Paris were instrumental in winning Allied recognition for the new state. When Dmowski returned to Poland following his triumph at Versailles, many felt that Piłsudski did not give him the respect and recognition he deserved.

In 1919 and 1920 Piłsudski tried to recreate the Polish-Lithuanian Commonwealth as a federation of Polish, Ukrainian, Lithuanian, and Belarusian states, and embarked on an alliance with Ataman Semyon Petlura's Ukrainian People's Republic. At the same time, the National Democrats believed in the creation of a "Poland for the Poles" and argued against what they saw as irresponsible adventures in Ukraine. The Polish-Soviet War pushed the two sides even further apart. Although the NDs briefly lauded Piłsudski's leadership when his troops reached the gates of Kiev, the Polish army's subsequent retreat put the Marshal's military abilities in doubt and led to scathing attacks on his competence as commander in chief. Even when Piłsudski turned the tide at the Battle of Warsaw, the NDs coined the popular myth of divine intervention and the "Miracle on the Vistula" in order to minimize his role in the victory. At the Peace of Riga, the National Democratic negotiator Stanisław Grabski purposefully gave up the Belarusian capital, Minsk, to the Soviets in order to render the implementation of Piłsudski's cherished federal arrangements impossible.[27] Piłsudski perceived Grabski's action as a betrayal of the cause for which many of his soldiers had died.

As the perceptive Henry Morgenthau Sr., head of the 1919 American mission to Poland, observed, antisemitism, or the so-called Jewish Question, played a critical role in this "family feud" between the Piłsudskiites and the National Democrats taking place within (non-Jewish) Polish society.[28] Yet, this observation is not always appreciated in the literature. Antisemitism, which can be distinguished from earlier forms of anti-Jewish sentiment by being directed not against the Jews as followers of the religion of Judaism but as a people (or ethnic group) imbued with certain traits and characteristics, is sometimes thought to have formed an integral part of Polish political culture in the interwar period.[29] Indeed, a considerable body of research from the last two decades of the twentieth century presents Polish nationalism/patriotism in all its facets as hateful, xenophobic, and deeply, perhaps inextricably, intertwined with antisemitism.[30] Thankfully, over the last quarter century, explicitly essentialist portrayals of Poland as the land of primordial, unbridled, or "nearly total" antisemitism have become rare, even if their echoes still persist.

More recent works have portrayed the development of antisemitic attitudes in Polish society as a contested and dynamic process. Many of these studies have focused on the role of specific political crises and junctures—such as the 1905

Revolution, the Russian Duma elections, the anti-Jewish economic boycott of 1912, and World War I—in the spread and radicalization of antisemitic discourses and sentiments.[31] Somewhat curiously, this approach has not been brought to bear on the study of interwar Poland. There is no doubt that in 1918, when Poland was suddenly "reborn" and appeared again on the maps of Europe, antisemitic nationalism was a powerful force in both culture and politics; more powerful, in fact, than some Polish historians like to admit.[32] But it was nowhere near hegemonic. It faced formidable rivals, championed by capable and charismatic political leaders like Piłsudski and the powerful "camp" of socialists, radicals, liberals, and moderate conservatives that coalesced around him. The role played by the "Jewish Question" in the December Events can help us not only construct an "eventful history" of antisemitism in interwar Poland but also contribute to the understanding of antisemitism more generally as a dynamic political phenomenon rather than a static ideology or primordial sentiment.

The December Events must be seen in the context of the bitter and protracted struggle over the meaning and future of Poland, in which the question of antisemitism played a critical role. The murdered President Narutowicz was a devoted partisan of Piłsudski and shared his civic vision of the national community. His murderer (Eligiusz Niewiadomski), on the other hand, claimed that the shots he fired on December 16 were actually intended for Piłsudski and for the inclusive vision of the Polish nation ("Judeo-Poland," as he derisively called it at his trial) the latter represented. Niewiadomski's words, as we shall see, were lauded by nationalist politicians and journalists. Thus, the story of the murder of Narutowicz plays a key role not only in the political struggle between the Piłsudskiites and the National Democrats but, more importantly, in the ideological conflict over the meaning of the imagined community of the nation and the place of the national minorities in that community.

The Radical Right, Political Assassination, and the Breakdown of Democracy

Moving beyond the disciplinary boundaries of Polish history, the December Events can be seen as one battle in what Mark Mazower has called the "European Civil War" between the left and the right, which unfolded during the interwar period.[33] When the Polish Republic adopted its democratic constitution in March 1921, Europe's faith in democracy appeared to be at an all-time high. As James Bryce wrote in his 1921 classic *Modern Democracies*, it appeared that Europe was ready to accept "democracy as the normal and natural form of human government."[34] But in less than a year, the liberal, left-wing, and progressive currents sweeping Europe in the wake of World War I appeared to be in retreat before a resurgent radical right, often modeled on Italy's Fascist movement, which captured power in Rome in October 1922.

Democracy's triumph proved to be ephemeral. Fascist regimes were eventually able to seize power in Italy and Germany and, depending on one's definition of fascism, in Portugal and Spain. In most countries of eastern Europe, the chief beneficiaries of the struggle between the radical right and the left were conservative authoritarians who, in the name of restoring public order, suppressed democracy and attempted to fend off the radicalism of both the left and the right. By the end of the 1920s, democracy had been extinguished in Hungary (1918), Italy (1922), Bulgaria (1923), Spain (1923), Greece (1926), Lithuania (1926), Portugal (1926), and Yugoslavia (1929).[35] In 1926, which could be aptly called the European "year of the coup," Marshal Piłsudski seized power in Poland to prevent the National Democrats and their allies from forming a government.[36] In the 1930s, Germany, Austria, Romania, Estonia, and Latvia also abandoned parliamentary politics, thus leaving Czechoslovakia as central, eastern, and southern Europe's lone surviving democratic regime.[37]

The timing of the December Events—a mere two months following the Fascist seizure of power in Rome—and the open admiration for Mussolini of many of its participants would seem to suggest a certain affinity between the events in Italy and Poland. This affinity, in turn, raises the question of the relationship between the National Democratic movement in the early 1920s and fascism. Scholarship dealing with authoritarianism and dictatorship in Poland has, not surprisingly, focused on Piłsudski's May 1926 coup and his so-called Sanacja regime. At the same time, scholars have been hesitant to apply the "fascist" label to any Polish parties, save for fringe National Democratic splinter groups of the late 1930s.[38] The adoption of some of Mussolini's political repertoire by the Polish right is thought to occur in the post-1926 period, as a response to Piłsudski's coup d'état.[39] In the 1920s, National Democrats are seen as essentially committed to parliamentarianism and democracy—a depiction that explains why Eligiusz Niewiadomski, the murderer of President Narutowicz, is often portrayed as a "fanatic" whose resort to lethal violence was far beyond the pale of normally accepted nationalist politics.

While it is universally acknowledged that the Italian Fascists did not embrace antisemitism until the late 1930s, hatred of the Jews could be found at the very core of the National Democrats' political program and cultural vision. The question of the relationship between antisemitism and ultranationalist, protofascist, or fascist movements in Europe is an important one. The two paradigmatic fascist movements, Italian Fascism and German Nazism, had, at least initially, drastically different approaches to the Jews. Yet, the Italian Fascists eventually embraced antisemitism, and in the late 1920s antisemitic ideology found itself at the very heart of east European fascist movements like the Romanian Iron Guard or Hungary's Arrow Cross.

In Poland, in contrast to Italy, the radical right's virulent political antisemitism preceded the commitment to authoritarian, let alone totalitarian, politics. A focus on the rhetoric and action of rank-and-file National Democrats during the December Events, as opposed to the realms of high politics and official ideology scholars have traditionally analyzed, can fundamentally change our assessments of the relationship between the National Democratic movement in the early Second Republic and both fascism and antisemitism, while contributing to the understanding of fascism as a transnational phenomenon.[40] The literature on European fascism is voluminous and abundant in definitions and typologies, which cannot be discussed here at length.[41] Nor is the goal of this book to construct (or pick) a definition of *fascism* and then work out whether the NDs were or were not fascist.[42] However, central to my understanding of fascism is Roger Griffin's notion that at the heart of the latter's "mythic core" lies a "palingenetic populist ultranationalism," or the idea that the national community is locked in a battle for survival with the forces of decadence and degeneration (the precise nature of which varies according to the fascist movement in question), and that victory in this battle will usher in a new age of national regeneration and glory.[43] This palingenetic myth can be found at the core of the National Democratic nationalism's mobilizing vision. The critical difference with Italy was that in the Polish case, as in that of Romania and Hungary, the "crisis" of the nation and the forthcoming "new order" were wrapped up almost entirely around one issue: the "Jewish Question."

Political assassination played an important role in the struggle between the left and the right, and the breakdown of democracy, throughout Europe. The years following World War I witnessed a sharp increase in the frequency of political murder, as well as in disturbing new trends in the public response to these events. Franklin L. Ford has referred to the "Terrible Twenties" as the "seedtime of modern terrorism."[44] Political murder was used as a weapon by both the radical left (especially the anarchists) and the right; its chief victims were democratically elected liberal politicians. In many cases, the gunmen acted alone, like Niewiadomski, or as a part of small "extremist" groups. Anarchists are blamed for the murders of Spanish premier Eduardo Dato (1921) and Czech finance minister Alois Rašín (1923), among others, while a Bosnian communist killed Yugoslav minister of internal affairs Milorad Drašković (1921). A lone, right-wing assassin gunned down Finnish interior minister Heikki Ritavuori (1922).

At the same time, murder was being increasingly used as a political weapon by larger- and better-organized nationalist terrorist groups. In 1924, Italian deputy and journalist Giacomo Matteotti was murdered by fascist Black Shirts, though assassination was not part of the Fascist state's typical repertoire of political action. More typical were the IRA (Irish Republican Army) and the Macedonian-Bulgarian IMRO (Internal Macedonian Revolutionary Organization), veritable "underground armies," which unleashed campaigns of hatred and terror within their respective countries and beyond their borders. Their most high-profile victims included Irish Prime Minister Michael Collins (1922) and Bulgarian Premier Alexander Stamboliyski (1923). The infamous White Terror, which followed Béla Kun's abortive Communist revolution in Hungary, led to thousands of murders, and even after it subsided, prominent Jewish Hungarians continued to be targets for assassination by right-wing nationalist groups like the Awakening Magyars.[45] But perhaps the most infamous series of politically motivated murders took place in Weimar Germany, where twelve prominent political leaders, and many less notable ones, were the targets of assassination between 1919 and 1924. Most of these attempts were carried out by right-wing, ultranationalist, and antisemitic former soldiers and Freikorps paramilitary members. Some of the most notorious ones were planned and coordinated by the secret, right-wing Organisation Consul, which was responsible for the infamous murder of German-Jewish politician, diplomat, and industrialist Walther Rathenau in June 1922.

At first glance, despite the clear uptick in political assassinations in the 1920s identified by Franklin L. Ford, it is difficult to discern a common theme in events as seemingly diverse as IRA's well-planned and coordinated campaign of terror and the seemingly random murder of Finland's Ritavuori by a lone, mentally unbalanced aristocrat. Yet, almost all these murders, whether carried out by lone "fanatics," small secret societies like the Organisation Consul, or well-organized underground "armies" like the IMRO or the IRA, are bound together by having occurred in what I would call a "culture of hatred." Even the latter two organizations, though ostensibly dedicated to irredentist causes, actually used violence primarily against their own compatriots (and in the case of the IRA coreligionists), who were deemed to have betrayed the nation. In the German case, the campaign of terror was aimed exclusively against internal enemies and (perceived) traitors.

Whether acting alone, in small groups, or as a part of larger organizations of terror, interwar assassins did so amidst widespread accusations of conspiracy and treachery, leveled by one part of society against another. This was perhaps least visible in the anarchist murders (though in Spain they took place during a nationalist conflict between Spaniards and Catalans), but it was very clear in Ireland, Bulgaria, and Hungary. In Weimar Germany, too, the murders polarized society to an unprecedented degree. While some, like that of Rathenau, mobilized supporters of democracy, others, like that of Matthias Erzberger, a Catholic politician and signatory of the Versailles Treaty, received "favorable attention" from mainstream German media.[46] Even the murder of Ritavuori, in relatively tranquil Finland, occurred while accusations of treachery were leveled by nationalist groups against the government for Ritavuori's conduct in the Karelian War. Understanding the murder of Narutowicz can help us conceptualize the relationship between discourses of hatred and political violence in interwar Europe and beyond.

The anatomy of the December Events can also help us understand another important feature of interwar European history, which is, perhaps, becoming increasingly relevant today: the fragility of democracy. While for most of the twentieth century, scholars have looked for structural explanations of the failure of democratic regimes, political scientists now acknowledge the importance of studying junctures, crises, and critical times, when the legitimacy and stability of democratic regimes is profoundly shaken. At times of crisis, agency and short-term strategies utilized by individual political actors can make a difference between the destruction and the survival of democratic regimes.[47]

The December Events contained two critical junctures at which the survival of democracy was in jeopardy. On December 11, at the height of the riots, the possibility of a right-wing seizure of power hung in the air. On December 16, following the murder of the president, it appeared that the left might stage a coup in order to take revenge on the National Democrats. Yet, in both crises, the decisions and actions (or inactions) of specific political leaders ultimately played a critical role in ensuring the survival of parliamentary democracy. An analysis of the specific decisions taken by the Polish elites in December 1922 can help us understand not only the ultimate failure of democracy in May 1926 but, perhaps equally important, the factors that can allow democracies to face the challenge of political extremists.

Sources and Structure

This book is based primarily on newspaper articles and accounts, memoirs (both published and unpublished), electoral pamphlets, parliamentary minutes and documents, and secret police reports. The press, in particular, constitutes a critical tool in understanding the discursive battles that shaped interwar Polish culture.

In the 1920s and 1930s, newspapers were at the very height of their influence in shaping the conceptual universe and life-world of Polish society because, on the one hand, increased literacy meant that they were accessible to a very wide audience and, on the other, they did not yet have competition from television or even the radio.[48] As Brian Porter-Szűcs has shown, these texts can reveal more than just the thoughts of the intelligentsia since they can "be read with an eye towards [the latter's] struggle with the heterogeneity of the social world, a reality with its own well formulated worldviews."[49] I have also used reports of speeches gathered by the secret police, as well as political pamphlets and brochures, in order to move beyond traditional ideological accounts of Polish politics and get closer to the level of street politics.

The narrative of the riots also relies heavily on the press. While the Ministry of Internal Affairs conducted an investigation into the riots following Narutowicz's election, and presumably collected interviews with eyewitnesses, it appears that these records were destroyed during World War II.[50] Police reports of the riots are conspicuously missing from the archives, most likely because the Warsaw police found themselves overwhelmed by the events at hand. But despite these issues, and the fierce partisanship of the Polish press, a relatively unbiased reconstruction of the riots is possible by juxtaposing diverse newspapers' accounts of the same events.[51] While it is true that the newspapers were obviously written by journalists, that is, members of the intelligentsia, during the December Events their focus was on reporting the events from the streets of Warsaw. As a result, the accounts allow us to reconstruct, albeit through a filtered lens, the actions and rhetoric of many ordinary Varsovians during these critical events and thus get closer to the level of popular politics than many studies of interwar Polish history (often focused primarily on political programs and on the realm of official ideology) have been able to go.

To understand the causes of the "December Events" it is necessary to first grasp the nature and intensity of the charges levelled against the president during his short week in the political spotlight. For this reason, the book does not proceed chronologically but begins with the story of the protests, riots, and murder that rocked Warsaw between December 9 and December 16 of 1922. Only then is it possible to analyze the roots of the hatred which reared its head on the streets of the Polish capital as well the unexpected impact of the violence on the development of democracy in Poland and the future of the country. The election of Narutowicz to the presidency marked an attempt by the national minorities to play a leading and constructive role in Polish politics. Consequently, the president's vicious repudiation by the right, and his ultimate murder, signaled the rejection of the minorities, and especially Jews, from the national polity by a large and vocal part of the electorate. This violent rejection had profound and generally unacknowledged consequences. While the right quickly recovered its poise and eventually accepted the president's murderer as one of its own, the left failed to deal with the journalists and politicians who instigated the murder and backed away from condemning the use of antisemitic propaganda in politics. Quite the opposite, left-wing and centrist parties became afraid of being associated too closely with "the Jews." While the murder of Narutowicz may have been a short-term setback for the right, it had a profound impact on the development of nationalist discourse in Poland and can help explain the extraordinary intensification of antisemitism that took place in the interwar period.

1

"Down with the Jews!"

The election of the first president of the Republic of Poland, scheduled for December 9, 1922, was promising to be a heated and controversial affair—though it is unlikely that anyone could have predicted the violence it would unleash upon the city of Warsaw. The field was crowded with five candidates, most of whom were relatively unknown to the public. One of these would be chosen by the National Assembly, a combination of the lower and upper houses of Parliament, which contained thirteen separate political parties. To complicate matters further, the National Assembly would continue to vote until one of the five candidates achieved an absolute majority of the votes, which left plenty of room for impromptu backroom deals and changing allegiances among the fractious and fickle deputies.[1] Yet despite all the appearances of chaos, the most important political cleavage in the election, and its symbolic importance, were probably clear to most Poles.

On one side of the political spectrum was the nationalist right, paying homage to the antisemitic National Democratic ideology of Roman Dmowski. Although technically composed of three separate parties (the National Populist Union, the Christian National Party, and the Christian Democratic Party[2]), the National Democrats, as they were universally known, had chosen a joint presidential candidate, Count Maurycy Zamoyski. Together, the right controlled some 40 percent of the seats in the National Assembly.

On the other side of the spectrum were the parties of the left: the Polish Socialist Party (PPS), the radical peasant Emancipation party, and a number of smaller groups, which together held some 25 percent of the votes (despite having won more than 30 percent of the popular vote). They all supported Marshal Józef Piłsudski, the independence fighter and former socialist who created the Polish army and ruled the country for the past four years as an unelected "Head of State"

(*Naczelnik Państwa*). Piłsudski, a charismatic leader widely seen as the architect of Polish independence, also had the support of the National Minorities Bloc (a loose alliance of Jewish, German, Ukrainian, and Belarusian groups) and the centrist peasant party "Piast," named after the first mythical peasant-king of Poland. Between them, Bloc and Piast controlled the remainder of the votes. It was widely expected that this coalition would beat the right in the presidential contest.

But less than a week before the elections, Piłsudski, probably the only man capable of uniting the fractious centrist and leftist parties, announced that he would not accept the presidency. His categorical withdrawal from the race was a tremendous blow to the left-wing parties, which proved unable to agree on a single presidential candidate prior to the voting. While the Bloc of National Minorities, alienated by the right's antisemitism, was expected to throw its votes behind one of the left-wing candidates, no one was certain which way the peasants would vote. There is little doubt that Piast would have voted for Piłsudski, but in his absence, all bets were off. In the run-up to the election, the National Democrats did their best to entice the wily peasant leader Wincenty Witos into joining their camp. Knowing that the left would need the support of minorities to get its candidate (whoever it would turn out to be) elected, the NDs also made it clear that they would not accept anyone chosen by "the Jews" (that is in cooperation with the Minorities Bloc) as a legitimate president of Poland. The "Doctrine of the Polish Majority," as this postulate became known, was intended to scare the peasants into *not* voting for the same candidate as the minorities. Faced with a mixture of sticks and carrots, Piast was rumored to be internally divided and still on the fence on the eve of the election. In the end, the peasant deputies' votes would likely make the difference between Zamoyski and one of the left-wing candidates being elected.

On the day of the election, there was no shortage of suspense, which was only exacerbated by the fact that choosing the new president took five separate votes and ended up lasting more than eight hours. Since newspapers bearing news of the results would not be out until the next morning, on the evening of December 9 a crowd of people, mostly university and high school students, gathered in front of the Sejm (Parliament) building to await the winner. According to the historian Janusz Pajewski, who as a youth also found his way there, the vast majority of those present expected Count Zamoyski to triumph. In the end, however, the peasants found it impossible to cast their lot with "the Count," and after numerous backroom maneuvers and machinations, the choice of the Assembly fell upon Gabriel Narutowicz, who was elected with the support of the left, Piast, and the national minorities.

Narutowicz, the descendent of a noble family from Lithuania, was a mild-mannered hydroelectric engineer who had spent most of his life in Switzerland. He left Poland in his youth returned only in 1919, giving up a prestigious post at the Zurich Polytechnic in order to put his world-renowned technical expertise in the service of the new country as minister of public works. Due to the unusual tact and polish he displayed as part of the Polish delegation at the Genoa Conference, in June of 1922 he was chosen by Piłsudski to become Poland's foreign minister. Although he was by all accounts universally respected by those who had worked with him, he was virtually unknown to most Poles. Among those who knew

Gabriel Narutowicz, the first president of the Republic of Poland. (Narodowe Archiwum Cyfrowe)

him, however, he had a reputation as a technocrat and moderate liberal with few enemies and no direct association with any of the mass-based parties of the left.[3] His associates remarked on his dignified bearing combined with considerable personal warmth, and often described him as a "true European gentleman."[4]

"We don't want this president!"

Narutowicz's moderate reputation made little difference to the youths gathered outside the Sejm. When news of his victory was announced, Pajewski heard cries of "Down with Narutowicz!" "Down with the one chosen by Jews!" and "Down with Witos!"[5] Yet, Pajewski, like the vast majority of Poles, including the police, the army, and most supporters of the new president, had no idea of the magnitude of the anger that would rock Warsaw in the following days. While some of the youths went home after learning the result, others lingered about. The next day, the *Gazeta Warszawska (Warsaw Gazette)*, a leading National Democratic newspaper, offered the following enthusiastic description of the events immediately following the election: "On the news that Narutowicz . . . will become president thanks to the votes of the Jews, Germans, and other 'national minorities,' from the breasts of the youth a single spontaneous cry went forth 'We don't want this president! We don't know him! Down with the Jews!' This cry ran through the streets of Warsaw and spontaneously a great march was formed."[6]

According to *Gazeta Warszawska*, the youths from Sejm formed the core of the march, but in the streets they were joined by large numbers of other Varsovians. The procession made its way down Nowy Świat Street and Ujazdowskie Avenue to the apartment of Józef Haller. Haller, a former general, had been the organizer and commander of the so-called Blue Army of Polish exiles, émigrés, and POWs who found their way to France. He was known for his nationalist views and National Democratic sympathies, and the "Blue Army," in keeping with Haller's own ideological commitments, had a reputation for antisemitic "excesses."[7] Since Haller was just about the only high-profile general with rightist sympathies, he had been courted by the National Democrats and had recently resigned his post in the army in order to enter politics.[8] He was duly elected as a deputy from Warsaw, and seemed to hold out the promise of providing the Polish right with something it had never had but desperately wanted—a charismatic military leader.

Haller did his best not to disappoint. From his balcony, he delivered a fiery speech to the crowds. "Today the Poland you have fought for has been trampled upon," he thundered, "and your instincts are a sign that the anger of the nation, of which you are the spokesmen, is rising like a wave."[9] *Gazeta Warszawska* and the lower-brow National Democratic daily *Gazeta Poranna* (*Morning Gazette*) did their best to cast Haller as the "leader" (*wódz*) of this wave of anger. "In a moving scene," *Gazeta Warszawska* reported, "people threw themselves to kiss Haller's hands," while chants of "Long live our leader!" filled the air.[10] This casting about for a "leader" was not accidental. The fascist March on Rome in Italy had taken place less than three months before the Polish elections, and right-wing newspapers were full of admiration for Mussolini and his movement. This was no coincidence, as many National Democrats hoped to take advantage of Narutowicz's election in order to emulate Mussolini's seizure of power.

From Haller's apartment, the crowd proceeded to the joint offices of the *Gazeta Poranna* and *Gazeta Warszawska*. According to the latter, "thunderous chants" of "Down with the Jews!" filled the air.[11] The protesters were greeted by Antoni Sadzewicz, editor of *Gazeta Poranna* and a National Democratic deputy. In his speech, Sadzewicz framed the election in a deeper historical narrative of supposed Jewish attempts to subvert the will of the Polish nation.[12] He concluded his oration by urging more protests on the following day. With that, the crowd dispersed. At the same time, a separate group attempted to launch a protest in front of the Ministry of Foreign Affairs, where Narutowicz was working, but was dispersed by police.[13]

While the outpouring of anger was ominous, it was not immediately clear what course the protests would follow in the coming days. Violent political demonstrations were not uncommon in Warsaw in the early 1920s. Even seasoned veterans of Polish politics, like Józef Piłsudski himself, did not initially take the protests seriously.[14] Unfortunately, police records of the days following the election of Narutowicz are conspicuously missing from the archives. This could be because the Warsaw police quickly found themselves totally overwhelmed by events or, equally likely, because they tried to cover up their own incompetence and (as we will see) tacit cooperation with the protesters. However, the last entry of the political police reports, dated December 7, 1922 (two days before the election), contains some interesting insights. The report discusses, in a very alarmist tone, the possible reactions of the left to a right-wing candidate being elected. Not a word was mentioned, however, about a possible reaction of the National Democrats to the election of a left-wing candidate—it does not seem the police believed that this possibility could result in serious violence.[15] Thus, when Warsaw went to sleep on the night of December 9, no one seemed to realize what lay in store in the next few days.

The right-wing press interpreted the results of the elections as wholly illegitimate and unabashedly called for action. While the Piast party was singled out in a series of scathing attacks, the overwhelming target of the National Democrats' indignation were the minorities or, more specifically, the Jews. The general tone was set by Stanisław Stroński's article in *Rzeczpospolita* (the Republic), somewhat mysteriously entitled "Their President."[16] While the title may sound cryptic to us, National Democratic sympathizers would have immediately known who "they" referred to—minorities and Jews. It was left up to the reader to juxtapose "them" against "us," presumably "real" Poles. According to Stroński, Narutowicz had been "imposed" upon the Polish majority by Jews, Germans, and Ukrainians. This fact "created a state of affairs which the Polish majority must stand against."[17]

The *Kurjer Warszawski* (*Warsaw Courier*), a right-wing paper not officially affiliated with the National Democrats, prophesied that the Zionist leader Yitzhak Grünbaum would now "be able to pull [Piast leader] Witos around by his nose."[18] The language used by the papers was suggestive and graphic. In a front-page article, *Gazeta Warszawska* claimed that "the rule of the Polish majority was murdered last night."[19] Personal attacks on the new president were also tailored to fit the narrative of Jewish domination of Poland. According to *Gazeta Warszawska*, Narutowicz owed his entire career to "Jewish financial circles" and his rise in the Ministry of Foreign Affairs to Professor Szymon Askenazy, the Polish-Jewish historian who, to the outrage of the National Democrats, had been selected by Piłsudski as Poland's first ambassador to the League of Nations.[20] According to *Gazeta Poranna*, Narutowicz "had made lots of money in Switzerland," a fact that was presumably suspicious in itself. Even more ominously, his wealth led to "the secret great power" of world Jewry taking a special interest in him.[21]

But perhaps most forcefully articulated was the narrative of Polish resistance to the "Jewish takeover" and the promise of an ultimate victory for the Poles in this epochal struggle. Indeed, if the National Democrats were motivated by *fear* of Jews, this was not the impression one got from reading their press, which appeared to be certain of ultimate Polish victory. In a front-page article entitled "Victory over Poland," *Gazeta Poranna* argued that "the fight for Poland and the right of the Polish nation would continue, and in this fight the Polish nation must be victorious."[22] Another article warned that Warsaw "will pick up the gauntlet thrown down [by the Jews] peacefully, with dignity, but with determination to carry the fight to the bitter end."[23] Yet another article called for a Poland that was "free from the Jews" and for "liberation from Jewish-Masonic influence."[24] All right-wing newspapers called for forceful protests against the newly elected president, implicitly stating that while the Jews had won a major battle, the Poles were on their way to winning the war. Embedded at the heart of this rhetoric, we can see echoes of the "palingenetic myth" of national rebirth through cleansing and confrontation with the forces of decadence that, according to Roger Griffin, lies at the cultural core of fascist movements.[25]

There is no doubt that the headlines of the right-wing newspapers fit perfectly into a script that had been articulated and relentlessly argued by the National Democrats for years: the Jewish takeover of Poland. While previously this plot had been rather vague and lacking in concrete evidence, now it burst into the open and became explicitly linked to a very specific political outcome. The whole conspiratorial narrative now hinged on a single issue—the election of the "Jewish president." The battle lines could not have been any clearer. On the one side stood the Jews and their "stooges," who had elected Narutowicz. On the other were those "real" Poles who tried to resist the Jewish conspiracy.

Indeed, this was the message of the National Democratic parliamentary leaders, which was duly reprinted in the right-wing dailies. In a special communiqué, signed by the leadership of all three right-wing parties, including luminaries such as Stanisław Grabski, Wojciech Korfanty, Juliusz Zdanowski, Stanisław Głąbiński, Józef Chaciński, Stanisław Stroński, and Edward Dubanowicz, the National Democratic parliamentary caucus claimed the following: "The Polish nation must feel the election of the very first president of the Republic [by the national minorities] . . . to be a serious insult to those generations who had fought for independence. . . . We cannot take responsibility in this unhealthy state of affairs and we will refuse any kind of support for a government nominated by a president imposed by foreign nationalities—Jews, Germans, and Ukrainians."[26]

Clearly, the press and the right-wing deputies were of one mind: Narutowicz, "their president," was an illegitimate imposition upon the nation. The "Polish majority" had been cheated out of its rightful place in running the country! Still, while there were plenty of people angry about the election results, the demonstrations that took place on December 10 were not quite as "spontaneous" as the National Democratic press would later claim they were. *Gazeta Poranna* and *Gazeta Warszawska* both urged Varsovians to show their displeasure with the election and even suggested rallying points for demonstrators. The Association for the Development of Commerce, Industry, and the Trades, universally known as Rozwój (Development), also played an instrumental part in organizing the students' anger.[27] Despite the lofty name and its membership consisting primarily of university students, Rozwój was dedicated almost exclusively to spreading antisemitism. It produced flyers and "literature," but its members were happiest staging street protests and beating up Jews.[28]

There was a considerable overlap of personnel between the National Democratic parties, the press (which not only stirred up public anger but also carried announcements of meeting points for specific demonstrations), and auxiliary organizations at the street level. *Gazeta Poranna* and *Gazeta Warszawska* were owned by National Democrats loyal to the movement's founder, Roman Dmowski. Antoni Sadzewicz, the editor of the former, was a deputy from the National Populist Union, one of the two National Democratic parties. Zygmunt Wasilewski, who ran the latter, was a close personal friend of chief Endek ideologue Roman Dmowski and a member of the National Democratic inner circle. *Rzeczpospolita* was owned and edited by Stanisław Stroński, the outspoken leader and deputy of the other Endek party, the Christian National Party. *Kurjer Warszawski* carried high-profile articles by senior National Populist deputy Władysław Rabski. Leading Rozwój activists, such as Tadeusz Dymowski and Konrad Ilski, were Sejm deputies representing, respectively, the Christian Democrats and the National Populists. General Haller was a Christian National deputy. Father Kazimierz Lutosławski, a sophisticated parliamentary deputy, prolific writer for *Gazeta Poranna*, spirited street orator, and rabid antisemite, was fully engaged on all fronts of the struggle for a "Polish majority." In sum, communication between the parliamentary leadership and the rank-and-file could travel quickly using a wide variety of channels as well as both personal and institutional networks.

The largest of the demonstrations to take place on December 10 started in the morning on the Third of May Avenue. The crowd, made up mostly of students, proceeded once again to General Haller's apartment on Ujazdowskie Avenue. This time the general was met with chants of "Long live Haller, the president of Poland!"[29] He, in turn, greeted the protesters with a speech calling for a social boycott of Jews and urging "determination and perseverance."[30] However, the general made no specific demands or promises. Perhaps, the rather conservative and unimaginative Haller wasn't ready to assume the role of the "leader" (*wódz*) that the right-wing youth were waiting for. Or perhaps, like many other National Democratic leaders, he was beginning to see the anarchy in the streets as a danger. At any rate, the speech seems to have fallen somewhat flat since, unlike his previous oration, it was not reprinted in the press.[31]

The marchers then proceed to the Sejm, where they chanted "Shame!" and "Down with him!"[32] The National Democratic deputy Father Nowakowski made a speech in which he claimed that "all evil in Poland was the fault of the Jews and their lackey Witos," the peasant leader of Piast. From the Sejm, the demonstrators moved up Nowy Świat and Krakowskie Przedmieście streets to the Europejski Hotel, where Narutowicz used to live.[33] On the way they passed the Italian mission, where they chanted "Long live Mussolini!" and "Down with the Jews!"[34] The Italian mission would continue to be a rallying place for demonstrators.

As the *Kurjer Poznański* (*Poznań Courier*) wrote: "It is no accident that the manifestations stopped in front of the Italian mission to cheer for Mussolini. The Nation has to follow the example of Italy. . . . The time for the great final effort has come—otherwise it may be too late."[35]

The warm feelings for Mussolini may be somewhat puzzling, because the National Democrats (still) officially stood for parliamentary democracy, while the Italian Fascists had not (yet) embraced antisemitism. In fact, however, the protesters' fascist sympathies foreshadowed an important cleavage in the National Democratic movement, between those who would remain faithful to the parliamentary system, like the old-school politicians Stanisław Grabski or Stanisław Głąbiński, and younger activists who would later embrace a more openly authoritarian, and eventually totalitarian, path.

After passing the Italian mission and briefly loitering around the Europejski Hotel, the protesters moved to Teatralny Square where they listened to speeches by Rozwój activists Opęchowski and Ilski. The crowds then dispersed, but another rally began at 4:00 p.m. at Rozwój's headquarters, located at 2 Żurawia Street. In addition to students, veterans of General Haller's and General Dowbor-Muśnicki's armies, known respectively as *Halerczycy* and *Dowborczycy* and notorious for right-wing politics, were prominently in attendance.[36] The crowd was treated to speeches by the Christian Democratic deputy Tadeusz Dymowski and the National Democrat priest, Father Kazimierz Lutosławski.[37] Dymowski outlined the political situation and the goals of the nationalist movement. Piast deputies, he argued, were "terrified" by the protests in Warsaw and in process of begging Narutowicz to resign. If the president proved intransigent, Dymowski claimed, Piast would join the right in boycotting the swearing-in ceremony. He also urged the students "to last one more day and organize a demonstration on a European scale." In conclusion, he promised to "settle the students' demands regarding the Jewish question," which meant instituting numerus clausus, and quickly hurried off to a meeting of ND deputies.[38]

Following the rally, a resolution was proclaimed in an attempt to articulate the demands of the gathered youth and their leaders. The language of the resolution is instructive, and it is worthwhile to cite it in full:

> The gathered Polish and Catholic people, shaken to the depths of their souls by the brazen audacity of the Jews and the Polish politicians controlled by them, who against the wishes of the Polish majority dared to impose their candidate upon the Polish nation, demand: (1) From Mr. Narutowicz that he not accept the insult

perpetrated upon the nation by his agreement and oath, and that he not accept the [presidency]. (2) From the "Piast" deputies, led by Witos down a perilous path, that they acknowledge their error in a manly fashion and turn back from the pernicious path they have set upon. (3) From the Nationalist deputies, that they decisively and uncompromisingly fight the demands of the Jews in Poland, until the complete liberation of our country from their shameful yoke.[39]

It is noteworthy that the exclusively evil motivations of Jews are taken for granted and, even more important, appeared to be beyond redemption. Witos and Narutowicz may be susceptible to threats, but the national minorities are not even worth threatening—it appears as if they are constitutionally incapable of playing a constructive role in the Polish political community, and unable to change their ways. The only way of dealing with them is to "fight them decisively and uncompromisingly" until Poland is "liberated."

After proclaiming the resolution and chanting patriotic hymns such as Rota, "well organized groups," each one numbering sixteen demonstrators draped in national flags, began leaving Rozwój headquarters.[40] For the most part, they repeated the agenda of the morning demonstration. Chants of "Down with the Jews!" were again uttered at the Italian mission and the Europejski Hotel. At the Ministry of Foreign Affairs, where Narutowicz was still working, a Rzeczpospolita journalist named Misiakowski gave a speech in which he claimed that Szymon Askenazy will become the new premier.[41]

The crowd then moved down the two biggest thoroughfares of Warsaw, Marszałkowska Street and Jerozolimskie Avenue, beating up people along the way. While the left-wing Kurjer Poranny notes that "anyone who didn't take off their hat quickly enough at the sight of the patriotic procession" was beaten up, there is no doubt that it was Jews who were singled out by the demonstrators and who suffered the brunt of the attacks. In fact, all Jews (or people identified as Jews) unlucky enough to be spotted by the marchers were beaten up. Trams were stopped in the middle of the street, and Jewish passengers thrown out and beaten. The police did not intervene.[42] Following these "excesses," as the press dubbed them, the demonstrators returned to their base at Rozwój.

While the organized protests ended in the evening, the violence was far from over and the mood in the capital was foreboding. According to Bernard Singer, "suspicious individuals" with carts and wagons intended for storing goods looted from Jewish stores appeared in the city.[43] Of course, who was and who was not a Jew was ultimately up to the rampaging youths. An unlucky priest, a certain

Father Popławski from a parish in the working-class suburb Wola, happened to be traveling on a tram on Marszałkowska Street. He presumably had a "Jewish appearance," and so was thrown off the tram and beaten up. When the attackers finally saw the priest's cassock sticking out from under his long coat, they apologized and offered their help. Father Popławski refused. "With two gashes on his head and soaked in blood," he proceeded on his way.[44]

Maciej Rataj, the marshal (speaker) of the Sejm who represented the peasant Piast party, took a walk through the city in the evening and was profoundly dejected by what he saw. Groups of youths roamed the streets "hunting for Jews" and chanting threats against the president. The police were doing nothing to stop them. On Wiejska Street, near the Sejm, Rataj observed the following "characteristic," as he called it, scene. A well-dressed man in a fur coat was having a chat with a night watchman (one of the least prestigious occupations in interwar Poland), with the former assuming the position of an expert and explaining the political situation to the latter. Rataj caught a snippet of the conversation. "They chose a thief-president, the Jewish stooge Narutowicz," the well-dressed man was saying.[45] The left had remained passive for most of the day, though according to *Kurjer Polski* (*Polish Courier*), groups of socialist workers occasionally brawled with students.[46]

Violence and the Politics of Fear

The reaction in the streets had an immediate impact on Poland's political class. The right, on the offensive in the streets, attempted to derail the constitutional process. While Narutowicz had already been elected, the swearing-in ceremony was set for Monday, December 11. According to some legal opinions, if there was no quorum (at least 50 percent of deputies and senators) in the National Assembly, the swearing-in ceremony would not be binding. With that goal in mind, the leaders of the right-wing parties decided that they would boycott the swearing-in ceremony and question its validity, thus putting further pressure on Narutowicz to resign.

As the violent crowds marched through the capital, the president-elect spent the morning working at his old post at the Ministry of Foreign Affairs. It was only in the afternoon that he met Maciej Rataj, the young but capable Piast deputy and marshal of the Sejm, to discuss the political situation. Rataj, who managed to maintain good rapport with both the right and the left through the crisis, told Narutowicz about the NDs' plans to boycott the swearing-in ceremony and attempted to impress upon him the gravity of the situation. He also reminded the president-elect that as a moderate and unknown technocrat, he could not even count on the spirited support of the left. "Do you have at least 100–1000 men in Poland upon whom you can rely unconditionally?" he asked. "I know that I do not," Narutowicz replied.[47] According to *Kurjer Warszawski*, Rataj also communicated to Narutowicz that he could not count on Piast's support and suggested that he resign.[48]

While the truth of the latter assertion cannot be corroborated (Rataj does not mention it in his memoirs), there is no doubt that the Piast party was in disarray, and desperately trying to back out of its earlier support for Narutowicz. As we have seen, the primary targets of the National Democrats' anger (and of the violence) were the Jews and the newly elected president. But Piast and its leader Wincenty Witos, accused of being traitors and "Jewish stooges," were close behind. The peasant party and its leaders caved in to the pressure with astonishing speed. Even though they had voted for Narutowicz just the day before, by the afternoon of December 10 many deputies had reversed their position. "As a result of the events taking place in Warsaw a strange consternation seized our club," Witos writes in his memoirs. Many Piast deputies "saw the resignation of Narutowicz as the only way out."[49]

Indeed, whether the reports of Rataj attempting to persuade Narutowicz to resign are fabricated or not, there is no doubt that his colleagues from Piast did exactly that. Later that day, Witos led a delegation of Piast deputies to meet with Narutowicz. Instead of congratulating the president, whom he had just helped elect, Witos argued "quite insistently," as he later put it, that it would be in the "interest of the state" if Narutowicz were to give up his new post.[50] Later on Sunday afternoon, the Piast parliamentary caucus issued a public declaration that can only be described as a cowardly capitulation to the National Democratic claim that only ethnic Poles had the right to choose the nation's president:

> Piast took the view that both because of foreign relations and due to the necessity of consolidating the internal situation, it was necessary that the candidate for the Presidency of the Republic gain, if not all, than at least a substantial majority of Polish votes.... Without casting blame on anyone in particular, it must be noted ... that the right threw down its gauntlet by choosing Count Maurycy Zamoyski, ... [and] Piast, as a democratic peasant party, did not find it possible to vote for Count Zamoyski, a representative of the aristocracy and the interests of the greatest land-owners. Therefore, Piast's vote for a candidate of the left was not the result of some deal reached with any of the Polish left-wing parties or let alone with the national minorities. Piast ... will continue to stand in defense of the law, and seek a consolidation of the Polish parties on the basis of building a Polish state.[51]

In short, Piast was trying to disassociate itself from having voted for the same candidate as the national minorities—thus implicitly accepting the National Democratic claim that there was something shameful in this very fact. If the National Democrats had chosen a more moderate candidate, the resolution implied, Piast *would* have voted for him. Piast's claim that finding a "Polish majority" was necessary "because of foreign relations" (*ze względu na zagranice*) is particularly bizarre, and sounds just as strange in Polish as it does in English.[52] Resorting to these kinds of justifications sheds light on the genuine fear of violence that must have gripped many deputies and on the desperate predicament the party found itself in.

There are a number of reasons for Piast's lack of backbone. First, the peasant party probably had the weakest backing of any political organization in the city of Warsaw, and no independent force of its own in the streets. The PPS had a strong and well-organized militia. Emancipation, though also a rural party, was closely intertwined with the Piłsudskiite movement and could count on its support and muscle. Even the Jewish Circle (Koło Żydowskie), as the Jewish parliamentary caucus was known, represented a large population that could perhaps be mobilized in self-defense. The Piast deputies, cut off from their rural supporters and unfamiliar with the big city, had no one to protect them, and it is not surprising that many were susceptible to threats of physical violence. Even months later, Witos was repeatedly warned by "friendly" National Democratic deputies "not to show his face in the city."[53]

But a more serious reason for the party's panic was the power of the discourse of the "Polish Majority." The attack of the National Democratic press on Piast was relentless. "No communiqués or justifications will change the fact that the peasants with their votes helped to elect the candidate imposed by the Jews as the first president of the Republic of Poland," *Gazeta Warszawska* thundered.[54] According to Father Lutosławski, writing in *Gazeta Poranna*, "Witos was marching under the command of the Jews." Now, however, Lutosławski continued, "Witos will have to learn that you can betray Poland in league with the Jews, but you cannot rule her against the wishes of the Polish majority."[55] According to the National Democratic *Kurjer Poznański*, by cooperating with the Jews, Piast "had crossed the Rubicon."[56]

Despite the violence in the streets and Piast's not so gentle "insistence" on his resignation, Narutowicz, by all accounts a mild and gentle man with little thirst for power, showed a surprising strength of character. "I cannot go back," he told Rataj, "that would be giving in to mob rule and would create a terrible precedent."[57] He also categorically refused Witos's insistent demands.[58] Following meetings with Rataj, Emancipation, and Piast, the new president met with

"Witos in Thrall to the Jews." The cartoon published in *Gazeta Poranna* on December 12, 1922, portrays peasant leader Wincenty Witos as a dancing bear. The chains are held by Jews, while Ukrainians act in a supporting role.

Piłsudski, who still wielded the temporary position of head of state, to discuss the transfer of power. Even this meeting did not go smoothly. Narutowicz wanted to extend the period of transition and for Piłsudski to remain in his current position for as long as one month. Piłsudski sharply refused this request, insisting that it was necessary to have a clear and unambiguous constitutional settlement in order to stabilize the political situation.[59] His will prevailed, as it often did. At the end of the day, Narutowicz found the time to return to his work at the Ministry of Foreign Affairs where, still in his capacity as minister, he signed a trade treaty with Japan, before returning to his temporary residence in the Łazienki Park.

The Inauguration

The inauguration and the formal transfer of power were planned for Monday, December 11. The three right-wing parliamentary clubs made a decision, not without some internal dissent, to boycott the ceremony and to question its valid-ity.[60] At the same time, the students and other National Democratic sympathizers in the streets received instructions to prevent the president-elect from reaching the National Assembly. It is impossible to determine exactly who made the final decision to deploy the "troops" in this manner, but there is no doubt that it was reached at the highest levels of National Democratic leadership.

News of a "great" demonstration prior to the swearing-in ceremony was printed in all the major right-wing newspapers. Rozwój, for its part, issued the following manifesto:

> Jewry, emboldened by its successes to date, has reached for the highest office in Poland. . . . The entire nationalist camp should courageously and vigorously look truth in the face and reject the Jewish-Masonic coup against the dignity and honor of the Polish Nation. . . . We call upon those deputies . . . who used Jewish support to push through their candidate, to return to their senses and turn back from the path which ultimately leads to giving up Poland to the feeding frenzy of the interna-tional secret Jewish-Masonic great power. . . . Come to the great Rozwój rally! Long live a Poland free from Jewish influence! Long live a Polish nation liberated from Jewish-Masonic influence![61]

By December 10, these posters, calling the youths out into the street, were plas-tered all over the city.[62] News also spread through cafes and among groups of youth. The left, predictably, claimed that much of this was the work of agitators.[63] In reality, however, the difference between "agitators" and regular citizens who accepted the NDs' claims and were outraged by the election of Narutowicz was likely blurred.

At any rate, the left, the government, and the police were all well aware of the demonstrations planned for December 11. The government was headed by Julian Nowak, a holdover from the previous Sejm and a colorless moderate conserva-tive whose chief asset appears to have been that he wasn't particularly offensive to anyone. At the end of the day, Nowak phoned his minister of internal affairs, Kamieński, who assured him that Monday's demonstrations would be contained and that police would maintain public order. Piłsudski later admitted to being distracted with "his own personal troubles and various life dilemmas," presum-ably related to his departure from power, and not paying enough attention to the violence in the streets.[64] Some workers requested a half day off of work on Mon-day, in order to participate in possible counterdemonstrations.[65] Emancipation issued a fiery proclamation in which it threatened that "for every right wing attack in the cities, the people will immediately answer with an attack in the country-side."[66] But overall, the reaction was muted. Even *Robotnik*, the usually militant PPS organ, merely expressed the confidence that "the authorities" will quell fur-ther demonstrations.[67]

The emotional temperature of the right-wing press on the morning of Mon-day, December 11, the day of the inauguration, was, if anything, even higher than on the previous day. "How dare the Jews impose their President upon Poland?" Father Lutosławski asked on the front page of *Gazeta Poranna*. It was a "shameful betrayal," he concluded. This sophisticated priest, social activist, scout-leader, medical doctor, and deputy ended his article with a call to action: "We call the national masses to fulfill their duty, and put all their energy into fighting the Jews in the economic, cultural, and all other realms, and to unite everyone in defense of the rights of the Polish nation."[68] But the students, who were the most militant supporters of the nationalist right, had already been primed for violence, and the decisive confrontation now moved from the press and into the streets.

As we have seen, the authorities were aware that large demonstrations were being planned with the goal of preventing Narutowicz from arriving at the Sejm, from his residence in Łazienki Park, for the swearing-in ceremony. While police records of these events cannot be located, it appears that the police wanted Naru-towicz to travel in an unmarked car, without an escort, along a circuitous route, so as to avoid the demonstrators altogether. According to *Kurjer Poranny*, the specific route was leaked to both the press and the demonstrators. In any event, it was rejected by the military authorities, who believed it to be dangerous and overly complicated.[69] At the last moment, Piłsudski, still "distracted" by personal issues, decided to enlarge the president's cavalry escort in case of rioting.[70]

Still, it seemed that a crisis might be avoided. The Sejm was decorated with flowers for the swearing-in ceremony. Large contingents of police, some on horseback, were stationed in front of the Sejm, along Wiejska Street, Ujazdowskie Avenue, as well as on Nowy Świat Street, Jerozolimskie Avenue, Bracka Street, and Książęca Street. Meanwhile, ever larger groups of youths began gathering in front of the Sejm, on Wiejska Street, along Ujazodwskie Avenue, and in the Three Crosses Square. Initially the police were able to keep the center of the streets clear, and the demonstrators confined to sidewalks. The headquarters of Rozwój again acted as a rallying point for the more politically engaged students. There, they were being formed into "detachments" and sent out to lead the crowds.[71] The demonstrators "moved in military formation … and were led by people bearing special insignia; almost all were armed with identical clubs and a large part possessed firearms."[72]

Police on the streets of Warsaw on December 11, 1922. (Narodowe Archiwum Cyfrowe)

Despite the large police presence, the situation quickly deteriorated. Acting rather passively, in many places the police found themselves behind the lines of the demonstrators. By 11:00 a.m., the entrance to Wiejska Street and the Sejm was entirely blocked off by the youths. Deputies who were trying to make their way to the Sejm for the swearing-in ceremony had to pass through the demonstrators before making contact with the police. The youths demanded identity documents from anyone wanting to pass, and reacted appropriately. While right-wing deputies heading to the Sejm were "greeted with ovations" and immediately let through, left-wing, Piast, and minority deputies were prevented from passing, were taunted, and, on more than one occasion, were beaten up.[73] Many were met with chants of "Jew! Socialist! Peasant deputy!" and attacked. Two Jewish deputies, Rabbi Kowalski and Senator Deutscher, and two peasants, Szydłowski and Cieplak, showed up at the Sejm with bloody faces.[74]

Jewish journalists were beaten up as well. If they tried to complain to the police, the latter would proceed to check their identification documents and pass them on to the students for another beating.[75] The Robotnik correspondent witnessed another journalist having his identification papers examined by a number of students. After poring over the papers, one of the students made the official pronouncement: "Many Jews have Polish last names." With that one sentence, the verdict was passed: The hapless journalist was declared to be a Jew and promptly beaten up.[76] Another journalist was beaten up because a "poor quality photo" in his documents prompted the students to label him a Jew.[77] Foreign ambassadors and dignitaries were also detained. Some like the head of the Italian mission were cheered. Others were insulted—the Japanese envoy had his hat knocked off.[78]

The epicenter of the demonstrations, however, was Three Crosses Square (Plac Trzech Krzyży). Located less than a five-minute walk from the Sejm, the square was large enough to hold thousands of demonstrators, and also lay on the route taken by many deputies and senators hoping to attend the swearing-in ceremony. It was so packed with people that many had to stand on the steps of Saint Alexander's church—according to subsequent testimony by police experts, there were around 15,000 demonstrators in the square.[79] Trams had to be steered away from their usual route, and take a detour down Marszałkowska Street. According to an anonymous witness cited by *Robotnik*, the demonstrators used a small candy shop to keep in touch with their headquarters at Rozwój. The witness recalled overhearing a phone call made from the shop, in which students at the square advised that "some rabbi had been beaten up" and asked for further instructions as to what to do with him.[80]

While there are no records of Piast or Jewish deputies offering resistance to the attackers, the socialists were in a somewhat different position. They were used to "running" Warsaw's streets, and in charge of their own well-armed militia. One of the most violent episodes started when senator and elder PPS statesman Bolesław Limanowski, PPS leader Igancy Daszyński, and leader of the party's Warsaw section Rajmund Jaworowski entered the Three Crosses Square. As someone cried "Daszyński is coming!" the crowd moved in and closed a ring around the three. Jaworowski, a former member of Piłsudski's revolutionary cum terrorist Combat Organization (Organizacja Bojowa), with ties to both high-level Piłsudskiites and the Warsaw underworld, quickly pulled out a Browning semiautomatic pistol. This momentarily forced the crowd back, and allowed the three to reach a doorway in one of the buildings encircling the square.[81] Luckily for them, this happened to be a textile shop, where the workers received them well and barricaded the door. Jaworowski managed to sneak out the backdoor and proceeded to get help.[82]

News of the incident quickly traveled around Warsaw. Two PPS deputies, Żuławski and Piotrkowski, decided to leave the Sejm and walk out into the street in order to demand the release of Daszyński and Limanowski. Piotrkowski proceeded to "energetically" denounce the demonstrators' tactics. According to *Gazeta Poranna*, he called them a bunch of "little shits."[83] Whatever exact words may have been exchanged, Piotrkowski was struck in the head with a blunt metal object and knocked unconscious. As he was being beaten, police stood idly by with only one officer, a certain Constable Kossowski, attempting to restrain the attackers.[84] Piotrkowski was eventually rescued by his comrade Żuławski, and with the aid of two policemen was dragged back to the Sejm, his face covered with blood. He was later transported to a hospital and there found to have a serious concussion.[85]

Meanwhile the emotional temperature in the city continued to rise. Tadeusz Caspaeri-Chraszczewski, an army captain and former member of Piłsudski's Legions, was trying to make his way to the swearing-in ceremony, and found himself unable to cross Ujazdowskie Avenue. The way was blocked by thousands of people, mostly high school students. Some were ripping park benches out of nearby Ujazdowski Park, and erecting a makeshift barricade to prevent the president from getting through. Caspaeri-Chraszczewski recalled being surrounded by a "roaring" sound of the chanting youth. "Jewish president!" "Mason!" "He's not a Polish citizen!" were some of the slogans that lodged in his mind. Dressed in his gala military uniform, he was eventually able to make it through the throngs.[86]

While students undoubtedly formed the backbone of the protests, middle-class and working-class Varsovians also actively participated in the demonstrations. Most sources estimate that about half of the people out in the streets were bystanders or curious onlookers.[87] However, given the high emotional pitch of the protest, many of these "curious bystanders" would eventually become eager participants. Piłsudski's wife, Aleksandra, who was also trying to make her way through the city that day, recalled: "I was unable to move in the throng of people. On one side of me was an elderly half deaf peasant woman, who kept asking me what's going on. On the other, was a fat, enormous servant girl. The latter, all red-faced, shook her whole body and waved her fists in the air, screaming: 'Down with Narutowicz! Down with the Jew! . . . The Jews will not rule us!' In the end, everyone around me screamed and swore in a similar manner."[88]

The state of affairs in the city was such that the cowardly Premier Nowak feigned illness and refused to accompany the president in his carriage, as protocol demanded. He later appeared at the Sejm in perfectly good health. At the last minute, the chief of protocol, Stefan Przeździecki, volunteered to take the premier's place. According to *Głos Prawdy* (*Voice of Truth*), the change of plans was so sudden and unexpected that Przeździecki had to borrow a top hat.[89] Narutowicz was fully aware of the situation in the city, but rejected advice to turn back.

According to his niece, who was with him at his Łazienki Park residence before he left, he took out his pistol, which he always carried with him, and laid it down on the table so as not to be tempted to use it in self-defense.[90]

Shortly before noon, the president's carriage, accompanied by two platoons of cavalry, left Łazienki Park. Along the entire route, hostile crowds surrounded the carriage, throwing snowballs and sticks at the president. "I remember very well," writes the historian Janusz Pajewski, "my fifteen year old middle school acquaintance . . . telling me with delight how he saw snowballs hitting Narutowicz in the face."[91] The police stood by passively. At one point the driver of the carriage was struck in the head with a brick. He later admitted that he wanted to "throw down the reigns and escape, leaving the President alone."[92]

At the corner of Ujazdowskie Avenue and Piękna Street, where a large barricade was erected out of park benches, the police fraternized with the demonstrators who, in turn, raised chants in their honor. Police allowed the student militia to stop cars, check their drivers' identity documents, and even throw snowballs at the people inside.[93] According to *Kurjer Poranny*, shortly after the minister of justice Makowski personally drove up to inform the police of the president's imminent arrival, the mounted contingent demonstratively left their post. The footmen remained, but though the unit commander gave orders to remove the

President Narutowicz, accompanied by Stefan Przeździecki, on his way to the swearing-in ceremony on December 11, 1922. (Narodowe Archiwum Cyfrowe)

barricade, pointing to four officers to carry out the task, they made no attempt to do so and stood idly by.

When the president's carriage finally arrived, the leader of the mounted escort led his horse into the benches and "with the horse's rear created an opening just large enough for the carriage to get through."[94] Taking advantage of the fact that the carriage briefly stopped, one of the demonstrators, armed with club, managed to climb up on it and get within striking range of the president-elect. Narutowicz later told his niece: "The club had an iron ball at the end. I thought: You're going to kill me just like that? And I looked him in the eyes. He lowered his eyes and the stick."[95] In the end, the police "pointed their bayonets at the demonstrators, only after some of the sticks thrown at the president starting falling on them."[96] Narutowicz later recounted that he could not forget the sight of police officers standing at attention and saluting him, even as they totally ignored the crowd throwing rocks and snowballs.[97]

The situation inside the Sejm reflected the passions raging outside. Agitated deputies from the left, powerless to stop the events in the streets, were looking for a way to release their frustration. The radical Emancipation deputy Zubowicz "looked for any available National Democrat, ready to beat him up."[98] Speaker of the Sejm, Rataj, personally had to break up a number of fistfights.[99] When the unconscious PPS deputy Piotrkowski was brought in from the street, a group of left-wing deputies attempted to break into the National Democrats' offices. According to Emancipation leader Stanislaw Thugutt, the incident almost ended in a shootout.[100]

Despite his travails in the city, Narutowicz arrived at the Sejm no more than half an hour late. His coat still bore the signs of snowballs thrown at him on the way, and there was a visible bump on his head.[101] The National Assembly was "strange and eerie," with almost half the deputies absent.[102] But from the gallery two National Democratic deputies raised heckles, yelling "Jewish king!" before being forcibly ejected by the wardens.[103] After that, the swearing-in ceremony proceeded without incident. According to his supporters, who were the only ones present, Narutowicz, though visibly moved, spoke the words of the oath forcefully and with great dignity. He was greeted by thunderous applause and chants of "Down with fascism!" "Long live Narutowicz!" and "Long live Piłsudski!"[104]

The Battle at Three Crosses Square

But the violence in the city was still intensifying. The PPS Warsaw regional leader Jaworowski, who managed to escape from the textile shop at Three Crosses

Square, eventually made his way to the Regional Workers' Committee, as the PPS Warsaw headquarters at Jerozolimskie Avenue was called. Many workers who had taken half the day off as a precaution were now ready to confront the nationalist youths, and a "rescue party" was organized with the aim of freeing Limanowski and Daszyński. Around 1:30 p.m., a march of workers bearing the red PPS banner made its way down from the Warsaw Committee offices to Three Crosses Square, singing the PPS anthem "Red Standard." As the march approached the square from the direction of Nowy Świat Street, the nationalist youths intoned the rival nationalist anthem "Rota," and prepared to meet the workers head on.

As the marchers entered Three Crosses Square, shots rang out, and many among the panicked crowd ran for cover into gateways and stores.[105] After the initial volley, the PPS workers and nationalist students charged each other. What then took place can only be described as a pitched battle. Most participants fought with "fists and sticks," but "from time to time gunshots could be heard."[106] After some fifteen minutes, police, who had been observing the scene passively, broke up the fighting by firing into the air. By 2:30 p.m. the square was quiet, with bodies of wounded strewn about. The workers led Daszyński and Limanowski out of their hiding place and, taking them into the middle of their march, escorted them to the Sejm.[107]

But the struggle was far from over—even as the battle at Three Crosses Square raged, new detachments of nationalist youth were being organized at Rozwój. On the way back from the Sejm, the workers exchanged gunfire with both the National Democratic youth and the police. As they retreated down Nowy Świat Street, another group of nationalists ambushed them and opened fire. This time, the PPS standard-bearer, a worker named Jan Kałuszewski, was killed. The bullet struck him in the back of the head.[108] Four others were wounded, among them the prominent PPS member and close collaborator of Piłsudski, Tadeusz Hołówko, who was shot through the cheek. This time, police did not intervene. With the PPS militia in retreat, a group of some 200 students marched to the offices of *Robotnik*, and started throwing rocks at the windows.[109] They were forced back after shots were fired from inside the building, though, this time, without any casualties.[110]

In the Sejm, with shots from Three Crosses Square resonating in the background, Maciej Rataj attempted to put together a joint resolution of all parties calling for calm. But the National Democrats refused to sign any resolution alongside the minorities, and demanded the latter's exclusion. The PPS, on the other hand, refused to collaborate with the NDs, and so the whole project came to naught.[111] Narutowicz remained trapped in the Sejm until an army detachment armed with machine guns cleared the students (and police) from Wiejska Street.[112]

While the events at Three Crosses Square were the fulcrum of the protests, and captivated the press, violence directed almost exclusively at Jews permeated the entire city center. Throughout the city core, groups of youths armed with sticks boarded trams, looking for "people with Semitic features."[113] Anyone identified as a Jew would, at minimum, have his hat knocked off. This introduction would usually be followed by a beating. Windows in the trams could also be smashed for good measure. In one incident, a group of youths boarded Tram 9, at the corner of Trębacka and Krakowskie Przedmieście streets, and spotted Wilhelm Meyer, an eighty-three-year-old German businessman who had the misfortune of looking "like a Jew." Meyer was beaten on the head with sticks, dragged out of the tram, and thrown headfirst into a wooden pole. A policeman intervened only once the beating was over, and escorted the bleeding man to a hospital.[114]

By 4:00 p.m., with increasing numbers of workers now having finished work, the PPS was able to put together a larger counterdemonstration. The march began in the working-class suburb of Wola and made its way down Bracka, Warecka, Nowy Świat, Jerozolimskie Avenue, and Marszałkowska Street. The workers' chants targeted "student fascists," especially as they passed the university and General Haller's residence. However, unlike any of the right-wing protests, the PPS march was escorted by a heavy police presence.[115] As a result, no violence took place.

By 8:00 p.m., the city was largely quiet, and most of the deputies were able to leave the Sejm without having to fear being attacked. A little later in the evening, everyone was gone except for the Jewish deputies and senators, who still feared attacks by right-wing youth. The orthodox deputies formed a minyan, and Rabbi Szapiro led the evening prayers. It was to be the orthodox rabbi's sole memorable act in his career as a Sejm deputy. Only late at night were the streets quiet enough for the Jewish parliamentarians to make their way home.[116]

2

From Protest to Assassination

By the morning of Tuesday, December 12, the violence was over. Large contingents of soldiers and police patrolled the streets. The socialists organized a general strike. There were no trams in the streets and no electricity or water in the city until evening hours, although right-wing newspapers reported with satisfaction that the gasworks continued to operate.[1] Outside the university, a small number of students gathered, chanting "It's time to drop all sentiments and begin an energetic action against the Jews!" However, this small rally failed to attract others and quickly petered out.[2]

The violence of December 11 appeared to have been a victory for the right and, at the very least, showed its capacity to mobilize the masses. Yet, the demonstrations failed to achieve any concrete political goals. While they may have scared Piast and Witos, Narutowicz's firm stance ensured that the "March on Rome" would not be successfully copied in Warsaw. The incompetent Minister of Internal Affairs Kamieński was promptly suspended, and replaced with the capable Ludwik Darowski. The latter in turn suspended a number of police officials, including the Warsaw commander, and proceeded to issue a public communiqué threatening to use the army in the event of further rioting. Late at night, Darowski personally spoke to the Warsaw PPS leader Rajmund Jaworowski and explained to him the consequences of any reprisals against the right. Whatever he said must have made an impression because, despite having been personally assaulted at Three Crosses Square, Jaworowski spent the morning of December 12 driving around the working-class suburbs of Warsaw calling on the workers to remain calm.[3]

The Revolution That Wasn't

To be sure, President Narutowicz deserves a large part of the credit for refusing to give in to the National Democrats' demands, despite the violence in the streets and the "forceful insistence" of centrist politicians, like Witos, who had voted for him. It must be remembered that the attitude of democratic elites can play a key role in extremist takeovers of democratic regimes. Fascist-style mass movements use violence not to stage coups or overthrow governments by force but to breakdown their legitimacy and create a power vacuum in which they emerge as the only guarantee of stability.[4] Neither Hitler nor Mussolini gained power through an outright coup. Rather, both were invited to form governments by segments among the previous regime's elite. Despite tremendous pressure, Narutowicz remained steadfast in his refusal to give in to the protesters.

But without taking anything away from the president's courage, other factors appeared to be at least equally important. Another critical difference between the Polish and Italian cases was the role of the armed forces. Unlike the Fascists, who could count on the friendly neutrality of the Italian army, demoralized by the bloody and hollow "victory" of World War I, the NDs could not count on the support of the Polish military.[5] On the contrary, they had every reason to presume that the latter, and especially the officer corps, would ultimately remain loyal to Piłsudski, the charismatic victor of the Polish-Soviet War.

Perhaps the most intriguing factor, however, was the National Democrats' failure of leadership. There was no Polish Mussolini in Warsaw who could be invited into the presidential residence or negotiated with. Indeed, after the bloodshed of December 11, many senior National Democratic (ND) deputies appeared to have become afraid of the jinn they had let out of the bottle. The conservative marshal of the Senate, Wojciech Trąmpczyński, was shocked by the anarchy in the streets and the inaction of the police. "Two water cannons would have gotten rid of the entire bunch," he remarked, expressing disdain for his more radical followers.[6] Similarly, Stanisław Głąbiński and Marian Seyda, two senior ND deputies, were "embarrassed by the demonstrations and wanted nothing to do with them."[7] This sentiment was even more prevalent among the decidedly less-radical Christian Democrats, whose representatives eventually met with Narutowicz.

Equally striking was the lack of cohesive leadership. In fact, the admiration so frequently expressed by young Polish nationalists for Mussolini is noteworthy because it underscored what was perhaps their movement's greatest weakness—the Polish right lacked a charismatic leader. The parliamentary leaders Głąbiński, Grabski, and Stroński were old-fashioned parliamentarians rather than charismatic street tribunes. They were not prepared for, and more importantly didn't really want, a coup d'état. Father Lutosławski, despite his violent demagoguery and vile antisemitism, was no revolutionary; in the final reckoning, he too was a legalist beholden to the constitution and the rule of law. Other National Democrats active in street politics, such as Rozwój organizers Ilski or Opęchowski, lacked either the vision or the charisma for national leadership roles. They singularly failed to take the reins, and turn mere riots into a genuine revolution.

Despite the high hopes placed in him, General Haller also failed to assume a leading role in the protests and provide a sense of direction and leadership. While he may have cut a decent figure in uniform, and was able to string together forceful patriotic speeches, Haller's memoirs bring to light a vain man of limited intellectual horizons and leadership abilities. Despite the students' "throwing themselves to his hands," Haller either failed to or, as he later claimed, simply didn't want to utilize the crisis as a means to organize a viable political movement under his leadership.[8]

Perhaps most conspicuous, however, was the silence of the man many considered to be the true leader of the National Democrats—Roman Dmowski. Indeed, since the early 1900s, Dmowski's name was virtually synonymous with the National Democratic cause. Dmowski not only had provided the National Democrats with the bulk of their ideology—penned in numerous articles and seminal books such as *The Thoughts of a Modern Pole; Germany, Russia, and the Polish Cause;* or *The Separatism of the Jews and Its Causes*—but also had served as one of their most successful and uncompromising political leaders. In the 1890s and early 1900s, he was instrumental in creating the National Democratic Party, from which virtually all Polish nationalists claimed their lineage. In the 1905 Revolution, he directed the NDs' strategy and was largely responsible for shifting their enmity from the Russians onto a new set of enemies—the Polish left and the Jews.

In confrontations with these new enemies, he did not shy away from violence. In 1905, he created the National Workers' Union (Narodowy Związek Robotniczy) and charged it with breaking strikes (sometimes alongside the Tsarist police) organized by Polish socialists. In the aftermath of the Revolution's failure, he competed vigorously for a seat in the Russian Duma. When these elections brought him into conflict with Warsaw's Jewish electorate, he almost singlehandedly masterminded the anti-Jewish boycott of 1912, which did so much to poison relations between Jews and Poles in Russian Poland, and to win for the latter a reputation for antisemitism throughout the world. He probably did more than any other individual to inject modern political antisemitism into Polish politics and culture. During World War I, he headed the Polish National Committee in France and was seen by the Allies, and especially the French, as the only legitimate leader of the Poles. Dmowski, in short, was not only the key Polish theoretician of political antisemitism, but also an eminent man of action who never shied

General Józef Haller, leader of the Polish Army in France and the most senior military figure with National Democratic sympathies. During the December Events, Haller was briefly seen as a potential leader by many nationalist youths, but he either failed or didn't want to use the protests to launch a bid for power. (Narodowe Archiwum Cyfrowe)

away from a fight with his rivals, whether through fair means or foul. One may well have expected him to see the December Events as his moment to step into the limelight and direct his followers into the final battle with their enemies.

Yet, reading right-wing newspapers from the stormy days of December 1922, one may justly be convinced that a man named Roman Dmowski had never existed or, at the very least, that he had never been a leading force in the National Democratic movement. Indeed, the election of Narutowicz found Dmowski on the small estate of Chludowo in the Poznań countryside where he had for all practical purposes temporarily retired from politics. He had not contested the 1922 elections in any capacity and did not seek a leadership position within either of the National Democratic parties. Part of his reticence concerned his inability to share a leadership role with the Galician parliamentarians, Grabski and Głąbiński, who had organized the National People's Union while Dmowski was in Versailles.[9] While this self-imposed political exile was partly due to health problems and sheer fatigue, there was also a deeper reason for Dmowski's reticence to take part in politics. According to those who knew him, in the years immediately following independence, the former National Democratic leader had purposefully taken a backseat in politics because he believed that "the world was entering into an era of international Jewry's power."[10] He also thought it prudent to wait out the leftist revolutionary currents still sweeping through much of Europe, before making a return to politics.[11]

It is the antisemitic aspect of his retirement that is most interesting. Indeed, Dmowski was a genuine believer in the conspiracy theories his movement expounded in the press. For example, he believed that "the Jews" were plotting against Poland at the Versailles peace talks and that David Lloyd George (who admittedly took a strongly anti-Polish line at the talks) was a "Jewish agent." Given the supposed ascendency of "Jewish interests" in world politics, and his own justified reputation for antisemitism, there is some evidence that by temporarily stepping away from politics, Dmowski wanted to shield Poland from the presumed ire of "international Jewry."[12]

It would be supremely ironic if Dmowski had indeed chosen not to take a public stance during the orgy of antisemitic violence that followed the election of Narutowicz because of his own antisemitic paranoia. Caught out in faraway Chludowo during the anti-Narutowicz riots, which moved with astonishing speed and were over within two days, Dmowski could not have taken an active role in leading the National Democrats to power even if he had wanted to. Whatever the precise causes of Dmowski's self-imposed exile from politics may have been, the National Democratic leader was conspicuously absent precisely at the very time when the right needed a single figure with the authority to unite it, and harness the anger against the "Jewish President" into a movement with a concrete political vision and program. It is not clear, however, whether at this stage of his political career Dmowski envisioned the creation of a truly radical authoritarian political movement. By the same token, we cannot know if he would have been willing to lead a bona fide revolution, even if he had been in Warsaw.[13]

Whatever the case may be, there is striking disjuncture between the National Democrats' rhetoric on the street level and the limited political objectives of their leadership. As we have seen, at the heart of the street politics of December 11 was the vision of crisis caused by enemies of the nation and the promise of a new Poland free of pernicious Jewish influence. The youth of the movement, with their quasi-military organization and an apocalyptic vision of the struggle between the nation and its enemies, were not dissimilar from their fascist counterparts in Italy. The calls for the nation to "awake" to the threat posed by the Jews are also reminiscent of other fascist movements.[14] There is no doubt that young Poles sensed this unarticulated cultural resemblance. This can perhaps explain their adulation for Mussolini, despite the fact that Italian fascists were not antisemitic, whereas the NDs had little aside from antisemitism in their political repertoire. The common denominator in their visions was the sense of a threat to the nation, and the promise of renewal—it was just that in Poland, unlike in Italy, this threat was embodied by the Jews.

But the resemblance to fascism, on the level of cultural schema and street politics, belied critical differences in the realms of official ideology and political strategy on the national level. One of the reasons why the March on Rome could not be replicated in Warsaw was that the National Democratic leadership stood firmly behind parliamentary democracy. The NDs were the largest group in Parliament and the authors of the recently adopted constitution. There is no indication that they even conceived of an authoritarian, let alone totalitarian, government. Aside from hatred for the Jews, their program could hardly be described as radical in any way. Even their opposition to Narutowicz was superficially within the bounds of the law—since according to the constitution, the president was the representative of the "nation," therefore Narutowicz, chosen by the minorities, could not be a legitimate president.[15] And while the youth exhibited instincts and a mentality that bore a striking resemblance to that found in fascist politics, the leadership, in a sense, lagged behind and was still enthralled with the idea of parliamentary rule. In sum, the young National Democrats were casting about in vain for a Polish Benito Mussolini, a leader with the vision to harness their energy into a meaningful political project. This may have been the reason for their love for the Italian Duce. In the end, however, a right-wing Piłsudski could not be found, and the revolutionary moment, if that was indeed what it was, had slipped away, its energy dissipated in violence against random "people with Semitic features."

By December 12, at any rate, the ND parliamentary leadership appeared to have decided that things had gotten out of hand. As Maciej Rataj put it, the party leaders came to the conclusion that they had "lost the reins" over the demonstrators and, frightened by the scepter of anarchy, were now attempting to reel their followers back in.[16] The official communiqué of National Democratic parliamentarians acknowledged that the election had "deeply disturbed the patriotic feelings of the Polish people," but called for "calm" and an end to the demonstrations.[17] The Christian Democrats, more moderate than their National Democratic coalition partners, issued their own communiqué in which they went even further in rebuking the demonstrators. The "interests of the state," they chastised the protestors, were ultimately more important than "slighted national sentiments."[18] In sum, then, the survival of the Polish democracy following the riots of December 11 can be adduced not only to the resolve of Narutowicz himself, but also to the ideological unpreparedness of the National Democratic leadership to capitalize on the opportunity that presented itself.

The right-wing press followed suit, and called for "calm."[19] But while virtually all right-wing newspapers called for peace and respect for the law, the emotions of anger and hate, and the apocalyptic image of a nation in crisis, which had underpinned the demonstrations, were continually stoked in the exact same vein as before. The contrast between the hateful rhetoric and the calls for "calm," "peace," or "restraint" could often border on the surreal. The perfect example is provided by the supposedly moderate National Democrat and theater critic Władysław Rabski, writing in the equally "moderate," by the standards of the ND press, *Kurjer Warszawski*:

Jesus and Mary! It is as if a lightning bolt pierced the stormy sky and revealed to Polish eyes the horrific larva of the red-bearded Satan. This Satan had the face of one of the [Jewish] senators from Nalewki [Street]. Jesus and Mary! From the deepest depths of the national soul sprang these words, as if we had suddenly seen Poland, a slave again, tied up by the red-bearded one and carried off, like a sheep, to the German market. But he could not lift her by himself. So Piast jumped in and helped him! Jesus and Mary! This was the scream of our consciousness, awakened by a sudden slap in the face and shaken by the coup against Polish pride, Polish law, and the rule of the Polish nation, terrified by the cynicism, stupidity and shamelessness of the leaders of the Polish peasants! Jesus and Mary! The street shook and became red with anger, spontaneously, incalculably, with sorrow in its soul. Peace! I beg of you. Hail to your sacrifice but the demon of anarchy is dangerous.[20]

In other words, while the rioters and demonstrators were mildly castigated for spreading "anarchy," their sentiments and hatreds were fully validated. And even as they somewhat belatedly repudiated violence, the National Democrats congratulated themselves for "turning the attention of Polish society to the goal of international Jewry to gain control of the government in Poland" and pointed out the need "for systematic warfare for the liberation of our cities, industry, trade, schools, universities, as well as the hearts and minds of those Polish workers and peasants, who . . . serve the foreign elements without even knowing it."[21]

The actions, or more specifically inactions, of the police received heavy criticism from the left-wing press. The right-wing press, in turn, praised the police for their "impartiality."[22] According to subsequent analyses by experts, the police had more than enough resources deployed to put an end to the demonstrations. Yet, they conspicuously failed to do so. A part of the reason for police inaction was simple incompetence. This was certainly the case with the minister of internal affairs, Kamieński, who despite having been well-informed hadn't even considered the possibility of taking any precautions against possible violence by the right.[23] Emancipation leader Stanisław Thugutt later said that Kamieński could not be held legally responsible for his inaction since "there is no provision in the criminal code for . . . a serious lack of intelligence."[24]

Nevertheless, the juxtaposition of assessments by the left and the right, combined with reports of police activity from diverse sources, would seem to indicate that the problem went deeper than incompetence. In the first place, as the head of the Warsaw section of the National Police 4th Department (Political Affairs) later testified, police authorities were kept fully appraised of all the planned rallies and demonstrations staged by the National Democrats.[25] Indeed, in a number of spots, section commanders took action against the demonstrators. While this prompted the latter to turn against the police, uttering chants like "Defenders of the Jews!" vigorous police action was nevertheless judged to achieve the desired result.[26] However, section commanders who undertook more energetic actions were quickly reprimanded and even "verbally abused" by their superiors.[27]

Some police commanders may have thought that a right-wing coup d'état was in the works, and wanted to get on the right side of history. There is also no doubt that many individual officers simply sympathized with the National Democrats and their demands. In fact, the Warsaw police was penetrated by a secret nationalist organization, the Polish Patriots' Emergency (Pogotowie Patryjotów Polskich) organization, which was exposed in 1924.[28] Superintendent (Komisarz) Henryk Gostyński, who was in charge of the police at Three Crosses Square, was a high-ranking member of the organization.[29] Thus, the inactivity of the police was not simply the result of incompetence but points to deeper sympathies with the radical nationalists within the force.

Three Shots at the Zachęta Art Gallery

But while the streets were calm, the discursive attacks on the new president continued unabated. In the press, Narutowicz was called a mere figurehead controlled by the true dictator, Szymon Askenazy, who supposedly used his powers to spread "Jewish-Masonic influence."[30] As we will recall, Askenazy, the bête noire of Polish nationalists, was a Polish-Jewish historian nominated by Piłsudski to serve as Poland's ambassador to the League of Nations. Perhaps the best-known article of the period, penned by Stanisław Stroński in the *Rzeczpospolita,* was aptly entitled "The Obstacle."[31] According to Stroński, Narutowicz was an "obstacle" thrown in front of the emerging "Polish majority" by Piłsudski who, himself, was too shrewd a politician to risk tarnishing his good name by associating it with the minorities. The object of Piłsudski's plan, according to Stroński, was to destroy Poland. An article bearing the same message, entitled "The Dam," appeared in *Gazeta Warszawska* the following day.[32]

At the same time, threatening telegrams continued to pour in to the president's office. By the end of the week, there was a thick "stack" of them piled on his desk. Some threatened "ritual [Kosher] slaughter" or a "miserable death." One contained arsenic. Another one simply urged the president to "abdicate." "At least this one was polite," he told his staff members with a smile.[33] Anonymous phone calls, often utilizing a fake Jewish accent, were also pouring in to his residence. When Narutowicz told Piłsudski of these unpleasant occurrences, the latter just laughed—it turned out that he had been periodically exposed to similar incidents throughout the entire duration of his tenure as head of state.[34] "The lice come out of everywhere!" Piłsudski exclaimed. Such were the costs of "laboring for the nation," he added. But, according to Piłsudski, the president could not accept the "dirt" of Polish politics. "These people are not Europeans!" he said of the National

President Narutowicz with his friend and distant relative Marshal Józef Piłsudski.
(Narodowe Archiwum Cyfrowe)

Democrats and their sympathizers. "They preferred living with someone else's boots on their faces."[35]

But if Narutowicz was deeply wounded by the continued attacks in the press, he didn't let this affect his political activity. On December 14, the president was able to arrange a formal transfer of power from Piłsudski. In an awkward ceremony, the bitter marshal insisted on demonstratively taking inventory of his belongings, to ensure that his enemies wouldn't later accuse him of misappropriating public goods. Although warm toward the president, Piłsudski had few kind words for other Polish politicians. "We [veterans] from the First Brigade[36] [of the Legions] know how to punch people in the face," he told marshal of the Sejm Maciej Rataj as he left his old residence at the Belweder Palace.

More importantly, between December 12 and 15, the newly elected president was able to meet with leaders of various political parties, including the National Democrats. Indeed, although Narutowicz had shown remarkable resilience in the face of the concentrated attacks against him, he appears to have concluded that Poland could not be ruled by an alliance of the center-left parties and minorities, despite this having been the parliamentary majority that brought him to power.[37] Rather, according to Rataj, the president was hoping to eventually create a coalition government of "all the Polish parties, stretching from the Emancipation to the Christian Democrats." He had already met with the latter, and was busily working on winning them for a coalition government. On the other hand, Narutowicz made no attempt to negotiate with the minorities.

It is highly unlikely that Narutowicz, who by all accounts subscribed to an inclusive conception of the Polish nation, actually changed his mind because of the riots.[38] Rather, his decision to ignore the minorities appears to have been motivated by the conviction that stability in Poland could be achieved only by reaching some sort of a modus vivendi between the left and the right.[39] In his last press interview, he explained that the role of the president "as he understood it" was to bring about "mutual understanding" between the "two great parties" that divided Polish society.[40] And the price of this understanding appeared to be acquiescence in some of the right's demands, including the rejection of the minorities' claims to participation in government. While the riots may have failed in their immediate objective of preventing the president-elect from assuming his office, they appeared to be successful in the larger and more important goal of winning his de facto acceptance for the exclusion of the minorities from the political process.

We will never know the full extent of Narutowicz's plans for the future of Poland. Somewhat deceptively, on December 16, the fateful day when the president was scheduled to open the annual art exhibition at the Society for the Encouragement of Fine Arts, popularly known as Zachęta (Encouragement), things appeared to be heading back toward normalcy. In the morning, Narutowicz met with his friend Leopold Skulski. The two discussed plans for a hunting trip, a hobby that was their shared passion. At the end of the visit, as if touched by some premonition, Narutowicz asked Skulski to take care of his children if anything were to happen to him.[41] Following the meeting, the president was scheduled to see Cardinal Kakowski at 11:00 a.m. However, the visit was delayed due to the arrival of a telegram with a plea for a pardon from a convicted murderer facing the death penalty. The president quickly signed the appeal and spared the man's life—it was to be his last political act.[42]

After a half hour chat with the cardinal, Narutowicz hurried to the Zachęta to preside over the opening of Poland's most important annual fine-art exhibition— it was a task traditionally carried out by Piłsudski. Premier Julian Nowak and a number of ministers, foreign diplomats, famous artists, and other dignitaries were already in attendance, waiting in the lobby of the Zachęta building when the president arrived. Painter Jan Skotnicki later recalled that just after the president's arrival, another painter, Eligiusz Niewiadomski, nonchalantly asked him, "Which one is Narutowicz?" When Skotnicki pointed out the president, Niewiadomski walked around the ceremonial ribbon and entered the gallery, ignoring the waiting dignitaries.[43]

Moments later, the president ceremonially cut the ribbon and entered the first room of the exhibition. There he stopped to chat with the English envoy William Max-Müller, who apologized for being ill during the inauguration and congratulated him on the election. "I think you should be offering me your condolences instead," Narutowicz jokingly replied in English. The president then continued his tour. On his left side walked the director of Zachęta, Karol Kozłowski, while Premier Nowak and Skotnicki, who acted as the tour guide, flanked him on the right. The English and American envoys along with the chief of protocol, Stefan Przeździecki, walked immediately behind the president.[44]

At approximately 12:10 p.m., as Narutowicz stopped to take a closer look at one of the paintings, Eligiusz Niewiadomski approached him from the back. Unnoticed, the painter stuck his pistol between Narutowicz's and Skotnicki's coats. Three quiet crackles, partially muffled by the fur coat, resonated through the gallery. Though shooting from the back, Niewiadomski aimed straight for

An artist's rendering of the murder of President Gabriel Narutowicz by Eligiusz Niewiadomski. Published in *Ilustracja Polska*, Decemeber 23, 1922. (Biblioteka Uniwersytetu Warszawskiego)

the president's heart, which, as a painter trained in human anatomy, he had no problem finding.[45] The gun was quickly pried from his hands, but the murderer did not resist. "I will not hurt anyone else!" he proclaimed.

Skotnicki, who was standing right next to Narutowicz as the shots went off, recalled the president's final moments: "I looked at the President, and noticed that he is looking at me with a surprised expression and swaying on his feet. Stefan Przeździecki and I tried to support him, but suddenly he fell on me. We dragged him to a couch but it was too short, so we had to lay him down on the floor. His eyes were open. He was looking at us, and, slowly and silently, leaving us."[46]

The poet Kazimiera Iłłakiewiczówna, who had worked for Narutowicz at the Ministry of Foreign Affairs, knelt down on the floor and cradled his head in her lap. She closed his eyes and held him until the police arrived. Przeździecki and a number of Narutowicz's other former employees from the ministry, where the staff was by all accounts devoted to him, formed a circle around the dying man, and a priest was quickly found to administer his last rites. In less than 15 minutes, the president was dead. As Iłłakiewiczówna waited with the dead body, she felt, perhaps unfairly, that the dominant emotions in the gallery were fear and anger, rather than compassion for the murdered president.[47]

As news of the murder spread through the building, the gallery erupted into chaos. A crowd of guests ran downstairs and out of the building, though individual reactions differed. The English envoy fainted. Sobbing uncontrollably, Julian Tuwim, one of the greatest poets of interwar Poland, had to be escorted outside. He would later write a poem condemning the National Democrats for fomenting hatred against the president. General Haller, who arrived minutes after the shots were fired, proceeded to tour the gallery as if nothing had happened. Cardinal Kakowski, who also arrived late, abruptly turned his carriage around and returned to his residence without entering the building or saying a word to anyone. Premier Nowak simply ran away and was nowhere to be found.

Skotnicki called out for a doctor, not to save the president (who was clearly beyond help) but to officially confirm the death and thus set the wheels in motion for an orderly succession of power. But the doctor who happened to be at the art gallery refused to issue a death certificate, presumably because he was afraid of getting involved in the whole affair. The ambulance that arrived quickly was also of little help. While the medics issued a death certificate, they refused to take the president's body, on the grounds that it was against regulation for an ambulance to transport cadavers. Fortunately, Minister of Internal Affairs Darowski and Minister of Justice Makowski took charge of the situation. The latter deputized a number of painters and janitors to secure the building. Phone lines from Zachęta to the outside were cut, in order to avoid the spread of panic. By about 2:30 p.m. a cavalry squadron arrived on scene to accompany the carriage bearing Narutowicz's body, draped in the Polish flag, to the Presidential Palace.[48]

The murderer, Niewiadomski, made no attempt to escape, though according to witnesses he could have done so easily, either immediately after firing the fateful shots or later, amidst the chaos. Indeed, according to some accounts, the confusion was so great that Niewiadomski was briefly left in one of the rooms entirely unguarded.[49] But instead of attempting to leave, he sat there motionless, with his lips set, legs crossed, and an impassive expression on his face. His goal, which would soon become apparent, was to save Poland from the tyranny of the Jews.[50]

Moderation Prevails

The assassination ushered in a period of chaos and constitutional crisis, which presented the left with the opportunity to take revenge on the National Democrats. The previous government, headed by Julian Nowak, had already offered its resignation on December 14. The new premier, former Minister of Internal Affairs Darowski, had not yet formally assumed his post. As news of the assassination spread through the city, the streets became empty and quiet. People, it seems, did not know what would happen next: How would the left react to the murder? For a number of days, persistent rumors that other important political figures had been murdered continued to circulate around the capital.[51] The administration and bureaucracy were thrown into utter disarray. Bogusław Miedziński, Ignacy Matuszewski, and Adam Koc, young Piłsudskiite officers who would go on to play key leadership roles in 1930s Poland, met at the General Staff in the Saski Palace to discuss the situation. According to Miedziński, they soon realized that "state institutions had ceased to function." Key government institutions, such as the Ministry of Internal Affairs and the Ministry of Foreign Affairs, did not respond to telephone calls. No one had issued instructions on how to deal with the assassination. Although they had no authority to do so, Miedziński and his colleagues sent officers to the Ministry of Foreign Affairs, the Ministry of Internal Affairs, and the State Police Headquarters providing information about what had happened, issuing instructions on how to deal with the crisis, and assuring that the situation was under control. According to Miedziński, no one asked for their credentials, and their directives were accepted without questioning.[52]

As Janusz Pajewski writes, for a few hours following the assassination "power lay in the street."[53] And there was certainly a chance that "the street" would seize power. At a stormy meeting of the Central Executive Committee of the Warsaw

PPS, Rajmund Jaworowski, head of the party's Warsaw section, announced plans to lead a march of workers into the city to take revenge on the right and "kill the people responsible for the murder."[54] Jaworowski, whom we will remember as the organizer of the PPS "rescue party" that engaged in a shootout with National Democratic students at Three Crosses Square on December 11, was certainly the man to lead such an undertaking. A devoted Piłsudskiite, former member of the Combat Organization of the PPS, and an intelligence officer in the Legions, he was a "half-idealist half gangster," who ran the Warsaw PPS like a personal fief.[55] Jaworowski was not only able to quickly mobilize large numbers of workers but, through his personal networks of patronage, had access to many organized criminal groups in the Warsaw underworld.

The bloodletting that would inevitably have followed was stopped, in part, by the national leader of the PPS, Ignacy Daszyński. Daszyński, an excellent speaker and a sophisticated veteran of the Austrian Parliament, represented a very different political tradition from Jaworowski's violent and conspiratorial past. Having learned of Jaworowski's plans, Daszyński followed him to the Central Executive meeting in order to bring them to naught. At the meeting, the socialist leader gave a "fantastic speech" arguing that the National Democrats had effectively committed "political suicide" and that inflicting violent punishment on them would amount to "turning them into martyrs." At the same time, Daszyński threatened to bring down the full measure of party discipline against any individuals who disobeyed him. In the end, Daszyński's mixture of "rhetorical magic" and threats prevailed, and the Warsaw organization reluctantly followed his lead. Still, according to Władysław Pobóg-Malinowski, "working class anger continued to simmer in the suburbs."[56]

Daszyński's intervention against a violent showdown with the NDs had an almost exact parallel in the Emancipation. Upon returning home from the funeral of Narutowicz, Emancipation leader Stanisław Thugutt was immediately called to address a gathering of a few hundred peasants who had just arrived in Warsaw from the country and had unspecified plans to take revenge on the National Democrats. Thugutt later recalled:

> When I arrived, they were debating about how to take revenge for the murder. The mood was such that even the most radical measure would have been approved. All this took place with a grim and fearsome sense of focus, without any unnecessary gestures or yelling. I jumped up on the tribune and began to calm everyone down, promising that the crime would be punished by the rule of law. These were the days of my peak popularity within the party and therefore no one contradicted me and

no one spoke after me; only occasionally it seemed that the whole room shivered and that I could hear some kind of deep and terrible groan of rage, and I wasn't sure whether these people might in the end trample me with their feet.[57]

Therefore, just like in the case of the PPS, the anger of the rank and file was successfully restrained by the parliamentary leadership. As Bernard Singer writes, the dominant message delivered by the parliamentary leaders of the left to the rank and file was one of restraint: "Comrades, do not let yourselves be provoked!"[58]

Piłsudskiites from the former conspiratorial Polish Military Organization (Polska Organizacja Wojskowa, or POW), who now constituted an influential though informal network, also made contingency plans for an armed showdown with the right. According to Tadeusz Caspaeri-Chraszczewski, former members of the POW were actively planning to undertake a "punitive action" against the right in cooperation with the PPS. Caspaeri-Chraszczewski was in contact with the radical Legionnaire (and future premier) Marian Zyndram-Kościałkowski, and the two discussed plans to punish the right and "deal with" General Haller for his "scandalous speeches." However, upon learning that the PPS had unexpectedly canceled its "action," POW members decided that they could not move forward "without the backing of the masses."[59]

Many Piłsudskiites later expressed a sense of regret at the failure to exploit the opportunity provided by the cold-blooded murder of the president to deal decisively with the right and bring the spiritual authors of Narutowicz's murder to justice.[60] Writing years later, even Thugutt himself wasn't entirely sure if pacifying his followers had been the correct decision.[61] In all likelihood, most Poles would have readily accepted a Piłsudski coup d'état on December 16, 1922, as a fully justified "restoration of public order" and an understandable response to "the unbearable provocations" of the right.[62] In other words, Pobóg-Malinowski suggests that the so-called "May Events" of 1926, in which Piłsudski seized power through a bloody military coup, could (and should) have taken place as the culmination of the "December Events" of 1922.

But the one man who possessed the authority to trump the flashy rhetorical flourishes of parliamentary leaders like Thugutt and Daszyński and who also possessed the charisma to unify the left in confrontation with the nationalist camp remained curiously silent. Indeed, Piłsudski's failure to exploit the opportunity to seize power is perhaps the most puzzling aspect of the assassination's aftermath. Piłsudski's biographer, Andrzej Garlicki, suggests that the most important factor in understanding the Piłsudskiites' failure to act was simply their surprise and unpreparedness.[63] More interesting possibilities, however, are suggested by a number of contemporaries who played key roles in the crisis following the murder of the president.

According to Piłsudski's opponents, like Generals Haller and Sikorski, the sly marshal hoped that his followers would arrange a coup for him, and that he would be able to seize power without getting his own hands bloody.[64] The same point is raised by Adam Pragier, a man intimately familiar with the Warsaw PPS organization, who claims that Jaworowski would not have proceeded with his plans to punish the right without direct backing from Piłsudski.[65]

More intriguingly, the same possibility is suggested by Piłsudski's close collaborator Bogusław Miedziński. According to Miedziński, following the president's murder, Piłsudski, who rarely gave explicit orders and expected his followers to act on their own initiative, was upset with a number of his close collaborators for their failure to act decisively and carry out a coup on his behalf.[66] According to another high-ranking Piłsudskiite army officer, the marshal was hoping for a clash between the PPS and the National Democrats, which would have allowed him to emerge as a nonpartisan arbitrator between the right and the left.[67] We will never know Piłsudski's hopes and plans following the murder. It is entirely possible that, contrary to what Miedziński guessed about the marshal's intentions, in 1922 Piłsudski was still committed to democracy and that he simply didn't want to stage a coup. Still, his refusal (or failure) to act will remain one of the most intriguing aspects of the "December Events," and presents a curious parallel to the right's failure to seize power a few days earlier. Again, Polish democracy was saved not so much because of its own strength but because of the lack of resolve of its potential enemies.

But the energetic actions of specific political leaders also constituted an important factor in democracy's survival, and whatever Piłsudski's plans may have been, the window for an armed showdown with the right was rapidly closing. Attempts to resolve the looming constitutional crisis were immediately undertaken by Maciej Rataj, the young and capable Piast deputy and marshal of the Sejm who, in accordance with the Constitution, temporarily assumed the position of head of state. At 1:30 p.m., a mere two hours after the assassination, Rataj called a special meeting of the Council of Ministers. Piłsudski was coopted into this process, and received a "special invitation" to attend the meeting despite no longer holding any official positions in the state.[68] At the meeting Rataj was able to forcefully resist the marshal's calls for Narutowicz's choice for premier, Darowski, to formally assume the post. Darowski, a decisive administrator with Piłsudskiite sympathies but no real power base of his own, seemed like an ideal candidate from Piłsudski's point of view. However, Rataj demurred and announced that further decisions would have to be postponed until a formal communiqué announcing his own assumption of the position of head of state was publicly issued. Thus, he left the question of the new government open and managed to avoid committing himself to Piłsudski's demands.[69]

With the communiqué duly issued, Rataj appointed General Władysław Sikorski as premier and communicated this choice to Piłsudski as a fait accompli.[70] Impressively, Rataj was able to win Piłsudski's assent for his choice of premier, despite the marshal's reservations about Sikorski, his most capable rival in the army.[71] Piłsudski himself assumed the position of chief of the General Staff. Sikorski, who would go on to lead Poland's government-in-exile during World War II, was perhaps the best military mind of the Polish army and had already distinguished himself in the Polish-Soviet War of 1920. He was considered to be a politically independent centrist—closer to Piłsudski than to the National Democrats, though not a Piłsudskiite. He also had a reputation as a decisive and strong-handed administrator. Now Sikorski and Rataj moved swiftly and efficiently to bring stability to the country and save the parliamentary system. By 10:30 p.m. on the day of the murder, when the Council of Ministers met again, Poland had a new government, and a state of emergency was declared in Warsaw.[72] While Piłsudskiites remained in influential posts, the government that came into existence was not under their control, and the window of opportunity for the left to assume power and force a showdown with the National Democrats appears to have closed.[73]

In fact, both Sikorski and Rataj were centrists who clearly wanted to steer a middle course between the demands of the National Democrats and the followers of Piłsudski, without being beholden to either group. They also worked hard to resist calls for revenge by the left and not burn bridges with the NDs. In his first address to the nation, Sikorski railed against "criminal fanatics whose murderous actions have covered us with shame." But he also took care to avoid openly blaming the nationalist movement for the murder, and in strong words cautioned the left against taking matters into its own hands.[74]

Gabriel Narutowicz, the first president of Poland, was buried on December 19, 1922, his body laid to rest in the catacombs of the Cathedral of St. John. The funeral mass was presided over by Cardinal Kakowski. The entire government, marshals of the Sejm and Senate, and numerous generals and diplomats were in attendance. Outside, the streets were lined with columns of infantry. The funeral procession was joined by members of numerous cultural organizations and groups of workers, bearing the banners of their trade unions. Peasants, whose traditional

Government ministers, with Premier Władysław Sikorski in the center, follow the president's coffin. (Narodowe Archiwum Cyfrowe)

The family of President Narutowicz and his best friend, former Premier Leopold Skulski, during the funeral procession. (Narodowe Archiwum Cyfrowe)

costumes represented lands from all over Poland, stood out in the crowd.[75] While the Post-Secondary School of Agriculture and Forestry sent an official delegation to the funeral, the conspicuous absence of official student delegations from the University of Warsaw and the Warsaw Polytechnic was noted by observers.[76] National Democratic luminaries Głąbiński, Dubanowicz, and Stroński followed the coffin in silence.[77]

As Stanisław Thugutt recalled: "The day of Narutowicz's funeral was terrible. The weather was so gloomy and misty that even at noon it was dark. On the sidewalks, from the Belweder to the Royal Castle, an impassive and unfathomable crowd lined the streets, and it was impossible to guess what was hiding behind that wall of silence."[78] Indeed, the question of what the Poles were thinking in the wake of the tragedy was an important one for the future of the country. On the one hand, it seemed possible that the terrible and senseless murder would shock the National Democrats and their sympathizers, and prompt them to reexamine the rhetoric that, it seemed clear to almost everyone, played at least some part in the murder. Perhaps the assassination would even lead to a new spirit of moderation and some kind of reconciliation between the highly polarized left and right. Or it could lead the Poles as a whole to reflect more deeply on the discourse of hatred propounded by the National Democrats and to shift their allegiance to other parties. However, as we will see in chapter 5 of this book, such hopes were quickly dashed.

3

Hatred and Electoral Politics

W hy did so many Poles come to view a presidential contest between two Catholic, Polish noblemen as an attempt by the Jews to take over their country? Why was it so easy for the nationalist right to portray President Gabriel Narutowicz, a close friend and associate of the popular and charismatic Marshal Piłsudski, as a "Jewish stooge"? And how can we make sense of the extraordinary violence unleashed by the election, which seemed to take even the leaders of the nationalist movement by surprise? Of course, there is little doubt that antisemitism played an important role in Polish political life since the beginning of the twentieth century, or that it had deep roots in certain aspects of Polish culture. Violence (especially, though not exclusively, political violence) was also endemic in the chaotic and unstable environment of post–World War I Poland. Indeed, some readers may see the December Events as yet another confirmation of the "Black Legend" image of early twentieth-century Poland as the benighted land of violence, antisemitism, and pogroms.

But such clichés are seldom helpful, and in this case too, the reality was certainly more complex than the Black Legend would suggest. In the first place, political antisemitism was actually a relatively new development in Poland. To be sure, popular prejudices against Jews existed among both the peasants and the nobility in the nineteenth century (as they did in many other European countries), but these attitudes very rarely found their way into *political* rhetoric or action.[1] Indeed, for the vast majority of the nineteenth century, the Polish national movement was supportive of Jewish emancipation and civic rights (which were denied by Tsarist Russia) for Jews. As late as the 1863 Rising, Polish national activists went out of their way to emphasize Polish-Jewish brotherhood and the full integration of Jews into Polish society.[2] Even the Catholic Church, justly criticized for stoking religiously inspired "Judeophobia," was highly critical of manifestations of antisemitism in political life.[3]

This picture began to change in the 1880s with the emergence of the National Democratic Party, headed by Roman Dmowski, which eventually made hatred of the Jews its central political plank.[4] In the aftermath of the 1905 Revolution, the National Democrats' ideology of national egoism, racial conflict, and hatred began to play an ever-increasing role in mass politics.[5] But the relationship between this discourse and violence was uneven. For example, in the 1912 elections to the Russian Duma, the National Democrats consciously played the antisemitic card and did their best to orchestrate a mass economic boycott of Jewish stores in Warsaw.

The relationship between electoral politics and the spread of antisemitism is particularly complicated. As Scott Ury has shown, the dynamics of electoral politics in Russian-ruled Poland radicalized the National Democrats and played a key role in the dissemination and intensification of their antisemitic discourse. Specifically, elections held under a skewed franchise, which gave Jewish electors an undue influence on choosing the single Duma deputy from the city of Warsaw, allowed the National Democrats to present the electoral contest as one pitting "Poles" against "Jews," thus ushering in the myth that "the Jews" were engaged in a nefarious conspiracy to usurp the Poles' right to political representation and self-determination. Yet, the relationship between antisemitism, electoral politics, and violence in early twentieth-century Poland was a complicated one. During World War I, for example, the NDs did their best to keep a lid on interethnic violence between Poles and Jews. Despite increased competition for scarce resources and a growing political conflict between the two communities, the 1916 municipal elections, held under German occupation, witnessed some cooperation between Polish and Jewish groups.[6]

The relationship between discourses of hatred and actual acts of antisemitic violence is equally complex. As Grzegorz Krzywiec has demonstrated, the National Democrats' antisemitic rhetoric continued to intensify over the course of World War I and the Polish-Soviet War.[7] Anti-Jewish violence reached an apex during the chaos of the Polish-Soviet and Polish-Ukrainian wars of 1919–1920. Most of this violence involved robberies and was not murderous, but some pogroms carried out by marauding Polish soldiers in the eastern *Kresy* region were deadly.[8] In the notorious L'viv pogrom, some 150 Jews were murdered by Polish soldiers and civilians following the capture of the city of L'viv from the Ukrainians.[9] Some military units, such as those of General Haller's "Blue Army," developed a particular reputation for anti-Jewish violence. However, it must be emphasized that the pogroms took place in the context of a general increase in violence, much of which was caused by the breakdown of state institutions, as well as the moral and economic destruction wrought upon Eastern Europe by World War I. Much of this violence was motivated by economic gain and not aimed specifically at Jews.[10]

However, even though the NDs' use of antisemitic propaganda continued to flourish and even intensify in independent Poland, actual acts of violence went into a sharp decline once relative peace was established in 1920. The consolidation of state institutions and the curbing of brigandage greatly decreased violence in general and antisemitic violence in particular. While the 1922 parliamentary elections (which preceded the presidential vote by three months) were marred by sporadic violence, little of the latter was directed against Jews. Rather, as may be intuitively expected, the violence that did occur most frequently took place between parties competing for the same vote. For example, clashes between communists and socialists were reported in numerous factories. And while secret-police reports fail to mention physical attacks on Jews by the National Democrats and their supporters in the run-up to the election, there are numerous reports of serious, violent clashes between rival Jewish groups.[11]

To understand the outpouring of antisemitic sentiment and violence against President Narutowicz, it is necessary to go beyond clichés about primordial Polish antisemitism and examine the complex and often entirely unexpected manner in which the antisemitic rhetoric articulated by the National Democrats was enacted in response to specific political events. In the following two chapters, I will build on Ury's contention that electoral politics in early twentieth-century Poland played an important role in the dissemination of political antisemitism, and explore how the complex interplay of antisemitic agitation, institutional constraints, electoral dynamics, and contingent events triggered the "perfect storm" that led to the December Events and altered the landscape of Polish nationalism. In this chapter, we will examine the struggle over the meaning of the "Polish nation" as it unfolded during the 1922 parliamentary elections, with special emphasis on the National Democrats' narrative of the Jewish takeover of Poland, which primed many Varsovians for violence. In chapter 4, we will see how the contingent outcome of the elections allowed the National Democrats to transform this narrative, and render it both more hateful and more powerful.

A New Politics in a New State

When Poland was recreated in November 1918, after more than a century of absence from the political maps of Europe, its borders, identity, and political system were all subject to multiple interpretations. Józef Piłsudski, the man who seized power in the political vacuum following the end of World War I, could have tried to impose his own answers to these questions, but for a variety of reasons, both pragmatic and ideological, he chose not to do so. Though he initially wielded dictatorial powers, in 1918 Piłsudski was a democrat by conviction (though perhaps not by temperament), and perhaps more importantly, he did not yet have the legitimacy to rule Poland by decree. One of his first decisions was to create an elected parliament, known as Sejm, which would be charged with drawing up a democratic constitution for the country. Thus, it was elected officials who, along with the soldiers fighting on numerous battlefields, would determine precisely what Poland would become.

The idea of parliamentary politics had old roots in Poland—the Polish-Lithuanian Commonwealth's Sejm was the most powerful, though certainly not the most effective, parliament in early modern Europe. But the Constitutional Sejm (Sejm Ustawodawczy) convened by Piłsudski in 1919 was a fundamentally new body, elected by a society with no experience of democracy. Free but chaotic elections were hastily organized in the former Russian Congress Kingdom, and brought forth deputies entirely unfamiliar with the workings of a parliamentary system.[12] But only some deputies were elected by universal franchise. The former Austrian province of East Galicia, which was still in the throes of fighting between Poles and Ukrainians, was represented by Polish deputies from the Austrian Reichsrat, who had been elected under a rather conservative electoral franchise. The Prussian provinces were also initially represented by Polish deputies to the German Reichstag. There were no deputies from the eastern Borderlands region (which would later become the palatinates of Volhynia, Polesia, and Nowogródek) or from Upper Silesia; both areas were sites of armed conflict between the Poles and their neighbors.[13] As a result of these multiethnic areas' absence, the Constitutional Sejm had almost no national minority representation, save for ten Jewish deputies and two German ones.

The Constitutional Sejm was polarized and chronically unstable. The right was dominated by the National Democrats. On the left were peasant, worker, and liberal parties of varying degrees of radicalism, all of which supported Piłsudski and recognized his leadership. The center, however, consisted of a number of parties with poorly defined ideologies and fluctuating membership. Deputies frequently switched their party loyalties, while parties appeared to be in a constant state of flux.[14] The lack of a clear majority on either the left or the right brought about a series of short-lived and unstable governments. Between 1919 and the Constitutional Sejm's dissolution in 1922, there were eight cabinets, and no stable ruling majority ever materialized.

The Constitutional Sejm was a unique creation, intended solely to prepare the constitution and lay the groundwork for the election of a "normal" Sejm, scheduled for October 1922.[15] All parties contesting the 1922 elections believed that the latter would usher in a new era of stability and majority governments. Not surprisingly, each one believed that *it* would constitute this majority.[16] Precisely for this reason, the constitution, finally ratified in 1921, left many matters purposefully vague—each party believed that it would be able to settle them to its own advantage following the first "normal" elections.[17]

The importance of the 1922 vote was further underscored by the recent Treaty of Riga, signed between Poland and Soviet Russia in 1921. The treaty ended the Polish-Soviet War and brought peace to the new state for the very first time in its existence, but at the same time, the treaty effectively destroyed Piłsudski's grand vision of creating independent Ukrainian and Belarusian states allied to Poland. The Poland created at Riga would be just under two-thirds Polish, and would include sizeable Ukrainian, Jewish, German, and Belarusian minorities. There would now be no escaping from the burning question: How would this new multiethnic state deal with its non-Polish citizens? This was one of the many matters that the 1919 Constitution had left deliberately vague and open-ended.[18] For these reasons, the parliamentary and presidential elections of 1922, the only

Marshal Józef Piłsudski (*center*) at the opening of the Constitutional Sejm on February 2, 1919. (Narodowe Archiwum Cyfrowe)

complete and free elections held in Poland until 1991, were bound to be of critical importance for the further development of political life in the Second Republic.

While each party assumed that the new elections would bring about a decisive majority and a stable government, in retrospect it appears obvious that these hopes were misplaced, not only because of the polarization of society and the fragmentation of political parties, but also because of the peculiar electoral system adopted by the 1919 Sejm. Since this system was to have a profound impact on the election results, and on the very creation of the controversial Bloc of National Minorities, it is important to consider its genesis. The 1922 parliamentary elections would be held under the D'Hondt system, used in Belgium, which tends to provide a roughly proportional representation, slightly skewed in favor of large parties.[19] However, thanks to National Democratic influence, the Polish electoral law introduced two additional provisions that were to play a fateful role in the elections.[20]

First, the Endeks (NDs) were able to map out voting districts in which urban areas were divided and small parts of them attached to rural districts. It was hoped that this arrangement would reduce the presence of both Jews and socialists (who made up large voting blocs in urban areas) in the new Parliament. Second, in addition to deputies elected in particular districts, each party could submit a national list (*lista państwowa*).[21] Deputies from the national list would be accorded proportionally (again with a slight bias in favor of larger parties) only to those parties that managed to introduce deputies from six or more electoral districts. The National Democrats and their allies on the right hoped that this measure would not only create a more stable government but also result in diminishing the representation of Jews, Ukrainians, and Belarusians.[22] This decision caused panic among the minorities, who believed that they would not be able to win any of the seats from the national list, and would therefore find themselves underrepresented in Parliament.[23]

The minorities' answer to this problem was the creation of the Bloc of National Minorities. By combining their votes into a single voting list, the disparate minority groups outsmarted the Endeks and not only optimized their share of seats under the D'Hondt system (which favored larger parties) but also received additional seats from the nationwide list. The Bloc combined most Jewish, Ukrainian, Belarusian, and German groups, with some exceptions especially among the Ukrainians and Jews.[24] It constituted a marriage of necessity between ideologically diverse groups, held together by little more than fear of Polish nationalism. As the Polish socialist Adam Pragier put it, the Zionist leader of Bloc, Yitzhak Grünbaum, assumed the role of the coordinator between "Prussian Junkers from

Pomerania, Belarusian half-Bolsheviks, Ukrainian nationalists, and [prenational] 'locals' from the Polesie region."[25] In light of the specific election results, this disparate group would eventually assume a key position in the presidential elections.

Yet another aspect of the constitution that would play a crucial, and unexpected, role in bringing about the crisis of 1922 pertained to the powers and election of the president. Because the right feared that the charismatic Piłsudski would become president, the Endeks and their allies wanted the powers of the latter office weakened. In fact, under the 1921 Constitution, the role of the president became largely ceremonial—executive power was vested in the office of the premier, who was responsible to the Sejm. Perhaps even more important, from Piłsudski's own point of view, was a provision that prevented the president from becoming the commander in chief of the armed forces, even in times of war. Instead, the armed forces were subordinated to the minister of military affairs, who in turn appointed the commander in chief. This proviso was included *specifically* to minimize the control Piłsudski could exercise over the military army in the event he was elected president.[26]

Instead of the direct popular election demanded by leftist pro-Piłsudski groups, which would have allowed the president to appeal to "the people" over the heads of the parliamentary deputies, the president was to be elected by a combination of the two houses of Parliament, known as the National Assembly (Zgromadzenie Narodowe). This provision was intended to ensure the ultimate supremacy of the Parliament over the president and was also intended to cripple Piłsudski. As we will see, these tactical decisions made by the Constitutional Sejm would later produce entirely unexpected results and turn the presidential election into a crucial symbolic contest between different conceptions of the imagined community of the Polish nation.

The Politics of Hatred

National Democratic ideology was formulated in the 1880s and 1890s by Roman Dmowski and his collaborators, Jan Ludwik Popławski and Zygmunt Balicki, in response to intellectual stimuli, most importantly Social Darwinism, emanating from beyond the borders of Poland. The discovery of the Darwinian philosophy of struggle between organisms and communities and the belief in the survival of the fittest led Dmowski and his collaborators to question what appeared to be "unrealistic" or "utopian" aspects of traditional Polish patriotism. Casting aside the old patriotic slogan of "For Your Freedom and Ours," the NDs came to see the world as "plagued by an unending war of all-against-all," in which weaker communities and social organisms were destroyed and only the strong survived.[27]

Given this diagnosis, Dmowski's goal became to ensure that the Poles would be among the winners rather than the losers of history, which had no meaning or transcendence and was ruled by little more than brute force.[28] This goal in turn demanded internal solidarity *within* the nation, and unity against all threatening "others."[29] While Dmowski certainly recognized that nationality is to a large extent socially constructed, he nevertheless believed that ethnicity was the foundation upon which national unity and strength would be built.[30] Poland, then, was to be a state "for the Poles," and all who refused to become Poles, in other words to subordinate their will to that of the nation (as the latter was defined by the NDs), were construed as enemies.

For the first two decades of its existence, the National Democratic movement remained confined to a relatively narrow elite of intellectuals, and had little impact on mass politics. In his early works, Dmowski devoted relatively little space and attention to the Jewish question. While his doctrine of national egoism emphasized conflict between *all* peoples and races, initially it was the Germans who were the Poles' main enemy in the struggle for survival. But the spread of National Democratic ideology and the radicalization of the NDs' antisemitism proceeded hand in hand. Events such as the 1905 Revolution, which for the first time witnessed the mass mobilization of Warsaw's Jewish community, or the Duma Elections, which appeared to pit Polish and Jewish middle-class voters in competition for the single seat available in Warsaw, turned the National Democrats' attention ever more obsessively toward the "Jewish question." And while in the beginning Dmowski may have used antisemitism instrumentally, by the end of World War I, he had clearly come to believe in the existence of an international Jewish conspiracy aimed at undermining the Polish nation. Although many Polish scholars draw a sharp distinction between the supposedly "moderate" National Democratic antisemitism of the early 1920s and its more radical version, which came to dominate nationalist discourse in the 1930s, we shall shortly see that by the time of the 1922 elections there was absolutely nothing moderate about the Endeks' hatred of the Jews.[31] However, the specific manner in which this hatred was articulated is critical for understanding why the election of Narutowicz resulted in such a spectacular and unexpected display of violence.

For the 1922 elections, the National Democrats organized themselves into a party called the National People's Union (Związek Ludowo-Narodowy).[32] The name was intended to help entice new members, who may have found the National Democratic brand overly polarizing, and represented a broader strategy to unify the right and center-right under the NDs' leadership.[33] The strategy was a new one and represented a certain shift of the balance of power within the National

Democratic movement. Indeed, while the new party recognized Dmowski's authority, key roles in the National Populist leadership were played by politicians from former Galicia, who had greater experience working within the parliamentary system. Most important among them were Stanisław Grabski and Stanisław Głąbiński, who jointly led the parliamentary representation of the National Populists from 1919 until 1926.

In order to maximize their take of the vote under the D'Hondt electoral law and the national list system, which was skewed toward larger groups, the National Populists entered into an electoral alliance with two like-minded parties. The first of these was known as the Christian National Party (Stronnictwo Chrześcijańsko-Narodowe). Its key politicians were Edward Dubanowicz and Stanisław Stroński. Dubanowicz, an old-time National Democrat who had been active in the National League since 1904, was virtually indistinguishable from his fellow Endeks from the National People's Union. Stroński, however, was a bit different. He was a renowned professor of French literature and also editor of the *Rzeczpospolita*, one of Warsaw's largest dailies. The Christian Nationalists as a group were more economically conservative than the National Populists (the former opposed land reform outright, whereas the latter were prepared to accept the parcellation of some great estates), but in all other respects, the two parties' profiles were nearly identical.[34]

The second like-minded party (and the third partner in the coalition) was the Christian Democratic Party (Stronnictwo Chrześcijańsko-Demokratyczne), which was led by the wealthy and charismatic Silesian politician Wojciech Korfanty. The Christian Democrats saw themselves as "centrist" and were closer to the church hierarchy than the Endeks were. In subsequent years, the Christian Democrats would go on to chart an independent course and could sometimes be counted on to side with the parties of the left, but in the early 1920s, the party "was still only gradually emancipating itself from its dependence on the National Democrats."[35]

In order to make maximal use of the D'Hondt system, the National Populists, the Christian Nationalists, and the Christian Democrats combined into a so-called voting bloc and presented a joint voting list to the electoral commission. This new entity was somewhat awkwardly labeled as the Christian Coalition of National Unity (Chrześcijański Związek Jedności Narodowej) and was dominated by the National Populists.[36] However, the terms *National Democrats* and *Endeks* also continued to function, thus emphasizing continuity between the National Democratic tradition and the new party structures.

To understand the mobilization witnessed during the December Events, it is necessary to move beyond the realm of high ideology and consider how the National Democrats' message was consumed on the "street" level. In the election campaign, the Christian Coalition of National Unity enjoyed a marked advantage over its rivals in its ability to produce electoral literature and propaganda, largely because it had generous financial support from a number of wealthy landowners and aristocrats.[37] A hitherto underutilized source for understanding National Democratic discourse on the popular level is constituted by a collection of propaganda flyers produced by the Coalition for the 1922 parliamentary election.[38] The leaflets were clearly aimed at the popular level; they are short and use simple language, and many contain the admonition to "read this and pass it on to a friend." While we obviously don't know how potential voters may have responded to the flyers, the very fact that the NDs chose to present their message in this manner is revealing of how they thought the voters *would* respond.

The leitmotif of the flyers is the call for "national unity," a theme that is expressed primarily through attacks on "the Jews," the eternal evil "others" of the National Democratic imagination. "The Jews" constitute the focus of the vast majority of extant flyers, which reveal a vision of the social world that is even more highly polarized and mythologized than the study of "official" National Democratic ideology or political programs would lead one to expect. What may be surprising is the specific manner in which the words "the Jews" were used as a rhetorical device that could be deployed against *any* other political force in Polish politics. This was done in two crude but rhetorically somewhat ingenuous ways, which are revealing of the emotive universe of the ND electorate. First, using a cliché that went back to 1905, socialists and other left-wing parties were depicted as being Jewish proxies.[39] Second, centrist and center-right parties were accused of breaking up "national" or "Christian" unity and thus indirectly helping Jews gain control of Poland. In this manner, the National Democrats were able to portray themselves as the *only* truly Polish party. This strategy focused on identity politics as opposed to concrete political demands and basically freed the NDs from the need to present *any* positive programs or policies.

For example, a flyer entitled "What Does Poland Need?" offered a catalog of grievances against "leftist" governments.[40] The remedy was straightforward: "As long as there is order in the treasury, good money, cheap credit, police cracking down on thievery and banditry, courts curtailing speculation, the railways running on time, and the development of educational facilities ... the nation will take care of the rest by itself." And the reason why these issues hadn't been addressed was even simpler—Polish parties were divided, and the nation itself was in a state of "economic slavery" to the Jews. Given this diagnosis of the plight of the Polish nation, the solution offered by the leaflet was equally straightforward. It consisted of three points. First, the government should support

"Christian enterprise." Second, Poland must become "a truly Catholic state" (whatever that meant). Finally, the "most important" point was "ensuring unity in the nation" and creating "a majority determined to defend the entire nation in the Sejm and Senate." If these conditions were created, the flyer implied, making the trains run on time would not pose a problem.

More sophisticated, and much more common, flyers utilized the bugbear of "the Jews" in order to directly attack specific (non-Jewish) political parties. One typical tactic, which had been a staple of the National Democratic arsenal since the Revolution of 1905, was to attack the Polish Socialist Party (PPS) by portraying its leaders as Jewish proxies. A typical flyer of this sort contained the following admonition: "The PPS is running *the Jew Feliks Perl*, the editor of the [PPS newspaper] *Robotnik* as its candidate in Warsaw. Polish workers, *are you not ashamed that a Jew should be your representative from the capital of Poland*? You now have proof as to whose command the socialists would like to see you under. Do you want our nation too, to be ruled by Leib-Trotskys and Radek-Sobelsons?"[41]

More sophisticated flyers, which appeared to discuss specific economic issues but, actually, did so only superficially, also inevitably ended up in the realm of myths, symbols, and identities. This is illustrated most clearly by a flyer that claimed to clarify the Coalition's position on rent controls.[42] The flyer's purported goal was to dement Socialist claims that the Endeks wanted to end rent controls in Warsaw. The message began rationally enough—it admitted that the Coalition *did* indeed propose to end "full" rent controls. However, the Coalition would do so only to replace "full" controls with "fair" ones, and the flyer argued that this was actually in the workers' economic interest. For example, if landlords were *unable* to raise rent, they would not invest in building new dwellings or in repairing existing ones, and thus housing shortages were bound to continue. But the clinching argument was left until the end. "Why would Socialists want to maintain rent controls?" the flyer asked rhetorically. Because the PPS "and the Jews who control it" want the housing shortage to go on! "But why?" the flyer asks. Only now, the true reason for the workers' economic misery became apparent. According to the flyer, "the Jews" were scheming to buy up all the dwellings cheaply while rent controls were in effect. Then, once in power, the PPS itself would eliminate rent controls in order to gouge the workers and destroy the Polish middle class. "And what will socialist papers write about it then?" asks the flyer rhetorically. The answer was clear: "Whatever [Polish-Jewish politicians] Perl and Diamand order them to!"

Other flyers equating Jews with socialism were much less subtle. One example was a flyer destined for use in the Senate election, which informed its readers that some 50,000 Jews had voted for the PPS and the National Civic Union (a center-left party of Piłsudski's followers) in the Sejm elections.[43] While it was not clear how this number was arrived at, the leaflet implied that voting for these parties must clearly be in the interests of the Jews. Having intimated that there was a link between Jews and the two parties, the flyer then posed the following question: "Do you want Poland to be ruled directly and indirectly by Jews?" If not, then there was only one answer according to the flyer: Vote for the Coalition.

Whereas the socialists were attacked for being controlled by Jews, or simply *being* Jews, parties of the political center were castigated for "splitting the Polish vote," which indirectly helped Jews gain control of Polish society. Thus, a flyer entitled "A Call to the Workers" claimed that "even today the Jews rule us ... secretly ... [but] if even more Jews and Socialists enter the Sejm and Senate, our future will be even worse."[44] It then went on to attack politically centrist parties for supposedly breaking up "our unity." A similar leaflet directed to "the tradesmen and merchants of Warsaw" attacked the centrist parties for splitting the Polish vote, which could possibly lead to a Jewish senator being elected in Warsaw.[45] From this particular electoral dynamic, the flyer extrapolated a global threat to the Polish nation. "Polish electors," it concluded, "defend Poland from universal Jewish invasion!"

A separate category of leaflets was directed at "Polish women." Although the left-wing government of Moraczewski extended voting rights to women in 1918, as in many European countries at this time, the Polish left was somewhat ambivalent regarding the participation of women in politics. The problem was that women were perceived to be more devout than men and thus were thought more likely to vote according to the recommendations of the Church. The National Democrats made full use of the left's hesitation on this question, but even here they could not resist resorting to the "Jewish Question." A typical pamphlet began with a quote from a socialist newspaper, "edited by the Jew, Haecker, and the socialist, Daszyński," which had criticized women's right to vote. "Polish women," the pamphlet went on, "if you do not want Jews and socialists to insult your feelings [and] mock your religious convictions ... vote for the Christian Coalition of National Unity."[46]

Only a handful of surviving electoral pamphlets published by the Coalition are free of attacks on Jews. However, the material still does not contain *any* positive or programmatic material, focusing, instead, on personal attacks against politicians of the left and center, most notably Piłsudski and the peasant leader Wincenty Witos, or against center-right parties, which are accused of splitting the "national" vote.[47] In the latter case, though the Jews are not mentioned by name, it was still clear that they would be the primary beneficiaries of the national vote being split.

The antisemitic obsession of the Coalition was so characteristic of the party that it was used *against* it by its rivals. A fake Coalition flyer, masterfully printed in the exact same style as the official ones, proclaimed the following:

> Vote for ... the Christian Coalition of National Unity, which represents every-thing in Poland that deserves the appellation of Polish. It is true that among its candidates ... we find a Mr. Feintuch-Szarski [a Jewish last name], but he is in the company of Bishop Teodorowicz, Father Lutosławski ... and others, so as to purposely demonstrate that even a Jew can be supported by the Coalition, ... provided that he can fulfill certain conditions, which make it possible for the Coali-tion to cover the high costs of electoral agitation, which is conducted, as we know, under the slogan "Down with the Jews!" But since Mr. Feintuch-Szarski is a rich banker from Cracow and willing to pay ... Long live Mr. Feintuch! Long live the Coalition![48]

It is impossible to tell exactly who produced this pamphlet or precisely what their intentions were aside from, obviously, embarrassing the National Democratic movement. But it is extremely telling that while the flyer used the phenomenon of antisemitism to attack the NDs, it certainly did not attack antisemitism itself. The authors of the fake pamphlet were playing with the stereotype. Nevertheless, their strategy illustrates a disturbing phenomenon—"the Jews" were beginning to be used, even by the left, as a rhetorical device to discredit one's political oppo-nents. In other words, rather than fighting the racist premises of the right, the left was beginning to manipulate them for its own purposes.[49]

The message of the powerful right-wing press was pitched at an only slightly higher intellectual level than the flyers. According to the National Democratic daily *Gazeta Warszawska*, the goal of "the Germans and Jews" was to bring Poland to ruin by supporting leftist or center-left parties. As *Gazeta Warszawska* saw it: "The Germans and the Jews ... are doing their best to become the greatest possible power in the Sejm, so as to thwart pro-national policies, and extend the power of leftist or center-left governments, which are leading Poland to disaster. It is the duty of every Pole to thwart the Jewish-German victory!"[50]

In other words, all real Poles had to vote for the Coalition—opting for any other party would only "split the Polish vote" and thus play into the hands of the "enemies" of the nation. The article followed this up with a sophisticated calculus of how Jews "steal" Polish votes in various electoral scenarios, and how not voting for the National Democratic list would *always* have the effect of bringing "more Jews" into the Sejm and reducing the number of Poles, no matter which party one voted for or what the electoral dynamic in the particular situation may have been. But despite the sophisticated electoral math, the bottom line was simple: Whenever a Pole voted for a non-ND candidate, he or she was splitting the "national vote," "harming the nation," and allowing a Jew to be elected.

All these arguments, though rhetorically aimed at Jews, were tactically directed against non-Jewish political parties. Most specifically, the goal of the National Democrats was to stake a discursive monopoly on being Polish. Reading newspapers like *Gazeta Warszawska*, *Rzeczpospolita*, or *Dziennik Poznański*, one comes away with the impression that the election was being contested by only two camps—"the Poles," meaning the nationalist right, and "the Jews," meaning everyone else. And the only real message of the right-wing press was to prevent the Poles from falling for any Jewish "deceptions" or "machinations," which was what the non-Endek political parties really amounted to. Obviously it is extremely difficult to accurately measure the impact of this propaganda campaign on voters. But the message was simple, relentless, and aimed at emotions rather than the intellect. The Endeks clearly believed that the only idea capable of mobilizing is a crude idea. As we will see in the next chapter, the elections proved them correct in many respects.

Antisemitism was a staple of National Democratic street politics long before the elections. In fact, it is extremely rare to find any mention of an Endek rally, demonstration, lecture, or any other event, in which attacking the Jews did not play a prominent part. A speech attacking the Jews was most often delivered at the very beginning of a rally, presumably to elicit an emotional response in the listeners and "warm them up" for the more quotidian speeches that followed. For example, at a rally of some 3,000 people held on September 21, 1921, the Warsaw National Populist activist Petrycki explained to the gathered crowd that Palestine could support only three million Jews, and not the five million who (supposedly) lived in Poland.[51] Therefore, it is not surprising, Petrycki argued, that the remaining two million would seek to create a "state within a state" in Poland itself. Unfortunately, he went on, "the government and society" did not understand this danger and were unable to fight it. With the crowd warmed up in this fashion, Głąbiński, one of the national-level Endek leaders, got up on the podium to give a less outlandish speech criticizing Piłsudski and his "clique" and demanding speedier elections. On the very same day, another rally began with a speech in which the Jews were blamed for the falling course of the Polish currency, which was followed by one denigrating Piłsudski as a "political fraudster."[52]

While the records left behind by police informants are not always detailed enough to allow me to fully substantiate this hypothesis, it seems likely that such an arrangement of the speeches was not accidental. It may very well have been that the antisemitic accounts of Jewish "frauds" and "conspiracies" against the Polish nation raised the emotional level of the audience, whose members were thus "primed" to interpret the actions of the government or even of the popular Piłsudski in a negative light. Police informants often described speeches simply as "criticizing the Jews," so it is not always possible to discern the specific accusations leveled by the speakers. But the extant evidence seems to indicate that the accusations were both numerous and creative. Aside from "causing infla-tion" and "attempting to create a state within a state," the Jews were also accused of "taking over" (zażydzanie) the economic life of particular regions, creating new political parties to break up Polish unity, supporting the schismatic Maria-vite Church, trying to break up Poland, or being in league with the Freemasons.[53] But the most common theme was the unity of the Jews and socialists. "Down with socialism and Jewish stooges!" was by far the most popular rallying cry heard at National Democratic demonstrations.

The contrast with other parties is striking. Speakers from the center-right, middle-class parties addressed economic issues in a substantive manner. The mass parties of the left and the center-left championed social legislation, such as improving working conditions or implementing land reform.[54] In the records left behind by the Warsaw branch of the political police, I have not come upon a single instance in which the National Democrats addressed a concrete social or political issue during the run-up to the elections.[55] Hatred of the Jews, and to a somewhat lesser extent of the left and of the followers of Piłsudski, appeared to be their only focus.

The Civic Nation

Contrary to what some scholars have argued, the National Democrats' ethnic nationalism was not the only mode of thinking about the nation in early indepen-dent Poland—in fact, during the period between 1918 and 1922, Endek national-ism faced a powerful and coherent alternative.[56] This alternative was articulated by a broad coalition of leftist and centrist parties and politicians grouped around the charismatic Marshal Józef Piłsudski. Known as the Patriotic Left[57] or, later, the Piłsudski Camp, in the 1920s this group included two mass-based parties, the Polish Socialist Party and the radical peasant party Emancipation (Polskie Stronnictwo Ludowe "Wyzwolenie"), as well as Piłsudski's followers from the armed forces and independent members of the left-leaning urban intelligentsia.[58]

Two other parties, the more conservative peasant party Piast (Polskie Stron-nictwo Ludowe "Piast," or PSL) and the National Labor Party (Narodowa Partia Robotnicza, or NPR), were not part of the Patriotic Left, but in the early 1920s, they were also counted among the supporters of Piłsudski.[59]

There is no doubt that the core of Piłsudski's followers vehemently rejected antisemitism and that they were not afraid to subject the practice to a forceful critique in the public sphere. Critiques of antisemitism were commonplace in Piłsudskiite publications such as *Droga* (*The Way*), *Rząd i Wojsko* (*Government and Army*), *Gazeta Polska* (*Polish Gazette*), or *Głos Prawdy* (*Voice of Truth*) prior to the 1922 elections. This should not be surprising given the prominent place accorded to human dignity and the positive valuation of the Polish tradition of *tolerancja* (respect for ethnic and religious diversity) by Piłsudskiite writers.[60] One the most explicit declarations of this sort was offered by Tadeusz Hołówko, a high-ranking PPS member and close collaborator of Piłsudski. "Our 'sympathy' for the Jews is simply the result of our spiritual culture and our respect for the rights of man, as such," Hołówko wrote. "We will never accept and we will never stop protesting against treading upon the human dignity of Jews."[61] Antisemitism was generally seen as "unethical" and morally base, and the language of shame (*wstyd, hańba*) was often invoked when discussing "excesses" committed by the National Democrats against Jews.[62]

The Piłsudski Camp was a loose coalition and did not articulate a single polit-ical program or a unified vision of the imagined community of the nation. PPS electoral agenda was concerned primarily with social legislation, while Emanci-pation championed land reform. And though both parties rejected antisemitism and were seen as "pro-Jewish" by their enemies, in their political rhetoric they paid little attention to the so-called Jewish and nationality "questions." The most serious challenge to the National Democrats' vision of the national community was articulated by the core of the pro-Piłsudski movement. Despite having the nearly unqualified support of the PPS and Emancipation, for the purposes of the 1922 election, the Piłsudskiites also organized two smaller parties, the National Civic Union (Unia Narodowo-Państwowa, or UNP) and the Civic Union of the Borderlands (Związek Państwowy na Kresach, or ZPK), which received the bulk of support from Piłsudski. Neither of these parties managed to win a single seat in the Sejm, and both ceased to function shortly after the election. Not surpris-ingly, they have been almost entirely ignored by the historiography, especially since they left historians virtually no sources to work with.[63]

Both the National Civic Union and the Civic Union of the Borderlands had considerable support among Poland's liberal elite and were backed by influential liberal newspapers, such as *Kurjer Polski* (*Polish Courier*) and *Kurjer Poranny* (*Morning Courier*) as well as the Piłsudskiite publications *Droga* and *Głos Prawdy*. Among their members were a large number of people who, while relatively unknown at the time, would go on to constitute the pinnacle of Piłsudski's Sanacja regime after the coup d'état of 1926.[64] Gabriel Narutowicz was one of the chief backroom figures in the creation of both parties.[65] For these reasons, the parties should not be dismissed, and understanding their origins, as well as their ultimate failure, is important in any attempt to trace the struggle over the meaning of the "imagined community" of Poland.

To a much greater extent than either the Emancipation or the PPS, the two smaller parties (UNP and ZPK) attempted to explicitly articulate an alternate discourse of the nation and counter the National Democrats' attempts to appropriate the latter. According to the Piłsudskiite *Głos Prawdy*, the smaller parties sought to give a voice to the middle classes and intelligentsia and "free" these groups from Endek hegemony.[66] As its name indicated, the National Civic Union was explicitly dedicated to working for a civic national identity.[67] Józef Lewandowski, a communist historian unsympathetic to the Piłsudskiite project, writes that the "only" real difference between the National Democrats and the National Civic Union, was the latter's liberal attitude toward the national minorities.[68] Far from being ephemeral, this difference reflected a fundamental disagreement regarding the nature of the imagined community of the Polish nation.

National Civic Union leaders imagined a Polish nation that was open to those who wished to join it, regardless of their religion or ethnic background. Speakers at the party's rallies forcefully condemned the politics of divisiveness, "beastliness," and hatred that, they claimed, the National Democrats were engaging in.[69] Unlike their PPS or Emancipation counterparts, party activists consistently addressed the dreaded "Jewish question" at mass rallies, and repudiated antisemitism more openly and forcefully than the Polish left ever would again, not only in their official program but also "on the street." For instance, the Civic Union speaker Julian Machlejd was attacked by the right-wing press for his supposedly pro-Jewish speech delivered at a Warsaw political rally. The offending remarks consisted of the assertion that if the Jews were treated well by the state, they would become loyal citizens.[70] Like the PPS, the National Civic Union also ran a number of acculturated Jews as its candidates.

The most important speeches on the subject of national identity were delivered by the National Civic Union's leading Warsaw candidates, Stanisław Bukowiecki and Jan Kucharzewski, on the fortnight of the election.[71] Kucharzewski argued that under the Partitions, the Poles accumulated "a large reservoir of hatred, mistrust, and bitterness" that had to be immediately "liquidated" instead of being directed "against the sons of our nation and the citizens of our own state."[72] While Kucharzewski did not address the Jews by name, his listeners would not have had any doubts as to who he was talking about.

Bukowiecki had no problem addressing the subject by name, not only in his high-brow publications but also in political speeches delivered at mass street rallies. His argument, made in a speech in front of some 3,000 people at the National Civic Union's final rally in Warsaw, is so interesting (and contradictory) that it is worth quoting at length:

> The Polish nation must be understood as a civic nation (*naród państwowy*), in the same way in which the Western states understand this term. . . . We must pull [the national minorities] into the orbit of national life to make sure that they become a component of Polish life, that they play an active part in it, and that they have the same obligations as Poles. This is fully compatible with respect for their language, culture, and so on, as long as we respect those differences and allow these people to live their life as they understand it. . . . The state cannot stand on the foundation of a never-ending internal conflict. This would deplete the strength of our nation, render our entire social life problematic and destroy us morally. This internal battle with the Jews is the gravest of dangers. The Polish nation cannot afford it.[73]

While the speech is admirable for its straightforward condemnation of antisemitism, it is important to point out a contradiction in Bukowiecki's argument, which will become important in explaining the subtle transformation of Piłsudskiite discourse in the aftermath of the Narutowicz assassination. Even as Bukowiecki argued for the creation of a civic Polish nation, he used a culturally (rather than civically) defined conception of the national community in his speech. Obviously, the "Polish nation" that could not afford the battle with "the Jews" did not (or at least not yet) include the latter. According to Bukowiecki, the goal of Polish policy was full assimilation (albeit without any coercion), but until then it was clear that he did not consider Jews to be Poles.

My intention in pointing out this contradiction is not to disparage the National Civic Union or to hold it up to a demanding and totally anachronistic standard of multiculturalism. Indeed, the Piłsudskiites were not alone in struggling between civic and cultural conceptions of the nation. Zionist politicians found themselves in the exact same predicament: On the one hand, they demanded to be included into the Polish nation, but on the other, they wanted to maintain a separate *national* Jewish identity based on ethnicity.[74] These contradictions illustrate the highly unstable nature of liberal and civic conceptions of the nation. In chapter 6 we will see that this instability, which is probably inherent in civic nationalism, would prove to be increasingly problematic for the latter's proponents in the wake of the Narutowicz murder.

It is also noteworthy to compare the complexity of Bukowiecki's thought and of his understanding of "national unity," with the simple, or even simplistic, message of "national unity" (understood as hatred of the Jews) articulated by the National Democrats. The National Civic Union's vision of the Polish nation required complex historical and conceptual explanations. These were always complicated, often convoluted, and could appear, as in this case, to be contradictory. The community imagined by the Endeks, on the other hand, was starkly simple and required no explanation. The simple slogan of "Down with the Jews!" could be enough to mobilize its supporters.

The second Piłsudskiite outfit, the Civic Union of the Borderlands, was even more explicit in stressing its connection to Piłsudski and in attempting to reach out to Poland's national minorities. Its flyers emphasized the party's connection to the marshal and promised equal rights for all nationalities, as well as land reform, universal education, and economic reconstruction in the Borderlands region.[75] Among its candidates were radical Warsaw Piłsudskiites such as Franciszek Paschalski, independent liberals like Narutowicz, as well as pro-Polish Ukrainian and Belarusian activists.[76] But despite many high-profile candidates and a close association with Piłsudski, both parties failed dismally at the polls.[77] The Polish right trounced them among the middle classes, the left beat them among workers and peasants, and the Bloc of National Minorities destroyed their hopes of appealing to the Ukrainians, Belarusians, and Jews. Indeed, as Hołówko pointed out, the future President Narutowicz, who contested the election as a representative of the Civic Union of the Borderlands, was defeated by the Bloc. From Hołówko's perspective, the Piłsudskiites' vision of a civic nation was rejected not only by the Poles but by the minorities as well.[78]

The failure of the Piłsudskiite parties can be attributed to a number of factors. Perhaps most important was their organizational weakness and the resultant failure to adequately mobilize what resources may have been available to them. Both parties entered the electoral game late and without adequate preparations at the grassroots level. They lacked established channels for mobilizing support, such as churches for the National Democrats or factory workers' councils for the PPS.

But another factor that may help us understand the two parties' failure was their very message. All other parties offered ready solutions to Poland's social and economic problems. These were quite different, and often absurd, but they at least claimed to be *solutions*. In National Democratic discourse, the removal of Jewish political and economic influence from Polish national life would solve, in an almost miraculous fashion, the vast majority of the country's political and economic problems The peasant parties promised land reform as the panacea for rural voters' troubles. For the PPS, the solution was socialism and progressive social legislation.

The National Civic Union and the Civic Union of the Borderlands, on the other hand, called for laborious state building, civic inclusiveness, intelligentsia leadership in political life, and eschewing opportunism and demagogy in politics. According to Piłsudskiite writers, no one else was able to articulate such a program "because they feared losing support among the masses."[79] The two parties' lack of fear appears to be a large part of the reason for their failure. In keeping with the ethos of the Legions, in which so many of them got their start, the Piłsudskiites, and Polish liberals more broadly, were ultimately elitists who refused to pander to the masses. Despite their democratic rhetoric, they had no taste for "right-wing chauvinism" or "left-wing demagogy," and believed that just as the National Democrats had no monopoly on the nation, so the mass-based parties of the left had no monopoly on "progress, radicalism, or liberalism."[80]

Even at political rallies they adopted professorial tones and lectured about the necessity of technocratic government or the complex historical causes of Jewish poverty in Poland.[81] National Civic Union flyers also failed to offer the catchy slogans and simple solutions to complex problems. On the "nationalities question," its flyers offer the following: "The Polish state is made up of two-thirds Poles and one-third national minorities. . . . The Polish nation must be understood as a civic nation. Our state is made up of a number of nationalities. With regards to these groups, we should aim to bring them into the orbit of national life, so that they feel that the Polish state is their state, and that they assume the same duties with regards to the state as the Poles."[82]

Such learned diatribes offered no solutions, let alone simple ones, for the problems faced by most Poles. This alone should explain the Piłsudskiites' failure at the ballot box in the era of mass politics. Still, failure in the elections did not mean that they lacked influence or that their quest for power would be abandoned. As Józef Lewandowski writes, "the influence of the National Civic Union activists was much greater than their popularity in society."[83]

Identity and Electoral Politics

In sum, National Democratic discourse at the "street level" was reduced to one simple message—hatred of the Jews. Moreover, contrary to what most Polish historians of the movement usually claim, there was very little that could be described as "moderate" about the Endek antisemitism of the early 1920s. In the run-up to the parliamentary elections, National Democrats blamed the Jews for absolutely everything that was wrong in Poland. The specific manner in which the rhetorical construction of "the Jews" was deployed by National Democratic politicians and journalists is critical to understanding the violence triggered by the election of Narutowicz. The NDs' relentless portrayal of the Jews as the culprits for all of society's ills, offered the Poles a plausible explanation of what was wrong with their country, a personal and clearly identifiable target for their anger, as well as a simple remedy—reduce "Jewish influence" and everything would get better. By rhetorically linking the Jews to the parties of the left, the National Democrats were also able to present themselves as the only authentic representatives of "Polishness." In Endek rhetoric anyone who didn't vote for the Coalition was effectively working to undermine the Polish cause and aiding the Jews in their ultimate goal of taking over Poland. As we will see in the next chapter, the narrative of a Jewish takeover would assume a critical, and unanticipated, importance in light of the specific results of the election.

The fact that most of the physical violence perpetrated by the National Democrats in the preelection period was directed at fellow Polish parties rather than at the supposed root of all evil, the Jews themselves, makes it clear that this strategy was used cynically and instrumentally for electoral purposes. But this demonization of the Jews, the portrayal of the left as "Jewish stooges," and the rhetorical exclusion of anyone but the National Democrats themselves from the imagined community of the Polish nation would soon result in much more extensive violence directed both at Jews and at anyone deemed to be associated with them.

The alternative to ethnic nationalism was presented much less forcefully, in part because it was much more complex. The electoral rhetoric of the mass-based parties of the left was rather narrowly focused on socioeconomic issues relevant to the latter's supporters, such as land reform and social legislation. But the failure of the National Civic Union and the Civic Union of the Borderlands, despite Piłsudski's immense personal popularity, resulted not only from their organizational weakness but also from the relative complexity of their message. In their longwinded, nuanced, and complicated speeches, articles, and books, supporters of Piłsudski and liberal fellow travelers belabored the virtues of a civic nation or the necessity of labor for the Fatherland. But they utterly failed to offer either a simple explanation of what was wrong with the country or a meaningful target for popular anger.[84] Their rhetoric lacked both the clarity and the conviction of that of the leftist parties, let alone the National Democrats. As we will see in the next chapter, this fact would play a decisive role in the days immediately following the parliamentary elections.

4

"The Jewish President"

I n the last chapter, we saw how the idea of a "Jewish" conspiracy to "take over" Poland was the key slogan and animating principle of the National Democrats' campaign during the Sejm elections. Yet this hateful rhetoric did not, at least in the short run, lead to violence against Jews. As we have seen, the National Democrats' (NDs') propaganda was actually, from a strategic perspective, targeted primarily at "Jewish stooges"—that is (non-Jewish) Polish parties competing directly with the Christian Coalition of National Unity for the votes of Christian Poles. In the context of this electoral contest, the NDs' primary slogan was the call for "national unity," which de facto meant exhorting all Poles to vote for the Coalition. What violence did occur, took place primarily between parties competing for the same vote. Indeed, the presumed Jewish conspiracy to "take over" Poland and the precise nature of the Jewish "threat" were quite vague and, aside from the exhortation to vote for the Coalition, were not tied to a clear call to action.

In the month-long period between the parliamentary and presidential elections, this somewhat vague conspiratorial discourse underwent a profound and critically important transformation, which can be understood only in light of the specific and highly contingent election results. The parliamentary elections returned a National Assembly in which the left and the right each controlled some 39 percent of the votes. The balance of power, and the keys to electing the republic's first president, appeared to lie with the National Minorities Bloc, in which the Jewish Circle played a leading role. This contingent outcome imbued the National Democrats' claims of a Jewish takeover of Poland with a new sense of menace and urgency. In this new political context, Endek politicians and journalists constructed an entirely new and starkly concrete narrative of a Jewish conspiracy to take over the very government of Poland, in alliance with the Polish left. This conspiracy came to be *embodied* by the materializing alliance between the National Minorities Bloc and the Polish center and left parties in the National Assembly. This coalition, according to the National Democrats, would be consummated during the presidential vote, with the election of a left-wing president with the aid of Jewish deputies and senators.

In order to counter this presumed conspiracy, the National Democrats developed what would quickly become known as the "Doctrine of the Polish Majority." This doctrine, which effectively stated that any government that included Jewish parties would be considered as "non-Polish" in its entirety, effectively set up a tripwire, the transgression of which would be immediately discernible to the National Democrats' followers as a sign that "the Jews" were indeed in the process of usurping the government of Poland from its rightful owners. In this chapter we will explore the emergence of the Doctrine of the Polish Majority, the left's attempts to counteract it, and the manner in which the particular combination of rhetoric and contingent events triggered violence in the streets of Warsaw and prepared the ground for the reconfiguration of nationalist discourses in Poland.

Piast, the Bloc, and the Keys to the Presidency

The elections of November 1922 created a Parliament that was split almost exactly down the middle between the center-left and the nationalist right. Between them, the parties supporting Piłsudski and the broadly understood left (the Socialists, Emancipation, and National Labor) had won some 27 percent of the popular vote. With the centrist peasant Piast party (still supporting Marshal Piłsudski at this point), this number went up to 40 percent. If one factored in parties that did not make it into Parliament (virtually all of which opposed the National Democrats and supported Piłsudski), the anti-Endek vote among Polish parties could be counted as being some 50 percent of the popular vote.[1] Nonetheless, under the D'Hondt voting system, which favored large parties, the left's and Piast's apparent victory translated into a mere 39 percent of the parliamentary seats for the center-left. The three right-wing parties, which managed to pull together a single voting bloc—the Christian Coalition of National Unity (Chrześcijański Związek Jedności Narodowej, or ChJN)—benefitted from the D'Hondt electoral calculus. With 29 percent of the popular vote, the right was able to claim 39 percent of the seats in Parliament—the exact same result as the left and Piast.

These results allowed both sides to claim victory. The Coalition, with its 216 deputies and senators, could claim to be the largest group in Parliament and the true victor. On the other hand, the left could plausibly claim to have won the popular vote. While the Piłsudskiite *Głos Prawdy* mourned the defeat of its champion, the National Civic Union, it took solace in the fact that the majority of Poles voted "for Piłsudski" and against the Coalition.[2] Still, according to the parliamentary math, the result was a stalemate with both the pro-Piłsudski center-left and the National Democratic right each controlling some 39 percent of the seats in the Sejm and Senate. The remaining 22 percent of the seats were held by the Bloc of National Minorities. It may be tempting to think of the Bloc as a natural ally of the Polish left. Indeed, an alliance of the Bloc and the center-left parties was the most obvious way in which a stable ruling majority could have been formed in the Sejm. And to someone uninitiated in Polish politics, such a coalition may have appeared to be an obvious choice. But there was also another possibility—the National Democrats could rule Poland if they were able to secure the cooperation of Piast, the most conservative of the center-left parties.

Parliamentary elections results and the popular vote

	Popular vote (%)	*National Assembly (%)*
Left	2,685,982 (30.7)	138 (25)
Right	2,551,582 (29.1)	216 (39)
Bloc & Minorities	1,940,255 (22.1)	112 (20)
Piast	1,153,397 (13.1)	88 (16)
Others	431,482 (4.9)	—
Total	8,762,698 (100)	554 (100)

"Bloc & Minorities" includes votes cast for smaller Jewish and Ukrainian parties along with those cast for the Bloc. In addition to a multitude of smaller parties, "Others" includes the Communists and the Polish Center (Polskie Centrum) party. Between them, these two parties received almost 400,000 votes. Although neither could be properly classified as part of the pro-Piłsudski left, both were closer to the latter than to the National Democrats.
Source: Nohlen and Stöver, *Elections in Europe: A Data Handbook,* 1500.

The first big test of which of these two possible coalitions would coalesce was provided by the presidential elections. These, according to the constitution, were to be carried out by the combination of the Sejm and Senate, known as the National Assembly. With the presidential election not scheduled until December 9, 1922, all parties had a full month to prepare their candidates, to choose coalition partners, and to make their case in the court of public opinion.

As the largest and most cohesive group in the Sejm, the Coalition could plausibly see itself as the victor of the parliamentary elections. Yet, it could not rule alone. And because of its aggressive electoral tactics, it had largely deprived itself of potential allies. It was absolutely unthinkable that the Emancipation, the PPS, or the Bloc would side with it. Support from National Labor was unlikely and, in any case, would not have been enough to form a majority government. The only option was Piast. Such an alliance was not entirely unthinkable. Although Piast advocated land reform and had supported Piłsudski in the past, it was seen as expressing the social conservatism of many Polish peasants. It also had little sympathy for the radicalism of Emancipation or the socialist demands of the PPS. The interests of urban workers, which the latter represented, were often at odds with those of the peasants. Finally, Wincenty Witos, Piast's formidable and charismatic leader, was known as a pragmatist and even something of an opportunist. It was widely believed that he would be willing to cooperate with either the left or the right, depending on what his party would get from the deal.

The Coalition began to court Piast almost immediately after the elections. In the new Parliament's first session, it helped Piast candidate Maciej Rataj become the marshal (or speaker) of the Sejm. In return, Piast dutifully supported the National Democratic candidate Wojciech Trąmpczyński for marshal of the Senate. The right-wing press greeted this development as a sign that a Piast-ND coalition was slowly coalescing.[3] But this kind of tit-for-tat horse-trading agreement would not work with regard to the presidency—after all, there could be only one president. Moreover, several important factors mitigated Piast from seeking too close an alliance with the National Democrats. Most importantly, while socially conservative, Piast demanded land reform and the breaking up of large estates in order to give land to smallholding peasants. The National Democrats, funded largely by landowners, opposed plans for land reform, and coming up with any compromise on the issue would not be easy. Another obstacle was the bad blood left over from the elections. When Piast attempted to make inroads among peasants in the National Democratic–dominated province of Poznań, the Endeks responded with terror and violence. Piast rallies and meetings were routinely attacked by mobs of Endek supporters (often led by priests), and during one visit to the province, Witos himself was hit in the head with a rock.[4] Finally, there is little doubt that in 1922 Piast still considered itself a part of the left.[5]

Therefore, in addition to any carrots that they could dangle in front of Piast, the NDs also needed a stick. Fortunately, from their perspective, the perfect stick was readily available. We will recall from the previous chapter that the dominant Endek narrative depicted Polish political and national life as being threatened by the Jews and their proxies or "stooges." Now, in the specific political context created by the election, wherein the left and Piast could not rule without the support

The opening session of the Sejm, November 1922. (Narodowe Archiwum Cyfrowe)

of the Minorities Bloc, this narrative appeared to be gaining coherence. In fact, the outcome of the election looked like it had been scripted to play right into the Endek myth of a planned Jewish takeover of Poland! The left could not rule Poland without help from the Minorities Bloc. By preemptively labeling cooperation with the Bloc as treasonous participation in the Jewish plot to destroy the nation, the National Democrats could prevent Piast, and perhaps even the rest of the Polish left, from seeking an alliance with the minorities and thus from ever attaining a stable ruling majority. The threat of being labeled "Jewish stooges" could therefore help bully Piast deputies into coming to terms with the right.

While components of rabid antisemitism and of rhetoric emphasizing the "Jewish threat" to the nation had been integral to National Democratic discourse during the parliamentary elections, in the period following the elections, they assumed an entirely new dimension. And with good reason—the only way the National Democrats could hope to win the presidency, and more importantly rule Poland, was by scaring the other parties, and particularly Piast, away from cooperating with the Bloc. Attacking the Jews now became a means to a *very* concrete political end—the presidency. The new tone and urgency were first evident in the National Democratic press. Four days after the Senate elections, in an article tellingly entitled "Us and Them," the mass market *Gazeta Poranna* wrote the following:

> The Jews have changed remarkably since the elections. . . . The Jews discuss the future government and politics with such liberty and certitude, as if Poland was already their cabal courtyard, where everything must take place according to Jewish will. . . . All their hopes rest upon this unassailable base—the belief that the left will never allow the [National Democrats] to govern, and that the left will be able to govern Poland only jointly with the Jews. . . . In the new Sejm they want to begin a transformation of Poland from a national state into a multinational Judeo-Poland. They are arrogant and pushy. They easily turn themselves into internationalists, progressives, neutrals, without ever ceasing to be Jews. We have known this for a long time. But will even a single party have the courage to rule Poland jointly with the Jews?[6]

Even though, in reality Jews constituted only 40 percent of the Bloc's deputies, with the remainder being divided between Ukrainians, Belarusians, and Germans, in an article entitled "The Great Jewish Offensive," *Gazeta Poranna* sought to demonstrate that the Bloc was in fact a Jewish creation designed to "declare war" on Poland.[7] The goal of this war was to take over the government and turn the country into a "Judeo-Poland." Other articles listed the old litany of supposed Jewish transgressions against the Polish nation, from controlling the foreign press to spreading pornography "so as to undermine the spirit of the nation."[8] But there was always a new element—the plan to take over the machinery of government with the aid of the Polish left.

The supposedly intellectual Endek weekly *Myśl Narodowa* (*National Thought*) pitched its argument at a slightly higher level. According to Father Kazimierz Lutosławski, the elections were a victory for "Polish nationalism" because they made "the entire nation feel the substance of the fundamental question of our time: to make Poland a national state."[9] Lutosławski claimed that the strong showing of the Bloc would lead to the rise of antisemitism and this would in itself be a victory for the right. He also added that Witos would be afraid to cast his lot with the socialists and Jews and predicted the formation of a coalition government between Piast and the Christian Coalition of National Unity.[10]

Not surprisingly, spurred by the right-wing press, both political and popular manifestations of antisemitism began to pick up markedly immediately after the elections. The tone of the National Democratic political rallies changed markedly. While during the election campaign Endek speakers dealt in vague and unspecified threats of Jewish and Masonic conspiracies, the latter now became starkly concrete. The new "danger," as an Endek speaker explained at a rally of some three thousand people a few days after the parliamentary election, was the Minorities Bloc and its attempts to subvert Polish politics.[11]

While university students were fairly quiescent during the parliamentary election campaign, a series of massive antisemitic demonstrations convulsed the campuses shortly after the elections ended. On November 24, 1922, a meeting of students from the University of Warsaw "unanimously" passed two resolutions: the first called for a "social boycott" of Jewish students, and included such provisions as not shaking Jews' hands and not talking to Jews. The second demand was to institute numerus clausus in Polish universities. National Democrat Stroński and Christian Democrat Chaciński made speeches supporting the student demands.[12] Following the meeting, some five thousand students marched to the Ministry of Education to present their demand for the institution of numerus clausus, chanting "Down with the Jews!" and "Long live numerus clausus!" and singing patriotic hymns.[13] Indeed, while the "social boycott" of the Jews was easy enough to implement (at least for hardened antisemites), the demand for numerus clausus gave rise to a massive campaign that mobilized thousands and, conveniently, brought the "Jewish question" to the center of national politics.

The campaign soon led to violence against Jewish students.[14] And it became a cause célèbre for right-wing newspapers and politicians, at both the national and the local levels. Local National Populist Union committees issued petitions supporting the "righteous demands" of the students.[15] Meanwhile, the National Democratic press supported the campaign with articles bearing titles like "A Healthy Instinct among the Youth."[16] According to *Gazeta Poranna*, the student rallies "offered indisputable proof that Polish society is waking up and beginning to realize the Jewish danger in Poland."[17] According to Zionist politicians, the students' antisemitic "transgressions" had the support of certain organs of the Polish administration.[18] It is impossible to ascertain whether or not this was the case, but it is beyond doubt that the students had the open support of the National Democratic parties and press.

Indeed, in the run-up to the presidential elections, the rhetoric of hatred put forth by the right-wing press intensified markedly. On December 3, nearly a week before the elections, in an article entitled "The Last Battle for Independence," Father Lutosławski argued that the Jews were a "fourth partitioning power" and that despite achieving independence, Poland was a "slave to the Jews."[19] "Down with the Jews," he continued, "must become our sacred rallying cry." Admittedly, Lutosławski claimed to discourage pogroms, which, "aside from being morally abhorrent," were politically "counterproductive" and helped Jews tarnish Poland's image abroad.[20] The main point, however, was that "we," (i.e., the Poles) would not tolerate "any discussions with the Jews" aside from figuring out how to facilitate their exodus from Poland.[21] The emphasis on "discussions" is important, and there is no doubt that it referred to the political talks that the Bloc was hoping to start with the parties of the left. Endek politicians and journalists beat this message home relentlessly. Official communiqués of the Coalition warned that Polish society "will turn its back on those who choose to work with the Jews."[22] According to *Gazeta Warszawska*, the Polish masses would never allow the Jews "to control the state."[23]

The Doctrine of the Polish Majority

In the intensifying atmosphere of hatred stirred up by the right-wing press and taken up by National Democratic student organizations with the blessings of senior right-wing politicians, a qualitatively new rhetoric was emerging. Specifically, the somewhat vague National Democratic slogan of "national unity" was very quickly being reworked into what became known as the "Doctrine of the Polish Majority." This doctrine was perhaps most succinctly explained in an article published in *Gazeta Warszawska* as early as November 15, and it was henceforth repeated explicitly and implicitly in virtually all right-wing publications. Here is how *Gazeta Warszawska* understood the fundamental issue at stake in the presidential elections:

> We write about this today—when no one can yet predict upon whom the Nation will bestow the presidency. And for this reason we must make one forceful objection: The [presidency] belongs, and can only belong, to the one chosen by the Nation [i.e., ethnic Poles], because according to the constitution supreme power in Poland belongs to the Nation and the president is but an organ of the Nation in the domain of supreme power. Let no one imagine that anyone but the Polish Nation itself has the constitutional power to bestow the presidency. No artificial majority, created against the Polish majority with the aid of the enemies of the nation [i.e., the minorities] shall wield power in the state. Reality based upon the wishes of the Nation would quickly smash to bits such dangerous delusions.[24]

In other words, the Doctrine of the Polish Majority amounted to the explicit exclusion of all people defined by the NDs as "non-Polish" from *any* political role in the state. And by this rhetorical sleight of hand, any governing coalition that *included* the minorities could be dubbed as "non-Polish" in its entirety. If the NDs were to succeed in persuading the electorate that any cooperation with the Jews amounted to treason, they would find themselves in a win-win situation. "We couldn't wish for anything better" than a coalition between the Jews and the left, wrote a *Gazeta Warszawska* journalist gleefully.[25] If the left refused to work with the Jews, the right would get to form the government. But if the left did opt to work with the minorities, it "would have to accept the responsibility for this decision" in the court of public opinion. Given the public's expected reaction, the article concluded, "we may even wish our opponents success."[26]

In sum, anyone cooperating with the Minorities Bloc was thereby a "Jewish stooge." According to Lutosławski, this applied even to Piłsudski himself, who could become president "only thanks to the Jews and their stooges." But perhaps this was not surprising since, according to Lutosławski, Piłsudski "not since yesterday has been a tool of international Jewry in its war against the Polish nation."[27] And while Lutosławski was more radical than some other National Democratic leaders, most notably Grabski and Głąbiński, he was not a loony, at least by the standards of his party. He was a mainstream, articulate, popular, and influential National Populist politician, and one the main architects of the Polish constitution.

Clearly, the Doctrine of the Polish Majority had a very practical political purpose. It was extremely unlikely that any of the Polish parties, with the exception of Piast, whose political program, aside from the commitment to land reform, was rather nebulous, would want to join the NDs in a coalition government. But Piast's natural allies, largely because of the peasants' emphasis on land reform, were on the left. The Doctrine of the Polish Majority, therefore, was created as a cudgel against Piast and was aimed to frighten the peasant deputies into rejecting any overtures from the left and the national minorities.

The pressure brought to bear on Piast, and personally on its leader Wincenty Witos, was substantial. According to the nationalist press, Witos "held the key to resolving the current political crisis."[28] But he would have to decide whether or not to "burn his bridges" not only with the right's parliamentary deputies, but with "nationalist public opinion as a whole."[29] If Piast chose to cast its lot with the Bloc, the National Democrats argued, Polish society would come to see the peasant party as traitors to the nation. This message was relentlessly beaten home in all the right-wing newspapers and brought to bear on individual Piast deputies.[30]

The imagery associated with the attacks on Piast leader Wincenty Witos was particularly interesting. In one cartoon in *Gazeta Poranna*, Witos was portrayed as the archetypal Polish peasant, sitting at a crossroads struggling to figure out which way to go.

According to the sign, one road led to "Poland," the other to "Bolshevik Land." The Zionist leader Yitzhak Grünbaum was portrayed as the devil, whispering into Witos's ear, presumably promising him power (in coalition with the Minorities Bloc), and urging him upon the path to Communism.[31] Interestingly, a Prussian soldier (the National Democrats' traditional enemy) could also be seen hiding in "Bolshevik Land," waiting eagerly for Witos's decision and presumably ready to reveal himself once the latter walked away from the national cause.[32]

"The Temptation of Witos." Zionist leader Yitzhak Grünbaum plays the role of the devil, trying to trick the gullible Polish peasant (Witos) onto the path leading away from Poland and toward Bolshevism. *Gazeta Poranna*, November 21, 1922.

The image played on stereotypes deeply embedded in Polish culture. Peasants were perhaps well-meaning but also naive and suspect to manipulation by the crafty, devious, devilish Jews. The choice now facing their leader was a binary one. There was only one legitimate road leading to "Poland." Conveniently, the only way for Piast to reach this destination was to follow the lead of the National Democrats and join them as a junior coalition partner. While the effects of images like the one discussed above are not possible to measure quantitatively, there is no doubt that they resonated deeply with many Poles, especially those who already believed that the Jews were attempting to control Poland. As we will see, the rhetorical and emotive power of the Doctrine of the Polish Majority would continue long after the specific institutional context, which produced it, had lost its importance.

But the notion that only an Endek-Piast coalition expressed the wishes of the "Polish majority" was based on a number of highly dubious premises and some outright falsehoods. Most obviously, it was predicated on the rejection of the claims of some 35 percent of the Polish state's citizens to any sort of "Polishness." Loyalty to Poland meant nothing; ethnicity meant everything.[33] In practice, the "Battle for the Polish majority," as the right-wing press quickly dubbed the presidential election, amounted to an orchestrated campaign of hatred against the Jews, and to a lesser degree the Germans and Ukrainians, and those political parties that showed any willingness to cooperate with them.

Moreover, an analysis of the popular vote reveals that a center-left coalition actually had the support of the majority of "ethnic" Poles, as these were defined by the National Democrats themselves. Based on the popular vote, a center-left coalition would have had the support of some 62 percent of ethnic Poles.[34]

Parliamentary election results and popular vote, without the Bloc

	Popular vote (%)	National Assembly (%)
Left	2,685,982 (39.4)	138 (31)
Right	2,551,582 (37.4)	216 (49)
Piast	1,153,397 (16.9)	88 (20)
Others	431,482 (6.3)	—
Total	6,822,443 (100)	442 (100)

In addition to a multitude of smaller parties, "Others" includes the Communists and the Polish Center (Polskie Centrum) party. Between them, these two parties received almost 400,000 votes. Although neither could be properly classified as part of the pro-Piłsudski left, both were closer to the latter than to the National Democrats.
Source: Nohlen and Stöver, Elections in Europe: A Data Handbook, 1500.

Therefore, the Endek position was highly inconsistent. On the one hand, the NDs rejected the constitutional provision that the majority of deputies in the National Assembly had the right to choose the president as "artificial" and not representative of the "Polish nation." But on the other, they chose to accept the equally legalistic and even more artificial allocation of seats in the Sejm and Senate, which clearly did not reflect the preferences of the majority of ethnic Polish voters. Finally, the National Democrats' obsession with the Bloc as a Jewish political party was also misplaced. To be sure, the Jews were the largest group in the Bloc, but they constituted no more than 40 percent of its deputies, the rest being made up of Ukrainians, Germans, Belarusians, and a small number of Russians.[35]

But despite these obvious inconsistencies, and the glaring fact that the majority of "ethnic" Poles supported the centrist and the leftist parties, subsequent events would show that the discourse of the "Polish majority" carried an immense power to mobilize. Indeed, the effectiveness of the discourse of the Polish majority illustrates the proposition, apocryphally attributed to Lenin, that a lie told often enough becomes the truth. The left would continue to point out that it had the majority of the Poles behind it. But, as we will see, its rhetoric was more complicated. It lacked catchy slogans, was based on an appeal to reason rather than one based on emotions, and was not driven home with the same relentlessness and intensity.

While the previous National Democratic call for "national unity" was rather vague and gained what coherence it had only in the face of an equally vague "Jewish threat," the Doctrine of the Polish Majority rendered this threat starkly concrete. Specifically, it came to be *embodied* by the materializing alliance between the National Minorities Bloc and the Endeks' other opponents in the National Assembly. By explicitly linking their (general) fear of a Jewish conspiracy to takeover Poland to a very specific political event (the emergence of an anti-ND coalition involving the national minorities), the Endeks effectively set up a tripwire, the transgression of which would be immediately discernible to their followers. Thus, the trigger for violence was set in place and ready to be pulled.

The Defense of the Civic Nation

Since it was clear that the National Democrats would never be able to work with the Bloc of National Minorities, one might assume that the left could be assured of the Bloc's support. As such, we may surmise, it had for all practical purposes won the election. In fact, however, the situation was more complicated. The entire spectrum of the left and the center-left parties, from the PPS to Piast, was dismayed by the Bloc's success. Even before the elections, the very existence of the Bloc was widely perceived as a manifestation of nationalist and anti-Polish sentiments among the minorities. Its creation was seen as the minorities' reaction to National Democratic attacks, but two wrongs did not necessarily make a right. As *Głos Prawdy* wrote, the Bloc had to be seen in the context of the "incessant barking of Polish, Ukrainian, Jewish, and German nationalists."[36] The real battle in Polish politics was between the "camp of democracy," and the "swamp of chauvinism"—and in this battle, the Bloc was unmistakably in the latter camp.[37]

The matter was also aggravated by personal politics and specifically Yitzhak Grünbaum's impetuous and highly abrasive political style.[38] Grünbaum had positioned himself and the Jews at the center of the Bloc and assumed a highly prominent role as its organizer and spokesperson. In doing so, he probably succeeded in making the Bloc even less popular than it would have been otherwise.[39] Finally, as the PPS daily *Robotnik* pointed out, there was no real community of interests between the Bloc and the Polish left, since the overwhelming majority of the Bloc's deputies "had nothing whatsoever to do with democracy, social progress, or the left." *Robotnik* went on to argue that Grünbaum's General Zionists were "the instrument of the Jewish bourgeoisie, and [as such] just as radically nationalistic and intolerant as the most radical National Democrats."[40] While there was obviously a good dose of hyperbole in this claim, it was true that the Bloc and the left had little in common ideologically.

Superficially, it may be possible to say that the Polish left and the Bloc both subscribed to a civic view of the nation. In reality, however, their respective views on the question of nationality and citizenship were very different. Left-wing Polish parties were prepared to give territorial autonomy to the eastern Borderlands and civic equality to all citizens regardless of ethnicity, religion, and so on. But they were emphatically opposed to notions of nonterritorial autonomy, which was what the Zionists wanted, or to territorial autonomy for the Germans in the west. The Zionists, on the other hand, who were largely responsible for organizing the Bloc, can only be described as a nationalist movement in that they demanded the official recognition of the Jews as a nationality, with corporate communal rights and nonterritorial autonomy. No Polish party or movement was prepared to accept these demands.

Still, these important considerations aside, there is little doubt that an unspoken factor behind the left's decidedly cool attitude toward the Bloc was the Doctrine of the Polish Majority. Too close an association with the Bloc could perhaps be politically damaging. Indeed, the National Democrats clearly took delight in the left's "dilemma." According to *Gazeta Warszawska*, "even the biggest enemies of 'Endek nationalism' were not sure if they should accept the presidency from Jewish hands."[41] But despite having little love for the Bloc, and for Grünbaum in particular, there is no doubt that prior to the presidential elections, Poland's left-wing press consistently upheld the right of national minorities to participate as fully fledged partners in the democratic process.

Indeed, the National Democrats' articulation of the Doctrine of the Polish Majority provoked an important public debate and prompted left-wing journalists to offer spirited rebuttals to the claim that the minorities had no right to participate in political life. The moderately conservative *Kurjer Polski* lamented the "inexplicable tendency" of the National Democrats to attack the Bloc by claiming that "every move" made by the national minority deputies "must be harmful towards Poland," and went on to point out that Gladstone frequently made use of Irish votes in pursuing his agenda in Parliament. If a powerful and "civilized" nation like Britain could utilize the votes of its minorities constructively, then surely Poland could do the same.[42] The article went on to offer the following image of the Polish nation: "Every individual . . . must be led to that great camp whose slogan is the strength and good of the state without regard for difference of language, [where all] can find protection under the buckler of the state, within their boundaries, specified by law."[43]

The socialist organ *Robotnik* went further in pointing out the absurdity of the National Democratic position: "Statistics tell us that almost 1/3 of the people of Poland are not Polish. . . . Therefore, it is a fact that the Polish Republic is not a state of only one nation. . . . The [National Democrats] proclaim: minorities do exist, they have 88 deputies in the Sejm, but we should act as if neither the minorities nor their deputies existed. Don't acknowledge them! Or rather acknowledge them but only so as to engage them in constant battle. The voices of the minorities must not count, neither in the choice of the President of the Republic nor of the government!"[44] The article then went on to attack the National Democrats' demands for numerus clausus, blamed Polish nationalist intolerance for the fact the Jews were currently "reinforcing their sense of national separateness," and argued that National Democratic antisemitism was modeled on Tsarist Russia. It concluded by noting that the Polish state would be "terribly weakened" if "the Polish nation was unable to deal with the question of national minorities."[45]

Droga was skeptical about the commitment of the National Minorities Bloc to the well-being of Poland, and saw the Bloc rather as the manifestation of Jewish, German, and Ukrainian nationalisms. But it nevertheless expressed the hope that the Polish left would reach an accommodation with civically minded elements among the national minorities.[46] The radical Piłsudskiite *Głos Prawdy* reminded its readers that the minorities were citizens and legal voters, even as it hedged its bets by stating that the majority of ethnic Poles voted "for Piłsudski."

At the same time, many left-wing journalists felt compelled to *acknowledge* the Doctrine of the Polish Majority, even while giving primacy to other considerations. On November 18, *Robotnik* wrote: "The Coalition's desperate cries that the Sejm and the senate have no moral right to . . . take the national minorities into account when choosing the Head of State . . . are laughable in the face of statistics. From a constitutional and civic point of view such nationalistic arguments, which are a poor disguise for . . . partisan reactionary interests, are inadmissible. However, in light of the election results among Polish society, they are a totally unsubstantiated conceit . . . because the Polish nation gave the majority of its votes . . . to parties of the left."[47]

The fact that even the NDs' most committed enemies felt the need to *also* present their argument in terms of the Doctrine of the Polish Majority (even as they disavowed it!) illustrates the instability of the civic or liberal conception of the nation and the rhetorical power of National Democratic discourse. Despite this, in the period between the Sejm and presidential elections, the left forcefully defended a multiethnic or civic vision of the Polish state and the right of the minorities to participate in politics as full partners, even, or precisely, as *national* minorities.

The Accidental President

The unlikely choice of Gabriel Narutowicz as the left's de facto candidate also had a considerable impact on the National Democrats' ability to present the Poles with a vision of an imminent Jewish takeover of their country, and it is important to understand the context that led to the selection of this unknown and unlikely candidate. Despite the considerable length of time that elapsed between the conclusion of the parliamentary vote and the presidential elections, which were scheduled for December 9, the latter caught the parties of the center and left totally unprepared. The reason for this was Marshal Piłsudski's announcement, made public only on December 4, that he would refuse to accept the presidency. In retrospect, Piłsudski's decision should have been anticipated—the constitutional prerogatives of the president had been stripped away by the National Democratic authors of the constitution precisely to make the office unattractive for him. Nevertheless, leaders of the major left-wing parties believed until the very end that he might be persuaded to run, and it was only the public and categorical rejection of this idea by Piłsudski, less than a week before the elections, that forced them to consider possible substitutes.[48]

This was no easy task. Piłsudski was probably the only person readily accept-able to the entire spectrum of center-left parties. Moreover, his popularity and charisma would render the role played by national minorities in his election relatively less important. While the National Democrats were not beyond calling the marshal a "tool of the Jews," voting for Piłsudski, even in the company of the minorities, would have a decidedly different flavor than voting for a less-popular candidate against the wishes of the self-appointed "Polish majority." Finally, Piłsudski's own instructions to his followers made the task of choosing a suitable candidate singularly complicated. In his farewell speech, Piłsudski outlined the qualities he believed his successor would need to possess. According to the mar-shal, the new president would have to be a man of compromise and not too closely affiliated with any single party.[49] This obviously disqualified party leaders and most well-known political figures, who not surprisingly found it difficult to stay neutral in the polarized environment of Polish politics.

It obviously would have made sense for the left to agree on a joint candidate. Indeed, the Socialists and National Laborites immediately announced their sup-port for any candidate agreed on by the two peasant parties, Piast and Emanci-pation. But such an agreement proved exceedingly difficult, due to a legacy of bad blood between the latter two. Emancipation wanted the left to elect a com-mon candidate, but since Piast's Maciej Rataj had already been elected speaker of the Sejm, it feared its rival Piast acquiring yet another high-profile office. Emancipation's leader Stanisław Thugutt rejected the candidacy of Stanisław Wojciechowski, a former Socialist and friend of Piłsudski from the early PPS days, because of his close association with Piast. He also rejected the suggestion of Jan Fryze, the influential editor of the *Kurjer Poranny*, that Witos become pres-ident while Thugutt himself get the post of premier.[50]

While there is no conclusive evidence of this, it appears that Witos, a politician of considerable talent and ambition, wanted the presidency for himself and was willing to cooperate with either the left or the right in order to get it.[51] At the very least, he seemed to be hedging his bets, and allowed his party to negotiate with the National Democrats. But while Witos may have been willing to have the National Democrats help *him* to the presidency, he rejected their continuous bar-rage of entreaties and threats and refused to support any of *their* candidates. Even as the National Democrats produced ever new "moderate" contenders, hoping that one of them would gain Piast's support, the wily Witos kept demurring and waited, in all likelihood, for his own candidacy to be raised.[52] His spokesperson kept all options open.[53] Who would blink first? The brinkmanship continued until the very eve of the election.

Kurjer Warszawski described the scene at Parliament on the evening of December 8 in the following words: "On the fortnight of the presidential election, despite the holiday, the Parliament was buzzing with political activity. From the early hours of the morning until late at night, the presidiums of all the parliamentary clubs were in session without any breaks, conferences between clubs took place, and in the backrooms we saw animation not seen even in the most heated moments of crisis in the old Sejm."[54] Piast, Emancipation, PPS, and National Labor held one more joint conference on the morning of December 9, with only hours to go before the election. The PPS evidently hoped to persuade the two peasant parties to agree on a common candidate, but to no avail.[55] In a spectacular display of either brinkmanship or incompetence, or perhaps a mixture of the two, the official candidates of the three left-wing parties were announced with only minutes to go before the election.

One of the most bizarre features of these discussions was that no one thought of including the Bloc of Minorities in the decision-making process. While there is no doubt that important and legitimate differences separated the Polish left from the minorities, the fact that the left did not even consider consulting the Bloc on tactical questions or invite its members to *any* shared deliberations is a testament to the power of the Doctrine of the Polish Majority and the fear of how the perception of working with the Jews might be interpreted by the Polish public. As Bernard Singer, the parliamentary correspondent of the Jewish *Nasz Przegląd* (*Our Review*), wrote, "the deputies of the Bloc dreamed of only one thing: getting close to the left, and making contact with the PPS, Emancipation, and so on."[56] And yet the call never came. Thugutt informed the Belarusians, Ukrainians, and Jews as to who would be his party's candidate no more than a few minutes before the vote, asking for their support and not providing any further details. While the Ukrainians and Belarusians immediately promised their support, the Jews raised a number of objections. But there was no time to discuss them—the bell signifying the start of the National Assembly session was "already ringing," and both Thugutt and his Jewish interlocutors had to run to take their seats.[57] This was more or less the extent of the cooperation between the Polish left and the minorities prior to the vote.

On the morning of December 9, 1922, when the National Assembly convened to elect the first president of the Republic of Poland, the deputies were presented with five alternatives. The National Democrats opted for Count Maurycy Zamoyski, then Polish ambassador to France. The candidacy of Zamoyski, unveiled on the morning of the election, was a last-minute change of plans—as late as the previous night, the NDs were still rumored to be putting forth the veteran Wojciech

Trąmpczyński as their candidate. Trąmpczyński was dropped only when the National Democrats realized that there was no chance of anyone but themselves voting for him. Zamoyski, it was hoped, would be different. Though a National Democrat, he was considered an amicable "man of compromise" and had friendly personal relations with Piłsudski and a number of his followers.[58]

It therefore appears that the last-minute replacement was intended to win over Piast. However, in what can only be attributed to a gross failure of political foresight, the National Democrats neglected to take into account the fact that, however moderate he may have been, Count Zamoyski also happened to be the largest individual landowner in Poland. At a time when land reform and the parcellation of great estates were the most burning questions for the peasant parties, his vast landholdings meant he would never be able to win support from Piast.[59]

Piast put forth the candidacy of Stanisław Wojciechowski, founding PPS member and close friend of Piłsudski in the early 1900s. By the 1910s, however, Wojciechowski had distanced himself from party politics, renounced socialism, and was engaged in the peasant cooperative movement. During World War I he worked closely with a number of National Democratic politicians and was seen as a compromise candidate. Emancipation, in turn, put forward the candidacy of Gabriel Narutowicz, a world-famous professor of engineering, who returned to Poland after decades of emigration in Switzerland to run the Ministry of Public Works, and later the Ministry of Foreign Affairs. Narutowicz was an ardent follower of Piłsudski, and a key backroom architect of the National Civic Union. While he was influential in political backrooms and held in high esteem by those who came in contact with him, he was virtually unknown to the general public.

Despite Narutowicz's ideas being more in line with those of Piłsudski, it was Wojciechowski who had the latter's support. There were a number of reasons for this. First, Wojciechowski's adventure with socialism was long over, and he was perceived as being only slightly to the left of center. He was tolerable to the left, had the backing of Piast, and had successfully cooperated with the National Democrats in the past. He had also been a close friend of Piłsudski and had no party affiliation or political base of his own from which to work. According to some, Piłsudski believed that he would be able to control him from behind the scenes.[60] Narutowicz, on the other hand, had shown fierce independence of judgment on particular issues, even in the face of personal pressure from Piłsudski.[61] In fact, there is evidence that Piłsudski attempted to exert pressure through "his people" in both the PPS and Emancipation in order to prevent the candidacy of Narutowicz from ever coming into being. In this case, Thugutt, generally a loyal Piłsudskiite, stuck to his guns and refused to drop Narutowicz.[62]

The Bloc of Minorities, spurned by the left, put forth its own candidate, Jan Baudouin de Courtenay, a renowned professor of linguistics and a political maverick, who had no chance of being elected.[63] The same was true of Ignacy Daszyński, the candidate of the PPS and the party's leader. Upon Daszyński's inevitable defeat, the PPS was ready to follow Piłsudski's directives and vote for Wojciechowski.[64]

As outlined by the constitution, the election would be an exceedingly complicated affair. If no candidate received an absolute majority, another identical vote would be held. If the second vote failed to produce a result, the candidate with the lowest number of votes would be removed from the list, and a third vote would be held. The voting would continue in this manner until one candidate reached an absolute majority of the votes. This arrangement is of critical importance, because the particular manner in which the votes were split later worked to strengthen the Doctrine of the Polish Majority.

As noon approached, the parliamentary clubs frantically prepared their formal candidacies. In the press gallery, journalists placed bets on who would be elected, with Wojciechowski and Narutowicz being the favorites.[65] The diplomats' gallery was nearly full. Through the window, one could see groups of onlookers huddled outside the Sejm to await the results. On the floor, the conditions were chaotic. Since the Sejm and Senate had never before met together, the room was overcrowded, and despite some extra chairs having been hastily brought into the building, there was a shortage of seating space.[66] The voting procedure, in which each vote took more than an hour and was followed by a thirty-minute break during which hurried huddles and ad hoc conferences were held, "stretched the deputies' nerves to their very limits."[67]

In the first vote, predictably, the parties all voted for their own candidates. But the nervous atmosphere only intensified.[68] During the break, in the backrooms and the cafeteria, rumors spread. According to some, the wily Christian Democrat Wojciech Korfanty managed to convince a portion of the right-wing deputies to vote for Baudouin de Courtenay—so that the runoff vote could be held between Zamoyski and the minorities' candidate.[69]

In the second vote, PPS abandoned Daszyński for Wojciechowski, thereby following Piłsudski's will, while the Bloc abandoned Baudouin de Courtenay for Narutowicz. It seems, however, that a number of German deputies backed the National Democratic candidate.[70] At any rate, while the Bloc deputies knew almost nothing about Narutowicz, they distrusted Wojciechowski because of the latter's willingness to engage in talks with the right. Daszyński was eliminated, while Baudouin de Courtenay held on with ten votes.[71] After the third vote, Baudouin de Courtenay was eliminated. The right steadfastly voted for their man Zamoyski.

At this point it should have become clear to everyone that the combined votes of Emancipation and the Bloc would trump those of Piast and the PPS, and that Narutowicz would make it into the final round to face off against Zamoyski, thanks to the votes of the minorities. Realizing this, Grünbaum, whose deputies were already being threatened by the National Democrats, asked Thugutt whether he was fully aware of "the stakes of the game being played, and what its consequences might be." Thugutt simply replied that it was too late to turn back.[72]

In the fourth vote, which would decide whether it would be Wojciechowski or Narutowicz who faced Zamoyski, Narutowicz's cause was further strengthened by nine renegade PPS deputies who, contrary to the decision taken by their party's leadership, wanted to prove their independence from Piłsudski.[73] It also appears that Narutowicz received the votes of four National Democrats, who believed that it would be to Zamoyski's advantage to face him rather than Wojciechowski in the runoff. In any case, both interventions were unnecessary—the votes of Emancipation and the minorities alone were enough to put Narutowicz through.

According to the right-wing press, the news that the runoff would be between Narutowicz and Zamoyski filled the National Democrats' backrooms with hope that Piast might now reconsider voting against the "Polish majority" and opt for the "national candidate."[74] Indeed, Piast found itself in an awkward position. Voting for Wojciechowski, a farm-cooperative activist and their own candidate, even in the company of the national minorities, would have been significantly different than opting for Narutowicz, an unknown Swiss-educated academic and reputed Freemason, whose victory over Wojciechowski had been assured by the Minorities Bloc. The alternative was no more appealing. Not only did Piast have little love for the National Democrats, but as mentioned earlier, Zamoyski was Poland's largest individual landowner—the bête noire of virtually all smallholders and middle-sized peasants. Given this situation, in the break preceding the final vote, Piast held an emergency meeting. After heated debate, a fateful decision was made.[75] Witos claims that he urged his party to vote for Zamoyski, but the rank-and-file deputies distrusted "the Count" and that sentiment carried the day.[76]

Thus Piast deputies were set to unanimously vote for Narutowicz. With that, Zamoyski's fate was sealed. Narutowicz carried the day by 289 votes to the latter's 227. Yet, the mood in the Sejm was far from jubilant. According to the somewhat tendentious report in the *Gazeta Warszawska*, the announcement of Narutowicz's victory was greeted with only scattered applause, even on the left half of the Sejm.[77]

Presidential election results

	First vote	Second vote	Third vote	Fourth vote	Fifth vote
Zamoyski	222	228	228	224	227
Narutowicz	62	151	158	171	289
Wojciechowski	105	152	150	146	—
Baudouin de Courtenay	103	10	5	—	—
Daszyński	49	1	—	—	—
Spoiled votes	4	3	3	4	29
Total	545	545	544	545	545

Source: Protokół Zgromadzenia Narodowego.

It is important to take a brief look at Narutowicz's political background and try to understand the mechanics behind his unlikely selection as Emancipation's presidential candidate. Gabriel Narutowicz was born in the village of Telesze (Telšiai) in Lithuania in 1865, into a noble Polish-Lithuanian family distantly related to the Piłsudskis. Their common background and sensibilities as nobles from the multiethnic eastern Borderlands would almost immediately draw Piłsudski and Narutowicz close.[78] Their personal life stories also shared many common features—both men were raised primarily by their mothers and, in the wake of the failure of the January Uprising, brought up in a very similar and intensely patriotic atmosphere that stressed the traditions of the Grand Duchy of Lithuania. In fact, Narutowicz's brother, Stanisław, was a signatory of Lithuania's declaration of independence and devoted his political life to the failed mission of creating a political space for Polish-speaking Lithuanians in that country.[79]

While Narutowicz and Piłsudski shared many formative influences, sensibilities, and a common vision of the Polish nation, their lives could not have unfolded more differently.[80] Narutowicz began studies in engineering in Saint Petersburg, but because of poor health, in 1886 he was sent by his family to Davos, Switzerland. He subsequently enrolled at the Zurich Polytechnic. Loose involvement in a socialist revolutionary group led to his being briefly arrested by the Swiss police. The incident itself was not significant, except for the fact that the Tsarist authorities issued a warrant for his arrest that effectively prevented him from returning home. Thus, Narutowicz stayed in Switzerland, where he became a professor at the Zurich Polytechnic and a universally respected specialist in hydroelectric engineering.

Consumed by his career, Narutowicz had no effective involvement in the Polish cause until the outbreak of World War I, at which point he became active in fundraising and propaganda work on behalf of Piłsudski's legionary movement.

Narutowicz took some time before making the fateful decision to give up his successful and comfortable life and "return" to Poland, a country he had never actually lived in—his home in Telesze was now part of the independent state of Lithuania. But patriotism appears to have triumphed in his heart, and in September 1919 he accepted the position of minister of public works in the Polish government. He would remain in this post, despite the ever-changing cabinets around him, until 1922. Following his impressive performance at the Peace Conference in Genoa in April 1922, he was asked to assume the post of the minister of foreign affairs. His work at the ministry won accolades from Piłsudski and his supporters.[81] In the elections of 1922, Narutowicz was involved in creating the National Civic Union and contested the election as part of the Civic Union of the Borderlands. Like the rest of that party, he was soundly defeated.

While Narutowicz was a fervent supporter of Piłsudski, he was not, as we have seen, Piłsudski's choice for the presidency. In fact, Piłsudski advised Narutowicz to turn down the nomination, and his operatives worked behind the scenes to ensure the success of Wojciechowski. The idea of putting forth the candidacy of Narutowicz was largely the handiwork of Emancipation's leader, Stanisław Thugutt. Indeed, outside the narrow coterie of Piłsudskiites and progressive Warsaw liberals, Narutowicz was almost entirely unknown. As Thugutt recollects, his selection of Narutowicz as the party's candidate raised some objections from the rank and file, because only a few of the deputies knew anything about him.[82] Even Thugutt himself had only a vague grasp of Narutowicz's stance on many issues. However, he believed that the latter was neither a socialist nor a populist but a "moderate Swiss radical," and thus fulfilled Piłsudski's requirement of not being an overly partisan candidate.[83]

Still Emancipation's choice of Narutowicz was particularly strange not only given Piłsudski's preference for Wojciechowski, which had been communicated to Thugutt rather clearly, but also due to the jarring disconnect between Narutowicz's persona as a worldly and sophisticated nobleman, and Emancipation's peasant base of support.[84] Nor was Narutowicz himself particularly eager to become a presidential candidate. Encouraged by Piłsudski, he initially resisted Thugutt's entreaties, claiming everything from poor health to the lack of knowledge of Polish politics. Only after putting up a "long and bitter fight," he conditionally agreed, saying: "I do not want to put forth my candidacy, but if Emancipation decides to do it, there is nothing I can do."[85]

As we have seen, Narutowicz's election was largely the result of contingent factors. Thugutt's eccentric and intransigent personality, the conflict between Emancipation and Piast, the Bloc's antipathy for Wojciechowski, and the Endeks' disastrous championing of Poland's most prolific landowner, all conspired to raise Narutowicz to the highest post in the country. Yet, while his victory was the result of a series of accidents, Narutowicz appeared to be the perfect target for the right's claims that the election had been fixed by "the Jews" and imposed upon the Polish majority. As Thugutt writes, Narutowicz "immediately made the impression of a man of very subtle and very deep culture of thought and character."[86] According to Piłsudski, he immediately stood among Polish politicians as a "true European."[87] This worldly and "European" persona and his dignified bearing rendered Narutowicz offensive to populist sensibilities, even for many on the left. As Pragier writes, many rank-and-file Socialists disliked Narutowicz because they believed that "he was too great a lord."[88]

If this was the sentiment on the left, we can only imagine how the right would perceive the new president. Given his Lithuanian and Swiss background and his worldly connections, Narutowicz was particularly easy to present "as some kind of overseas devil or Elder of Zion."[89] Wojciechowski, a more plebeian figure, elicited more familiarity and sympathy among populists on both the left and the right. While there is no doubt that, with the possible exception of Piłsudski, any candidate chosen with the aid of the National Minorities Bloc would have been the target of widespread protests by the NDs, Narutowicz was tailor-made to act as the lightning rod for the right's anger. His accidental election was only the last in a series of contingent factors that conspired to trigger the violence of the "December Events" and set the scene for the murder of the president himself.

5

The Unrepentant Right

Historians are almost unanimous in their agreement that the murder of the president by the "madman," as he is usually referred to, Niewiadomski was an embarrassment and a political setback for the nationalist movement in Poland.[1] Despite having been so vocal in their opposition to the illegitimate "Jewish president," the National Democrats did not attempt to utilize the murder in order to stage a bid for power. Quite the opposite, the initial reaction of the right-wing press appeared to be outright panic. Writing in the highbrow nationalist weekly *Myśl Narodowa*, one of the key literary figures of the right, Adolf Nowaczyński, explicitly sought to refute charges made by the left and the minorities, both of which believed that the murder was a long-term political victory for them. In his article, Nowaczyński cited Apolinary Hartglas, a leader of the Zionists, who wrote: "The president of Poland fell. But along with him fell the [National Democrats] who revealed to the world their true, disgusting faces. The idea of the [civic] state will step over the dead body of the NDs, and continue to flourish."[2] The same sentiments were expressed at an important socialist rally by the Polish Socialist Party leader, Ignacy Daszyński, who argued that by murdering the president, the National Democrats had "committed suicide."[3]

In order to refute these charges, the primary strategy espoused by writers like Nowaczyński was to distance themselves from the murderer and to portray the latter as a mentally unbalanced renegade. "The madman," wrote Nowaczyński, "who committed this heinous murder did the worst favor and the most terrible harm to the ideals and interests of the [nationalist] movement, which in a moment of failure of all his mental faculties, he may have thought he was trying to help."[4] In sum, Nowaczyński pleaded that Niewiadomski not be taken as a representative of the National Democratic movement as a whole.

Indeed, in the first few days, all right-wing journalists appeared to be doing absolutely everything in their power in order to disassociate themselves from the murder and its perpetrator. Their condemnation of Niewiadomski was as scathing as it was unanimous. *Gazeta Warszawska* immediately proclaimed that all Poles were "deeply touched by the heinous assassination."[5] Similarly, Stanisław Stroński who had just a few days before branded Narutowicz as "their [i.e., the Jews'] President" now claimed him for the *entire* nation.[6] "Today, the whole nation sees in the murdered president of the Republic not a representative of their own or the enemy political camp," he wrote in the *Rzeczpospolita* in a stunning reversal of his earlier position, "but a representative of the state and, even more so, the victim of a crime which calls for universal condemnation."[7] Yet, this attitude of contrition, if that is indeed what it was, did not last long. In fact, the process of turning Niewiadomski from a "madman" to a nationalist hero, took place in a matter of weeks. In this chapter I will examine this surprising transformation and explain its significance for understanding the future of Polish politics.

The murderer: Eligiusz Niewiadomski poses in front of a painting of his wife, Marie de Tilly. (reprinted with permission of Małgorzata Karolina Piekarska)

The Madman

Whether the sense of outrage expressed by right-wing journalists like Stroński was sincere or not may be debated, but there is no doubt that fear of retribution from the left played at least some role in their initial reaction to the murder. Left-wing newspapers were adamant in their claims that Niewiadomski was doing nothing more than acting upon the calls of the right-wing journalists, and that the latter bore true responsibility for the murder. "We will not stop talking about this," wrote Stanisław Posner in the Socialist *Robotnik*. "We will not let you forget that you are the guilty ones."[8] Meanwhile, in *Kurjer Poranny*, Piast deputy Antoni Anusz demanded that it was not the "blind instrument" but the "hand that directed it" that deserved punishment for the crime.[9]

To deflect criticism of this sort, *Rzeczpospolita* expressed the hope that the "authorities" would lead a thorough investigation into the crime and reject the temptation to exploit it for political purposes.[10] *Gazeta Warszawska* also immediately attempted to distance itself from Eligiusz Niewiadomski, "a man whose state of mental health had been dubious for a long time."[11] There was also a concerted effort to show that Niewiadomski was not to be identified with the National Democratic movement. *Gazeta Warszawska* pointed out he had once had a physical altercation with Antoni Sadzewicz, the editor of the fellow National Democratic newspaper *Gazeta Poranna* (*Morning Newspaper*), in order to show that he should not be considered a National Democrat.[12]

The right-wing press was correct on two accounts. First, contrary to what most of Narutowicz's supporters initially assumed, it soon became clear that Niewiadomski acted alone and was not linked to a wider right-wing conspiracy.[13] Secondly, he was not a member of any of the National Democratic parties or organizations. While for the purposes of this chapter Niewiadomski is interesting mainly insofar as his actions and character were evaluated, interpreted, and judged by other Poles, it is nevertheless important to briefly consider the trajectory of his life.[14]

Though Niewiadomski was not actively involved in politics, he cannot be described as being unknown. In fact, the man who shook the very foundations of the Second Republic had enjoyed a distinguished career as a painter and an art critic. Niewiadomski was born in Warsaw in 1869. His mother died when he was two years old, and thereafter he was raised by his older sister Cecylia. After finishing high school, he studied art in Warsaw before attending the Saint Petersburg Academy of Fine Arts in 1890. By all accounts he was a distinguished student, and in 1892 he won a government fellowship to continue his studies, as well as a number of other prizes. In 1895 he spent a year in Paris studying fine arts and exhibiting his work. At that point, according to his own account, he strongly sympathized with socialism.[15] Upon returning to Warsaw he continued painting, taught technical drawing at the Polytechnic, and became involved in art criticism, writing reviews for influential publications like *Tygodnik Ilustrowany* (*Illustrated Courier*) and *Kurjer Warszawski* (*Warsaw Courier*). Like many painters of his day, Niewiadomski became an avid mountaineer. He hiked in the Tatra Mountains and painted numerous alpine landscapes. In 1898 he married Maria Natalia de Tilly. His son, Stefan, was born in 1900, and daughter, Anna, in 1902.

Niewiadomski's political views were gradually moving away from socialism and toward nationalism, and in 1897 he joined the National League. Returning from his trips to the Tatra mountains, he smuggled issues of illegal National Democratic publications into Russian Poland. In 1900 he became involved in organizing the Towarzystwo Oświaty Narodowej (Society for National Education), a secret organization created by the National League in order to spread its ideas among workers and peasants. Thus, in many respects, Niewiadomski's political involvement mirrored that of many other National Democratic activists who would later rise to leading positions in the movement.

But this political trajectory was suddenly derailed. On the night of April 2, 1901, Niewiadomski was arrested by the Tsarist secret police, after issues of National Democratic publications were found during a search of his apartment. He spent a few days in the Pawiak Prison, and then four months at the Warsaw Citadel. For many Polish political activists, especially, though not exclusively, among the left, time in a Russian prison was a constant occupational hazard. Yet, this relatively brief contact with the Russian penal system seems to have had a powerful effect on Niewiadomski. Although he was released after a relatively short time for lack of evidence, Niewiadomski immediately resigned from the National League. In fact, for all appearances he gave up political activity altogether. From 1901 until 1918, he continued to teach, paint, and write. During this period he became involved in a number of artistic and personal controversies and earned a reputation for being touchy and quick to anger. But, until Poland regained its independence, he was never again involved in politics.

During World War I, he played no role in the struggle for independence. In March 1918, he secured a position as a civil servant with the Ministry of Culture and Art of the German-sponsored Regency Council (Rada Regencyjna). But when Poland became an independent state, his courage appeared to return. During the Polish-Soviet War he volunteered to join the army, and received a position in the Second Bureau of the General Staff, which dealt with counterintelligence. He promptly resigned from his position because, as claimed at his trial, he was shocked by the Second Department's incompetence and inability to deal with subversive communist activity.[16] He was then transferred to a reserve infantry formation and, upon his own request, sent to the front.

Following the end of hostilities, he returned to a position at the ministry, but resigned in November of 1921 when funds for his department were cut, and returned to teaching. Again, he did not become involved in the National Democratic movement or in any other form of political activity. As an active and well-known painter, and a member of the *Zachęta* society, he had no problems gaining access to the exhibition where he would commit the fateful murder.

Therefore, the right's disavowals of Niewiadomski could appear to be credible. He had not belonged to the National League or any of its affiliates since 1901 and had a reputation for being emotionally unstable. But while one might have expected the murder to provide an opportunity for the right to moderate some of its more extreme claims, especially those concerning the supposedly "illegitimate" nature of Narutowicz's election, this was not to be the case. In fact, the image of Niewiadomski as a "madman," which proliferated in the right-wing press in the first days following the assassination, would soon undergo a profound transformation.

But before the mechanics of this process are discussed, it is necessary to frame it in its political context. To be sure, the panic that gripped many National Democratic writers after the murder of Narutowicz had a solid grounding in reality. The anger of the left was palpable, and a violent retaliation for the murder of Narutowicz was a very real possibility. However, as we have seen, the anger felt by many rank-and-file Socialists and Piłsudskiites was successfully contained by senior parliamentary leaders like Ignacy Daszyński and Stanisław Thugutt, who remained beholden to democracy and the constitution. As a result, the left squandered its chance to seize power and force a violent reckoning with the NDs. Instead, it was the moderate centrists, led by Rataj and Sikorski, who tentatively emerged as the rulers of post-Narutowicz Poland. The new premier, Sikorski, was not interested in confronting the National Democrats. In his very first address to the nation, he made it clear that his government would not exact vengeance for the murder of Narutowicz and sternly warned that attempts by the left to do so would not be tolerated: "Despite the understandable anger with which society is reacting to the murder of the President, I demand that everyone unconditionally keep their peace. The government has fulfilled its duty. The ones guilty of this perfidious murder will meet just and lawful punishment. But at the same time, any kind of vigilante action will be stopped with full determination."[17]

In keeping with his speech, no one was arrested for inciting the president's assassination, and the efforts of the prosecution focused on the one man who carried it out.[18] There can be no doubt that upon hearing Sikorski's words, nationalist writers like Stroński and Nowaczyński, who were accused by the left of inciting the murder, breathed a sigh of relief.

The right's recovery of poise and its reaffirmation of the principles that had led to the murder are extraordinary, and can be traced through an analysis of Niewiadomski's depiction on the pages of *Gazeta Warszawska*, Poland's leading National Democratic newspaper. On December 17, in a front-page article entitled "The Tragic Conflict," *Gazeta Warszawska* presented a position that was significantly different from the fearful disavowals of Niewiadomski published a mere day earlier.[19] To be sure, the paper reiterated that the murder "was in nobody's interest." However, it also acknowledged that the nation was governed by its own laws and subject to its own "actions and reactions," which were beyond the control of any political forces or organizations. Since the election of the president, the key question facing all of Polish society was whether the nation would have its sovereignty "taken over" by the Jews. This new slavery was not, like the partitions, "external." Rather, it had been created by the "willing compromise of the Poles with the enemy." The president, according to *Gazeta Warszawska*, was a casualty of the nation's "reaction" to this state of affairs, and "became a victim of this conflict not as a person but as a symbol."[20] Of course, *Gazeta Warszawska* still condemned the actual act of the murder. However, it was gradually moving toward portraying the latter as something natural and inevitable, beyond the active agency of any political party or actor.

Just as Narutowicz was being deprived of his individuality and rendered into a "symbol" of Jewish control, so Niewiadomski was also beginning to undergo a somewhat slower process of symbolic metamorphosis in the National Democratic press. In this process, his individual act and motivation came to be imbued with, and eventually subsumed by, a broader and deeper symbolic meaning. Thus, a mere day after the murder, *Gazeta Warszawska* no longer portrayed the murder as the "irresponsible" reaction of a "lunatic," but as the more or less natural "reaction" of society as a whole.[21] The process of rehabilitating the murderer, and turning him into a symbol of Polish resistance to the Jewish threat, was beginning to take shape a mere day after the murder.

On December 18, *Gazeta Warszawska* explicitly drew the "link between the murder and the election of the president [by the Jews]."[22] Again the newspaper stopped well short of endorsing the action, but by positing a clear causal relationship between the two events, it effectively accomplished two rhetorical goals. First, such a framing of the issue was a clever defense against the culpability of the nationalist movement. If the election of the president by the Jews would *inevitably* result in the nation "recoiling and expressing its outrage" in unpredictable ways, then the right-wing journalists and politicians could not be blamed for the murder. Thus, it was a mistake for the left to blame "everything on intermediary factors, such as articles and speeches." The latter were merely *symptoms* of public outrage, and not the *causes* of the murder—which was itself also a symptom of the public anger at the role played by the Jews in the elections.

Secondly, by portraying the murder as the natural result of the manner in which the president had been elected, rather than of its own agitation, the right also reconfirmed the rectitude of its own claims regarding the illegitimate nature of the minorities' participation in the electoral process. It was as if the National Democrats were saying "we told you so." Only a new president elected by the "Polish majority," the article concluded, would be able to "pacify public opinion" and put everything back on the right track.[23] Thus Narutowicz continued to be portrayed as an illegitimate president, and the violence that accompanied his election was unfortunate, but natural.

Rzeczpospolita was perhaps more circumspect about portraying the murder as "natural," but, if anything, it was even more forceful in its defense of the Doctrine of the Polish Majority, which had been articulated to delegitimize the election of Narutowicz, and claimed that the minorities had no right to play any role in Polish politics. As Stroński wrote on the day following the murder, "if the right defends with its entire might this one simple and sacred rule, and defends it legally, openly, proudly, and uncompromisingly, then how dare [the left] blame it for the covert actions of one unbalanced and unsound man?"[24]

To make good on their commitment to the Doctrine of the Polish Majority, the leaders of three right-wing parties issued a public communiqué to Piast, in which they called for a "conference with the goal of finding a Polish majority" for the election of the next president. Somewhat embarrassingly, the communiqué referenced Piast's panicked statement from December 11, in which the peasant party had done its best to disassociate itself from the election of Narutowicz and "the Jews," and belatedly place itself in the camp of the "Polish majority."[25]

Gazeta Warszawska's ideological reaffirmation of the Doctrine came on December 21, 1922, in an article entitled "The Rule of the Nation State."[26] According to the article, most likely written by Dmowski's close collaborator Zygmunt Wasilewski, the fundamental conflict in Poland was not over socioeconomic questions or broadly understood political matters, but over the role of nationality in politics. According to the author, the country could currently be divided into two camps. On the one side were those who believed that only Poles had the right to rule Poland. On the other, were those who "openly proclaim the thesis that all citizens of the Polish state have the right to rule Poland, not only formally but even morally." This was the key issue over which the battle lines had been drawn in Polish politics since 1918. "The election of the president," the article concluded, "was only an episode in this fundamental conflict," the outcome of which would decide the nation's future.[27]

The very same day, Stanisław Głąbiński delivered a "program speech" to the deputies of the National People's Union, the National Democrats' primary electoral vehicle, in which he announced the party's political priorities. The speech is fascinating, both in what it tells us about the absolute lack of impact that the Narutowicz assassination had on the National Democrats and, more generally, on the role of identity in nationalist political thinking. According to Głąbiński, the most important issue facing the country in the future was "that Poland remain a Polish and Catholic state, because this rule is the rock foundation upon which our entire future will be built." To this end, Głąbiński announced that his party would ensure that all matters of fundamental state importance, such as changes to the constitution or presidential elections, would require the majority of Polish votes, regardless of the votes of "other nationalities." In the same vein, he promised that the National People's Union would fight to make Polish the official language in all state offices (which it de facto already was) as well as ensuring that Poles were represented in state offices, concessions, and any business dealing with the state, "at least in proportion to their numbers in the country." He also left an open door for numerus clausus in higher education, though he did not make a specific promise to implement it.[28]

The next critical issue facing Poland in the coming years was signing the Concordat with the Vatican. The high priority given to this proposal may seem somewhat surprising given the gravity of the economic and administrative challenges facing the country, but it most likely represented an attempt to reach out to the Roman Catholic hierarchy, which was still skeptical of nationalism and may have been further put off by the recent violence.[29] The third challenge was the full integration of the eastern Borderlands with "the fatherland." In particular, Głąbiński promised to take better care of the "hitherto neglected" Polish population of the multicultural region. On a more ominous note, he also noted that "separatist propaganda masquerading as the call for territorial or national autonomy must be stopped."[30]

Only after these three points, did the speaker move to the question of foreign relations (he advocated a continued alliance with France). And only at the very end of his speech did he address economic questions and, to boot, did so in a manner that demonized the national minorities. Rather than dwelling on tangible economic issues, Głąbiński concluded his speech with promises of rectifying the "sickly state of our cities." The problem with the cities, according to this moderate leader, was that the latter were "filled with a non-Polish element which is often the enemy of Poland."[31]

The Polish right had not—as Hartglas and Daszyński had hoped—committed political suicide. In fact, judging from the reaction of the right-wing press and the leading politicians, it is obvious that the assassination of Narutowicz had absolutely no impact on National Democratic thinking as far as the Doctrine of the Polish Majority was concerned. Indeed, as we shall shortly see, even the qualified criticism of Eligiusz Niewiadomski would soon be replaced by quite a different attitude toward the murderer—one of reverence and respect.

The Trial

The trial of Eligiusz Niewiadomski proved to be one of the most important and galvanizing judicial proceedings in the history of the Second Republic, as well as a test for the country's still relatively new justice system. Ordinary Varsovians lined up for hours in the hope of getting tickets to the proceedings, but almost all had been given away to state officials.[32] The left, in particular, wanted to ensure that the trial would not be interpreted as unfair or biased against the accused. Sikorski's government wanted to avoid "antagonizing the still agitated, though now somewhat calmed" public opinion.[33] To this end, Kazimierz Rudnicki, the prosecutor in the case, received special instructions from the minister of justice, Makowski, to avoid making any statements that could be interpreted as making the whole National Democratic movement culpable in the murder.[34] The same considerations prompted Rudnicki and the Supreme Justice, Franciszek Nowodworski, to follow regular procedure and avoid bringing the case to trial immediately. Rudnicki believed that there could not be even "a shade of doubt . . . that the trial had taken place in conditions not in accordance with the law."[35]

The trial was somewhat complicated by the fact that Leopold Skulski, Narutowicz's friend and hunting companion who had become the ward of the latter's children, brought forth a civil case against Niewiadomski. His attorney, Franciszek Paschalski, demanded the symbolic compensation of one Polish mark for Narutowicz's children as a "recompense for the moral loss inflicted upon them by the murder of their father."[36] In accordance with Polish law, the civil and criminal cases were tried at the same time.

Niewiadomski demanded the death penalty for himself and initially didn't want to take on a defense counsel. However, Stanisław Kijeński, a well-known Warsaw lawyer and National Democratic sympathizer, was able to persuade the murderer to use his services. Kijeński, who, as it turned out, was highly sympathetic to Niewiadomski's plight, told the latter that he would act as an "advisor," help him navigate the thicket of legal complexities, and allow the accused man's own voice to be heard.[37]

The facts of the case were absolutely clear, and the examination of a number of witnesses and experts brought absolutely no new factual information to the proceedings.[38] Niewiadomski readily admitted to "breaking the law" and was prepared to assume the consequences of this act, but he did not acknowledge his moral "guilt."[39] Indeed, the historical significance of the trial, which is not readily acknowledged by historians, resides in the symbolic realm. The question around which the trial revolved pertained to Niewiadomski's motives and his guilt in the moral, rather than legal, sense. As all the sides realized, what was really at stake was not the legal verdict, which was never in doubt, but the interpretation and meaning of Niewiadomski's act. For Niewiadomski, the trial provided an opportunity to explain his motivations to all Poles. For Rudnicki and Paschalski, it provided the opportunity to publicly condemn and discredit these very motivations. The judge in this symbolic trial, the only one that mattered, would be public opinion.

Niewiadomski was eager to explain his actions and "shed light" on the "genesis" of the murder. Rather than limiting himself to stating his guilt, he immediately launched, with the court's permission, into an eloquent, though occasionally rambling, explanation of his decision to kill President Narutowicz. According to his testimony, Niewiadomski had originally intended to kill Piłsudski. The idea first occurred to him in 1918, when the Lublin Government of Piłsudski's followers attempted to introduce radical social reforms in Poland, but it was further cemented in his mind by subsequent events.[40]

What were the reasons for Niewiadomski's hatred of the man who was, even by many of his political enemies, acknowledged to have had an enormous impact on the "rebirth" of Poland? According to Niewiadomski, Piłsudski was "not without heroic qualities." But he was also, and this was the reason for Niewiadomski's hatred, the creator of "Judeo-Poland."[41] Indeed, Niewiadomski's actions make no sense without reference to his pathological antisemitism. To understand the link between Piłsudski and the Jewish plot to undermine Poland, we must delve deeper into Niewiadomski's worldview, which he proceeded to elaborate upon during his speech.

In brief, Niewiadomski faulted the Jews for creating and popularizing socialism, and infecting the latter with "materialism, the spirit of hatred, and lies." The Jews and socialists, according to Niewiadomski, always hated "the national idea." Thus, it was no surprise, he claimed, that they hated Italian fascism, which he

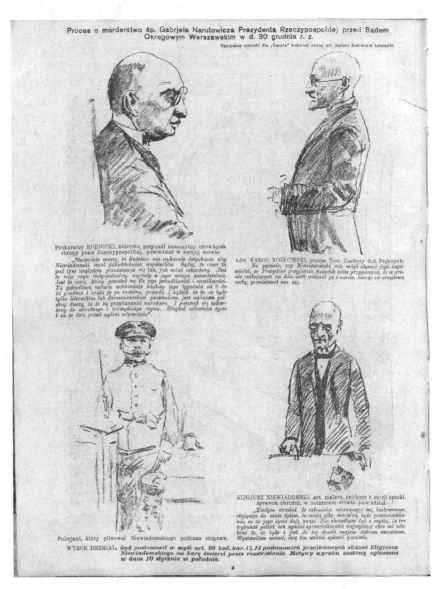

Proces o morderstwo śp. Gabrjela Narutowicza Prezydenta Rzeczypospolitej przed Sądem Okręgowym Warszawskim w d. 30 grudnia r. z.

Specjalne rysunki dla „Świata" wykonał znany art. malarz Kazimierz Lasocki.

Prokurator RUDNICKI, któremu przypadł zaszczytny obowiązek obrony praw Rzeczypospolitej, powiedział w swojej mowie:

„Stwierdzić muszę, że śledztwo nie wykazało dotychczas, aby Niewiadomski miał jakichkolwiek wspólników. Sądzę, że rzecz tą pod tym względem przedstawia się tak, jak mówi oskarżony. Jest to więc czyn indywidualny, wyrosły w jego mózgu samodzielnie. Jest to czyn, który powstał na tle jego pobudliwości i wrażliwości. Ta pobudliwa natura wchłaniała oddychy tego tygodnia od 9 do 16 grudnia i brała je za rzetelną prawdę. I sądzę, że to, co było tylko literackim lub dziennikarskim paszkwilem, jest nakazem polskiej duszy, że to są przykazania narodowe. I posunął się oskarżony do okrutnego i bezmyślnego czynu. Zdeptał człowieka życie i za to dziś przed sądem odpowiada".

Adw. KAROL KOZŁOWSKI, prezes Tow. Zachęty Szt. Pięknych:

Na pytanie, czy Niewiadomski nie mógł słyszeć jego zapowiedzi, że Prezydent przyjeżdzie, świadek sobie przypomina, że w gronie czekających na dole osób widział go i nawet, biorąc za urzędową osobę, przedstawił mu się.

ELIGJUSZ NIEWIADOMSKI, art. malarz, profesor h. storji sztuki, sprawca zbrodni, w ostatniem słowie powiedział:

„Kiedym strzelał do człowieka nieznanego mi, bezbronnego, stojącego do mnie tyłem, to moją siłą moralną było przeświadczenie, że za jego życie daję swoje. Nie chciałbym żyć z myślą, że ten trybunał polski, ten symbol sprawiedliwości najwyższej chce mi odebrać to, co było i jest do tej chwili mojem dobrem moralnem. Wystawiłem weksel, chcę ten weksel spłacić uczciwie.

Policjant, który pilnował Niewiadomskiego podczas rozpraw.

WYROK BRZMIAŁ: Sąd postanowił w myśl art. 99 kod. kar. i § 15 postanowień przejściowych skazać Eligjusza Niewiadomskiego na karę śmierci przez rozstrzelanie. Motywy wyroku zostaną ogłoszone w dniu 10 stycznia w południe.

4

Artist's depiction of the trial. Clockwise from top left corner are Public Prosecutor Rudnicki, Defense Attorney Kozłowski, Eligiusz Niewiadomski, and a policeman tasked with guarding the murderer. *Świat*, January 20, 1923.

loved.[42] The link between Piłsudski and the Jews was indirect. According to Niewiadomski, in 1918 Piłsudski had the power to do anything he wanted to in Poland. He should have, according to Niewiadomski, given the country a program of "work, battle readiness, discipline, and strong government." Instead, the left-wing governments that Piłsudski had allowed to take power caused "social discipline to break down" and brought the country nothing but "anarchy." Thus, instead of giving Poland a "strong government," he continued, Piłsudski allowed fully free elections, which "put the fate of the country into the hands of cowherds and farmhands."[43] Niewiadomski adduced all these failures of Piłsudski and his fellow socialists to the fact that the Jews had imbued socialism with "their racial elements which led to the degeneration of moral values."[44]

In other words, Piłsudski, who should have broken with socialism (and its pernicious Jewish influence) decisively, failed to do so. Quite the opposite, under his watch the Jews continued to increase their domination of Poland. That was his greatest sin. To illustrate his point, Niewiadomski proceeded to provide supporting evidence gathered from his own involvement in public service. He complained of corruption, inefficiency, and waste, and bemoaned "the thousands of officials" producing an "endless number of useless papers." Piłsudski wasn't "directly responsible" for all this, but he had "set the tone" for the "lack of creative will" that characterized the state apparatus.[45]

Niewiadomski proceeded to get somewhat more specific and drew an even more explicit link between Piłsudski and the Jews, based on the recollections of his service in the Polish army's counterintelligence unit. Here, he argued, Piłsudski's responsibility was "direct." In the army, Niewiadomski was shocked by the incompetence and ineptitude that surrounded him. His supervisor, Witecki, was "overweight and frequently late." One of his colleagues, Szafrański, had "gold signet rings on his fat hands." And another one was a Jew! Some of typists and secretaries also were Jewish. And "some Jew from Białystok or Grodno" was in charge of going through potentially subversive correspondence written in Yiddish.[46] According to Niewiadomski, this man was a German spy—and yet, the counterintelligence service was "powerless" and could not arrest him.[47]

The list of seemingly random grievances—many, though not all, of which involved Jews—went on. Some Jew who was a student at the Warsaw Polytechnic was caught with communist propaganda leaflets. Niewiadomski believed that he should have been shot on the spot. But his supervisor, Rotmistrz Dalewski (who was not Jewish), decided to confiscate the flyers and let him off. There was a shortage of pens and paper in the army. A certain Horowitz, apparently a high-ranking communist, was detained at the Citadel prison for a while. But then he was transferred to a POW camp, and was able to escape! One time, Niewiadomski was given an encrypted notebook to decipher, which turned out to be a list of communist sleeper agents in the Polish army. He deciphered it, but the notebook turned out to have been four months old and was no longer useful. And so he went on, with trivial anecdote following trivial anecdote. "Who was responsible for all this?" he asked rhetorically as he drew closer to the end of his speech. His answer was simple: "Piłsudski."[48]

Narutowicz, Piłsudski's successor, was to have a "lighter hand." "A light hand," Niewiadomski concluded, is what is required by "thieves, speculators, bandits, embezzlers of public goods, peasants not wanting to pay taxes, Jews, plotters . . . , all enemies of Poland." This, according to Niewiadomski, was why Piłsudski chose Narutowicz as his successor. "The rest is well known," he declared and fell silent.[49] The genuinely puzzled prosecutor Rudnicki retorted that on the basis of Niewiadomski's remarks he "currently understood less about the motives and causes of the murder than he did before."[50]

According to his account, Niewiadomski was fully prepared to kill Piłsudski and had even chosen the time and the place for the deed. Specifically, he was planning to shoot the marshal during the opening of an art exhibition about Warsaw in the era of King Stanisław on December 6. It was only that very morning that he learned that Piłsudski would not seek the presidency. He then realized that killing Piłsudski *after* he had just given up power would "weaken the nationalist idea," and that his action would be interpreted as that of a criminal or a madman. Still, he was aware, quite presciently as it turned out, that despite not having accepted the presidency, Piłsudski "will continue to occupy a central position in the state, that he will help direct its fate, and that during the decisive confrontation, he will stand at the head of street thugs, paramilitaries, and regular army units in the fight against the national camp." Thus, Piłsudski's decision not to seek the presidency threw Niewiadomski into a state of despair.[51] Senior National Democratic leaders would later express regret that Niewiadomski killed Narutowicz instead of following through with his original plan.[52]

At any rate, the link between Piłsudski and the Jewish domination of Poland, as well as the reasons behind Niewiadomski's plan to kill the marshal, were established. But Skulski's attorney, Paschalski, wanted to know more precisely how these motives eventually turned into the plan to murder Narutowicz, and he asked the accused about how he had come to that decision.[53] Compared to his rant about Piłsudski and Jews in the army, his statement on Narutowicz was relatively brief and focused. In fact, Niewiadomski reiterated, almost word for word, the Doctrine of the Polish Majority, as it had been put forth by the mainstream right-wing newspapers. The murder, he claimed was: "One of the episodes in the fight for the nation, the fight for the Polishness of Poland. As such, my action is its own defense, and speaks for itself. . . . I believe that as a human being, as a professor, as a husband, and as a father, Narutowicz was a good, noble, admirable person. . . . For me he existed not as a human being but as the symbol of a certain political situation. . . . He was a symbol of shame. My shots removed this badge of shame from the forehead of Poland. Through my deeds spoke not partisan fury, but the conscience and the offended dignity of the nation."[54]

Niewiadomski's statement was virtually indistinguishable from the charges leveled against the president in the press. Terms like "the fight for the Polishness of Poland" (*walka o polskość Polski*) or the "shame" (*hańba*) supposedly inflicted upon the nation by Narutowicz's election were staples of the right-wing papers. There is absolutely no doubt that Niewiadomski's language was virtually identical to that of *Gazeta Poranna*, *Gazeta Warszawska*, or *Myśl Narodowa*. His act was a defense of the Doctrine of the Polish Majority, as it had been defined and popularized by those papers.

Niewiadomski further reiterated these sentiments in his final remarks, which he was allowed before sentencing. He also framed his action in a larger political context, and expressed his hopes for the long-term consequences it would have: "I do not evince contrition. In fact, I evince a certain hope that the echoes of my shots will reach the most distant patches of Polish soil, that they knock to all homes, and all hearts, that they find their way to the camp of our opponents [i.e., the left and followers of Piłsudski], those who are bewitched and do not know whom they serve, to noble and young hearts, and awaken in their consciences doubts as to whether they are serving the right cause."[55]

Given these self-incriminating statements, as well as the public nature of the murder, the final verdict was never in doubt. Niewiadomski was duly sentenced to death by firing squad (though one of the three judges dissented on technical grounds and argued for the penalty of life imprisonment). What is interesting for our purposes, however, is how Niewiadomski was judged by society and, more specifically, by the National Democratic right.

Reading his speeches today, it seems quite clear that, aside from the moral valuation we might place upon his beliefs, Niewiadomski's thinking was not altogether sound. His rambling speech associating Piłsudski with the Jewish conspiracy to ruin Poland, in particular, raises serious questions. As Prosecutor Rudnicki aptly pointed out, from anecdotal evidence describing the shortcomings and failures of an admittedly imperfect state apparatus, Niewiadomski drew global and totally unsubstantiated conclusions. To cite one of the most ludicrous examples, the fact the Second Department employed Jewish typists did little to prove that Piłsudski was helping "the Jews" create a "Judeo-Poland."

There is no doubt that Niewiadomski was stubborn, willful, and disdainful of people whose views were different from his.[56] Aside from speculation in the press, a full-length book appeared in 1923 claiming to analyze Niewiadomski's mental health and concluding that he suffered from schizophrenia.[57] But while the right-wing press had *initially* dubbed Niewiadomski a "madman," it greeted his remarks at the trial extremely favorably. In fact, despite their seemingly paranoid and out-rageous claims, for the National Democrats, Niewiadomski's speeches at the trial actually helped to *refute* charges that he was insane. Strange as it may seem to us, they marked the beginning of a process in which Niewiadomski would be turned from a "lunatic" into a "noble soul."

The first person to publicly defend Niewiadomski was, not surprisingly, his defense attorney, Stanisław Kijeński. The fact of this defense is not surprising since that was, obviously, Kijeński's job. But Kijeński did not have to fully iden-tify himself with Niewiadomski's position. He could have defended the man even while acknowledging that his actions were misguided. But Kijeński did no such thing. In fact, the specific line the defense took may give us some pause. In his closing remarks, the defense attorney argued that:

> Narutowicz was the . . . victim of his own lack of knowledge of national life, and the lack of knowledge and understanding of the strange circumstance which propelled him to the most important position in Poland. . . . There had never been a deed such as [Niewiadomski's] in the history of Poland. But then Poland had never found herself in circumstances as exceptional as those in which Niewiadomski saw her. Poland had never been sucked up by foreign elements in this manner. Niewiadom-ski saw that in every field we are being derailed and thrown out of the saddle. This is the tragedy of his deed, and the tragedy of his deep, loving, pained heart. . . . In his speech, Mr. Niewiadomski said that he saw that Poland was being turned into a Judeo-Poland, and that the government was creating favorable conditions for this development and its growth. . . . This fact also deserves consideration in the judg-ment of Niewiadomski's deed.[58]

While questions concerning Niewiadomski's mental health may never be con-clusively answered, Kijeński was one of the best Warsaw lawyers, and certainly wasn't a lunatic or madman. Moreover, he must have been fully aware that his words would reach a national audience and likely put his reputation at stake.

Yet, in the previously cited speech, Kijeński made a number of claims that are virtually indistinguishable from those of Niewiadomski. First, Kijeński portrayed Narutowicz as the victim of his own ignorance. Had the president understood his nation better, the argument went, he would never have accepted the election under such circumstances. By "blaming the victim," Kijeński was arguing that the situation was such that something bad was *bound* to happen to Narutowicz. He was, therefore, subtly removing the agency from Niewiadomski and portraying the murder as the presumably *natural* result of Narutowicz's acceptance of the presidency from Jewish hands.

Kijeński's second claim is even more radical: Poland had *never* been controlled by "foreign elements to the extent that it was today." Let us not forget that the defense attorney was making this claim a mere four years after the country had regained its national independence. Yet, according to Kijeński, independent Poland was actually *less* independent than under Russian, Prussian, and Austrian rule. This extraordinary argument prompted Prosecutor Rudnicki to ask whether this was a "lapsus linguae" on the defense attorney's part.[59] But it wasn't. As Kijeński explained, during the Partitions people at least had the "ideal of Poland" to look up to. But today, he went on, that very ideal had been subjected to a "terrible shame." Niewiadomski, according to Kijeński, felt this shame "along with millions" of other Poles. The battle against "external enemies" was less serious than against the "internal enemy who has taken root among us."[60]

Finally, Kijeński fully endorsed Niewiadomski's claim that "Poland was being turned into a Judeo-Poland, and that the government was creating favorable conditions for this development and its growth." Moreover, while this "fact" didn't justify Niewiadomski's action in the *legal* sense, it certainly had an impact on the moral judgment that society ought to pass upon the murderer. Niewiadomski had acted out against a *genuine* threat and a dishonor to Poland. In doing so, he admittedly broke the law. But precisely in this very conflict between justice in the legal and justice in the moral sense lay "the tragedy of his deed, and the tragedy of his deep, loving, pained heart." As we will see, this line of interpreting the motives behind the murder of Narutowicz would soon be taken further by the right-wing press.

The day after the verdict was announced, *Gazeta Warszawska* reprinted the full text of Niewiadomski's rambling first speech about the links between Piłsudski and the Jewish conspiracy against Poland. As we remember, among other accusations, which can only be described as ludicrous, the murderer in his speech blamed Piłsudski for the fact that Jewish secretaries were employed by the army's counterintelligence unit. Niewiadomski's final words, in which he expressed a total lack of remorse for his deed, were also reprinted. The defense attorney's remarks, which fully endorsed Niewiadomski's worldview, were also printed in full, but those of Rudnicki and Paschalski were very briefly summarized.[61]

But perhaps the right-wing newspapers' tacit endorsement of Niewiadomski's outlandish claims should not be surprising. After all, while the evidence provided by Niewiadomski was spurious, the charges themselves were neither new nor outside the political discourse of the National Democratic movement. In the days preceding the presidential election, writing in the prestigious *Myśl Narodowa*, Father Kazimierz Lutosławski forcefully argued that Piłsudski was "a tool of international Jewry in its battle with the Polish nation."[62]

Gazeta Warszawska's commentary on the trial stopped short of praising Niewiadomski—that would come later. It defended his deed in an elliptical fashion, motivated in part by fear of censorship.[63] Still, the message was clear:

> Blood. The law has been satisfied and so is the law-abiding sense of a civilized society. The accused himself respected this sentiment by asking for the death penalty. But the dramas of national life do not die in the archives. They live in the minds of contemporaries, in their thoughts and imaginations, and become legends for future generations. ... The relationship between the deaths [of Narutowicz and Niewiadomski] is one of action and reaction. Individuals are subsumed by the flow of life which flows over graves, but if nationalist [*narodowa*] thought does not pull out a vital lesson from this tragic conflict, then learning history is in vain. ... Life knows no limits and from the grave it begets new life.[64]

The "vital lesson" in question was left to the imagination of the reader, but any reader of *Gazeta Warszawska* would immediately know what it was. Niewiadomski was descending from the national stage and into the realm of "legends," but the lesson offered both by his death and by that of Narutowicz was clear—Poland could not be ruled against the will of the Polish majority. The author's reference to "action and reaction," then, referred as much to the death sentence carried out against Niewiadomski being a reaction for his crime, as to the death of Narutowicz being the result of the nation's reaction to his violation of its cardinal rules.

The Noble Soul

Even before his execution, which would complete the process of turning him into a nationalist martyr, Niewiadomski was slowly being turned into a legitimate spokesperson of the National Democratic idea. On January 4, 1923, *Gazeta Warszawska* fully claimed Niewiadomski's views as its own:

Who cares that in his trial Niewiadomski had said [exactly] what the nationalist dailies were writing? What is important is that what the dailies were writing was what the Polish people were thinking and feeling. These dailies are the voice of the common people and not of [some] conspiracies. Niewiadomski, working on the basis of well-known and commonly accepted principles, came to a tragic and incorrect conclusion. . . . Nonetheless, those who refuse to see and understand the legitimate basis of this incorrect conclusion offer bad counsel. . . . [T]he nation brings its accusation against [Piłsudski and his followers] through the mouth of [Niewiadomski]. It is true that . . . Niewiadomski reiterated in his speech many of the accusations made by the nationalist press. He reiterated them in circumstances which shook the nervous system of the entire society, which made an impression in the wide world, and which will be remembered for many generations.[65]

In other words, *Gazeta Warszawska* now argued that Niewiadomski's views were the same as its own and, even more important, the same as those of "the Polish people." Similarly, the "moderate" National Democrat Władysław Rabski believed that "10 million Poles" shared Niewiadomski's views.[66] Even his deed was no longer a "heinous assassination"; it was merely a "tragic and incorrect" application of legitimate and praiseworthy principles.[67]

Finally, *Gazeta Warszawska* implicitly accepted Niewiadomski as its own spokesperson. The extraordinary, dramatic, or "tragic," to use the favorite adjective used by all right-wing papers, circumstances surrounding the murderer's trial lent his message a gravitas that, it was hoped, would resonate in Poland and the world "for generations." In other words, though it still disassociated itself from the actual act of the murder, the right accepted Niewiadomski as its spokesperson and was grateful for the soapbox that the trial effectively provided for the spreading of its gospel.[68]

The same transformation could be seen among National Democratic intellectuals and highbrow journalists. Adolf Nowaczyński, the "artist-thinker" of the National Democratic movement, who had called Niewiadomski a "lunatic" in the days following the murder had radically changed his mind a mere three weeks later.[69] Now, Nowaczyński argued, no one could possibly dare utter the epithets "madman, fanatic, or irresponsible" in relation to Niewiadomski. Rather, he continued, "the spirit which [Niewiadomski] displayed [when taking it upon himself to kill the president] cannot but provoke admiration for its strength and capacity for sacrifice." Niewiadomski's speech given at the trial was "not only a historical document from the current political moment, but a monument to a man of great character.[70] There seemed no end to Nowaczyński's cloying praise for the murderer: "A hard soul, a noble soul! . . . A man as pure as a tear. A heroic character, unknown in our society, whose great soul renders all of us, on both the left and right, [moral] midgets. Today . . . sadness grips us not for the one who fell accidentally, this pedestrian president, with whom Poland had no emotional bond, and who had simply become one of the symbols of the titanic struggle between the Christian world and Jewry [but for Niewiadomski]."[71]

Nowaczyński also reiterated Niewiadomski's hope that the murder would change the political landscape of Poland and bring the followers of Piłsudski to understand certain aspects of the National Democratic critique. Specifically, Nowaczyński had high hopes that even Piłsudski, who (he generously admitted) also possessed a "noble soul," would be moved by "what Niewiadomski had to say about the Semites." At this point, Nowaczyński revealed what he believed was the *main* divide between the followers of Piłsudski and the National Democrats— the former's lack of understanding for the latter's antisemitism. Niewiadomski's words, Nowaczyński hoped, would open the Piłsudskiites' eyes to this issue. He wrote: "This isn't about the national minorities with whom we all want agreement, peace, and harmony: the Germans, Ukrainians, and Belarusians. This is about that one national minority, the demon of humanity, this singular anti-Christian minority, the disease known as Jewry, the demon with which Europe and the entire world are now leading a struggle to the death. Hopefully, these commandments from [Niewiadomski's] testament will etch themselves into the memory of Piłsudski and all who believe in Piłsudski."[72]

Needless to say, Nowaczyński's hopes of Piłsudski's imminent conversion to Niewiadomski's gospel of antisemitism were dashed. The "artist-thinker" of the right promptly found himself under arrest, while his article was confiscated by the censors.[73] Nevertheless, his suggestion that a rapprochement between the National Democrats and the Piłsudskiites was possible if the latter embraced antisemitism seemed to anticipate the creation of the antisemitic Camp of National Unity (Obóz Zjednoczenia Narodowego) by some of Piłsudski's followers in the late 1930s. What is more important for the present purposes is to note that, in Nowaczyński's view, Niewiadomski's antisemitic speeches at his trial fully rehabilitated the murderer and made it possible for the right to embrace him as a sort of tragic hero.

Still, the process by which Eligiusz Niewiadomski would become a fully-fledged martyr of the right could only be consummated by his execution. The right-wing press by and large accepted the death penalty as a legitimate punishment, and only Stanisław Stroński raised a mild legalistic objection on the pages of the *Rzeczpospolita*.[74] But it was precisely the execution and the funeral that turned Niewiadomski into a martyr and a cause célèbre. Extensive details of the execution were reported on the front pages of right-wing newspapers with pathos that undoubtedly would have pleased the murderer himself.

The execution was scheduled for the morning of January 30, 1923. "At 6 am," *Gazeta Warszawska* reported, Niewiadomski enjoyed a conversation with Stanisław Kijeński, who reported that the murderer was "in excellent spirits" and "even joking around." He then met with a priest, Father Sontak, and received him with "great warmth and gratitude." At 6:30 a.m., a car with an armed escort left the Warsaw Citadel and proceeded to the execution place just outside the gates. As a precaution, the Citadel was encircled by a ring of troops.[75]

Somewhat comically, the car carrying the prisoner broke down, and Niewiadomski walked the last stretch of the way "in a firm stride." He asked the guards not to hold him, since he "didn't want people to think that he required being held down." The murderer then spoke to another priest, received a blessing, and kissed the cross. Six soldiers were delegated to the execution, and Niewiadomski asked that he not be tied to the pole and that his eyes remain uncovered. His wish was granted.[76] According to the *Gazeta Warszawska* relation: "He stood firmly, and asked the soldiers to aim at his head. Then he calmly took off his coat, hat, and glasses and tossed them aside. He stood erect, smiled, and held up a flower he had received from his family."[77]

According to *Rzeczpospolita*, he left behind a little note asking that the funeral be simple "since he never liked to reach for distinguished places and would like to maintain this style."[78] Just before the shots went off, he cried, "I die for Poland, which is being destroyed by Piłsudski!" These last words could not be printed due to censorship, and only emerged in subsequent days. After his body was laid to rest in a shallow grave, the gates of the Citadel were opened, and a "pilgrimage" consisting of people who had waited outside the army cordon, most of them poor and working class, entered to pay their respects to the deceased.[79]

Gazeta Warszawska's eulogy for Niewiadomski was written by Dmowski's friend and collaborator Zygmunt Wasilewski. It marked the culmination of the astonishingly quick rhetorical transformation of the murderer from a "madman" to "a man of great character." Wasilewski wrote:

> He was righteous, idealistic and sensitive, but demanding and strict with himself. . . . His character was also described as straight arrow. He evinced great strength, openness, and courage. . . . During the trail he proved . . . that he governed his will precisely and with full awareness of his fate. We had before us the model of a strong character, imposing principles upon his actions. The deed, for which he met

a terrible punishment, was a catastrophe. But the spiritual type which had manifested itself in the process must win admiration for its strong makeup and capacity
for sacrifice. Even [nonnationalists] must marvel at his psychic state, in which the
interests of the individual were completely subsumed by those of the nation. In this
sense, his speeches at the trail will remain not only a historical document of the
current moment, but the memento to a man of great character.[80]

It is important to further highlight the somewhat complicated strategy behind
Wasilewski's rhetoric. Wasilewski still condemned the murder itself as a "catastrophe." But this catastrophe was the result of Niewiadomski's spiritual purity,
his identification with the nation, and his dedication to a moral standard that was
ultimately higher than the law. Morally, Niewiadomski was in the right, even if
from both the legal and the tactical perspectives he had to be condemned. In this
sense, Wasilewski and the National Democrats were simultaneously able to both
claim Niewiadomski as one of their own and to disown him. They claimed him
on the grounds of his moral purity and dedication to the nation, and disowned
him on the grounds of the illegal and politically harmful character of his actions.

But ultimately, for Wasilewski, there was no doubt as to history's verdict on
Niewiadomski: "A child reading Niewiadomski's words 100 years from now will
not be able to understand why a man of these views, feelings, and character, was
put to death in his own fatherland, by the will of the state, and with his own
assent. . . . With his sacrifice he gave witness to the idea of the nation."[81] In other
words, if the right could not *fully* claim him today, Wasilewski intimated, it was
for complicated legal and tactical reasons, which future generations would not
even be able to comprehend. But in the long run, history would vindicate Niewiadomski. Stripped of its complicated legal and tactical context, and evaluated
solely on moral grounds, the murder was ultimately an act of righteous sacrifice
for the nation. From this perspective, the murder's life was, in Wasilewski's pre-
sentation and no doubt in Niewiadomski's own imagination, a tribute to the ideal
of "sacrificing individual existence to the struggle against the forces of degeneration which had seemingly brought the nation low," which constitutes the idée
fixe of cultural manifestations of fascism.[82]

The fact that the authorities did their best to keep the funeral of Niewiadomski
secret is an indicator that the government saw it as a potential source of embarrassment or, worse, a rallying point for the nationalist opposition. The date of the
funeral, February 6, 1923, was announced late on the evening of the previous day.
Furthermore, permission for the funeral was given only on the condition that the
body would be exhumed at 4:00 a.m. and that the hearse would leave the Citadel

by 6:00 a.m. If these conditions were not met, the funeral would not take place. The hearse had to avoid main streets and proceed by a circuitous route outlined by the security services in order to avoid attention.[83]

The sympathetic proprietor of a large funeral parlor, a certain Seweryn Staniszewski, offered his services for free. According to *Gazeta Warszawska*, this was only one of the "many proofs that the public adequately appreciated the deceased's greatness of soul and character."[84] Niewiadomski was laid in a closed coffin with two roses, one red and the other white. At the gates of the Citadel, a large group of people awaited with wreaths and flowers. Before reaching the Powązki Church, horses were unharnessed from the carriage and a group of volunteer youths pulled the hearse into the church, where the crowd sang the nationalist anthem, *Rota*.[85]

According to *Gazeta Warszawska*, by the time the procession reached the Powązki cemetery, it numbered some 10,000 people. The crowd, mostly made up of "poorer classes," lined the entire path from the church to the gravesite. Numerous wreaths were carried in front of the procession, and flowers and fir branches were thrown in its path. One particular wreath singled out by the *Gazeta Warszawska* correspondent bore the encryption: "From the Polish Women of America—All Hail the Immortal." In a further display of public respect for the murderer noted dutifully by the newspapers, one of the men present, a military veteran, took a medal off his chest and tossed it into the grave.[86] As the coffin was lowered into the ground, the *Rzeczpospolita* correspondent noted, "One thought grabbed everyone: a thought of this solemn and sad moment, and a sadness, which knows no words, united all hearts."[87] Later in the day, the grave was visited by "throngs of mourners." They brought flowers and wreaths, which were piled so high on the grave that they were visible from far away "among the trees and the cemetery statues."[88]

The right's fascination with the figure of Niewiadomski continued to the point that he became the object of a veritable cult. Masses for the murderer's soul proliferated. On February 11, less than a week after his funeral, the Polish Episcopate had to issue a statement calling on the clergy to cease abusing masses for the souls of the dead.[89] Writing in the 1930s, Piast leader Wincenty Witos noted: "Even today . . . Niewiadomski's grave is a place of pilgrimages and the anniversary of his death brings many of his admirers there. It is noteworthy that among them one can find members of all the social classes of Warsaw. . . . By the manner these people conduct themselves it is clear that they consider him to be at least a saint."[90]

While awaiting his execution, Niewiadomski finished a book on art history and penned an "open letter to the nation." Right-wing newspapers published the

The grave of Eligiusz Niewiadomski shortly after his funeral. (reprinted with permission of Małgorzata Karolina Piekarska)

latter, which, for the most part, was a restatement of the paranoid views the murderer had expressed during his trial.[91] In the letter, Niewiadomski, once again, attempted to frame his act in historical perspective:

> My death is the necessary culmination of my deed. My deed will only flower once watered with my own blood.... I had to hit Poland with a lightning bolt to awaken those who believe that Poland is already a reality, that the time of sacrifices and striving is over, and that it is possible to put our weapons down. What our eyes are looking upon is not yet Poland. It is still the Poland of Piłsudski—Judeo-Poland. Real Poland still has to be built. This process is now starting. My hopes were not in vain. Whatever is Polish and healthy in the camp of the left heard my voice. I die happy that the work of waking Polish consciences and unifying Polish hearts will be fulfilled.[92]

Niewiadomski's hope that whatever was "Polish and healthy" in "the camp of the left" was eerily prescient in its anticipation of the acceptance of antisemitism by many of Piłsudski's successors. But his impact on the right was already evident at the moment of his death. As we have seen, the "Doctrine of the Polish Majority," in the name of which Niewiadomski claimed to die, became enshrined in the program and politics of the Polish right. The murder of the president did not stop this process. Conversely, by reaffirming the doctrine even in the face of its most extreme and murderous implications, the right emerged from the crisis with a renewed sense of its own righteousness.

Niewiadomski himself became a nationalist hero. Maciej Rataj wrote that despite being executed, Niewiadomski was "not morally destroyed" in the public imagination.[93] This is an understatement. While the right initially recoiled at the act of the murder and attempted to distance itself from its perpetrator, that position changed very quickly. The very same Adolf Nowaczyński who had called Niewiadomski a "madman" on December 23, praised him "as a man of great character" less than two weeks later. In light of the right-wing newspapers' praise of the murderer, the adulation heaped upon him by the masses of Warsaw should not be surprising either.

But perhaps the most amazing feature of this process is that it occurred because of, rather than despite, Niewiadomski's paranoid and rambling speeches delivered during the trial. It was these speeches, in which the murderer supported his bizarre claim that Piłsudski was creating a Judeo-Poland, and the equally bizarre evidence, which won him the admiration of the right-wing intellectuals and the public. Clearly, the murder of Narutowicz was *not* an embarrassment or a setback for the National Democratic right. Scholars who have made this point seem to have been unduly influenced by the *immediate* reaction of right-wing newspapers and politicians to the assassination. But a mere three weeks after the fact, Niewiadomski and everything he stood for had been fully rehabilitated. Far from being ashamed of him, right-wing journalists openly expressed the hope that Niewiadomski's deeds and words would have an influence on the followers of Piłsudski and bring them around to accepting antisemitism. As we will see in the next chapter, these hopes were not quite as far-fetched as they may initially appear.

6

The Defeat of the Civic Nation

We have seen in the last chapter that, despite superficial appearances to the contrary, the right did not use the murder of President Narutowicz as an "opportunity for reflection."[1] Quite the opposite, the National Democrats' response to the murder illustrates the reaffirmation of their commitment to political antisemitism and the newly formulated Doctrine of the Polish Majority even in the face of their murderous consequences. How would the rest of Poland's political class react to the murder? As Bernard Singer writes, "the tragic death of the president temporarily drew together the center, the left, and even the national minorities."[2] Some on the left expressed the hope that the death of Narutowicz "would not be in vain" and that it would "wash off the mud which had been heaped upon the President."[3] Therefore, it was not unreasonable to expect that the indignation felt by many of the deputies after the cold-blooded murder would rally Piast and the left, and perhaps prompt them to arrange some sort of agreement with the national minorities in order to shut the National Democrats out of power. In reality, however, the very opposite took place.

Piast, Antisemitism, and Land Reform

The capitulation to the Doctrine of the Polish Majority, and the drift to the right, was most easily discernible in the case of Piast. As Władysław Pobóg-Malinowski writes, until 1922 Piast and its leader Witos "marched under the banner of co-operation with Piłsudski." But the December Events, Pobóg-Malinowski argues, changed all that. "Witos, frightened, believed that Poland was in a state of anarchy and sought some stabilization. He concluded that the impunity of the right is a sign of its strength, and of the weakness of the left, and that power is on the side of those who kill with impunity rather than those being killed."[4] There is no doubt that even before the actual assassination, many Piast deputies were profoundly shaken by the riots in Warsaw. Their desperate attempts to dissociate themselves from Narutowicz a mere day after having played the decisive role in his election are ample testimony to this.[5] Nor were their fears unjustified. Most Piast deputies were peasants from far-flung corners of Poland, and had no supporters in Warsaw to protect them. The riots of December 11 must have convinced them that the police, as well as the organs of the state in general, could not be relied upon for this purpose.

However, explaining Piast's newly found willingness to cooperate with the right solely in terms of a visceral fear of violence would be unfair to the party's leaders, who were both less cowardly and more sophisticated than they appear in Pobóg-Malinowski's account. To fully understand Piast's turn to the right, and the role that the murder of President Narutowicz played in this turn, it is necessary to examine the political thought and practice of Maciej Rataj, Piast's second most powerful leader. Although he was the son of poor peasants, who by his own admission spent most of his childhood years herding cows, Rataj would become one of Poland's most intelligent, articulate, and perceptive politicians. During the years 1919–1926, he wielded considerable influence, which was based

Maciej Rataj, Marshal of the Sejm. Rataj played a critical role ensuring a smooth and democratic succession during the stormy December Events. However, the experience appeared to convince him that the Doctrine of the Polish Majority was too powerful to be opposed in the public forum. (Narodowe Archiwum Cyfrowe)

not only on his position as marshal of the Sejm but also on his reputation for moderation and nonpartisanship. As Bernard Singer wrote with a dose of irony: "Rataj won the hearts of all. . . . Deputies from the right visited his office as if going to confession. In difficult moments, when [a vote of nonconfidence against him loomed in the Sejm] the PPS came to his rescue. . . . With time, he became known as the embodiment of nonpartisan patriotism."[6]

Rataj explained his understanding of the central problem facing Polish politics in a conversation with moderate Endek leaders Stanisław Głąbiński and Marian Seyda, which took place on December 12. Rataj asked Głąbiński, who was deeply disturbed by the riots of the previous day, what the National Democrats planned to do next. Głąbiński answered that the NDs would become the parliamentary opposition. To this Rataj replied: "There are two possibilities in this regard. Either no parliamentary majority will arise (since the majority that elected Narutowicz was accidental), in which case whom will you oppose!? The state!? That is the politics of angry children. In the other case, you will push Piast to cooperate with the minorities in order to win the antisemitic card, in which case Piast will respond to your antisemitic slogans with a radical social program ('Take the land now!') and will defeat you, because the peasant won't care whether the land is being given to him by a Catholic or a Jew."[7] To Głąbiński's shocked response that this would be terribly detrimental to the interests of the Polish state, Rataj retorted that if the National Democrats "cared about the state, they should not push Piast towards cooperation with the minorities."[8]

Rataj's formulation of the alternatives facing Polish political life is striking not only for its insightful analysis but also for the congruence of his thinking with David Ost's recent theorization of the role of anger in politics.[9] Ost argues that political narratives that seek to explain and channel political anger can be broadly divided into those that focus on economic or structural explanations of "what is wrong" and those that offer explanations based on identity. In his exhortation to Głąbiński, Rataj effectively described the choice between these two types of narratives as the primary question of Polish politics. As we have seen in chapter 3, the National Democrats offered an explanation based on identity politics—the Jews were the fundamental problem facing Poland. This narrative could be deployed with some effectiveness against Piast, if the latter entered a coalition that included the Bloc of National Minorities.

However, fully ready at Piast's disposal was an economic narrative capable of successfully mobilizing the majority of Polish voters against the National Democrats. According to Rataj, the demand for "a radical social program," and more specifically land reform based on the forced parcellation of large estates, ultimately possessed a greater power to mobilize voters than political antisemitism. In a head-on confrontation, the marshal of the Sejm claimed, economic self-interest was a more powerful mobilizing force than the call for racial hatred.[10] But despite being the son of poor peasants and the deputy of a peasant party, and despite having expressed strong disapproval for antisemitism in his private memoirs, Rataj *himself* apparently opted for an alliance with the purveyors of ethnic hatred rather than facing the potentially disruptive effects of radical land reform.

Even the assassination of Narutowicz, which brought to light the dangerous and destabilizing consequences of the hatred found at the core of the Doctrine of the Polish Majority, failed to shake the moderate marshal's conviction that radical social reform was a greater danger than political antisemitism. In fact, in the days following the murder of Narutowicz, when the election of his successor was being discussed, Rataj became a forceful advocate of the "thesis that the new presidential candidate must win with the majority of Polish votes."[11] The new presidential vote, scheduled for December 20, was initially promising to be just as chaotic as the election of Narutowicz had been. While the PPS and the National Labor Party announced that they would vote for any candidate jointly agreed upon by Piast and Emancipation, the two peasant parties once again had difficulties reaching agreement. On the night of December 19, it was rumored that Piast itself could not decide between Premier Władysław Sikorski and Stanisław Wojciechowski, while Emancipation was still considering as many as eight different candidates, with the former National Civic Union activist Jan Kuchazewski leading the field.[12]

Yet, behind the scenes, Rataj was working hard and holding numerous meetings with representatives on both the left and the right to find a candidate acceptable to the "Polish majority" in the Sejm. After a number of consultations, he was able to narrow down the list of candidates to Wojciechowski and Sikorski—both of them centrists, closer to the left but considered acceptable to the right. The marshal had considerable success with his project and claims to have succeeded in persuading the "moderate" Socialists Daszyński, Barlicki, and Moraczewski that only a candidate supported by a "Polish majority" could succeed in bringing about political stability.[13] While Emancipation leader Thugutt initially threatened to purposefully find a candidate entirely unacceptable to the right, he admitted that deep down he had no stomach for another battle against the "Polish Majority."[14] "Theoretically," he wrote, "it would have been possible for us to once again have our candidate elected in the fifth round of voting, but I felt that neither I nor the country could take the terrible stress of another five round election."[15] In the end, despite making threatening noises to the contrary, Emancipation and Piast agreed upon the candidacy of Stanisław Wojciechowski, a centrist who enjoyed both personal historical ties to Piłsudski and good relations with the National Democrats.[16]

So if Rataj's call for the president to be elected by the "Polish majority" failed, it was the right and not the left that was to blame. Only at 11:00 p.m. of the night before the election did the leaders of the three right-wing parties decisively announce to Rataj that they would be "unable" to vote for Wojciechowski and proposed their own compromise candidate, the conservative Morawski.[17] It would appear that this late decision reflected a victory of the rank-and-file National Democratic deputies over the parties' more conciliatory leadership.

Thus, the vote promised to be one pitting the left against the right, with the left again relying on the support of the national minorities. Again, no left-wing politicians visited the minorities to discuss tactics or choice of candidates. Only Piłsudski sent his envoy, Marian Zyndram-Kościałkowski, to inform the minorities of the left's choice of Wojciechowski and to ask for their votes.[18] But even at the very last moment, Rataj had not given up his quest to make the new president appear more Polish and less Jewish. Mere hours before the election, the Galician Zionist leader Ozjasz Thon received a surprise visit from the marshal of the Sejm—it was the only visit by a Polish parliamentarian to the National Minorities Bloc during the run-up to the election. Yet, the purpose of Rataj's visit was not to ask for the Jewish vote. It was, in fact, the very opposite! During the brief discussion, Rataj asked the Jews *not* to vote for Wojciechowski and, instead, to formally declare their own candidate.[19]

Having a Bloc of Minorities candidate in the election would have accomplished two of Rataj's objectives, both related to the Doctrine of the Polish Majority. First, and most obvious, it would have removed the odium of having been the "Jewish candidate" from Wojciechowski. Second, the presence of another candidate would have allowed a runoff between Wojciechowski and Morawski. This would have given at least some National Democrats one more opportunity to cast their votes for Wojciechowski, thus possibly allowing him to become the candidate of the Polish majority in the runoff.[20]

In the end, all these machinations came to naught. The minorities uniformly voted for Wojciechowski, as did all Piast deputies, despite many of the latter being "terrified" of the possible consequences and "fully ready" to cast their lot with Morawski.[21] As a result, Wojciechowski was elected by the very same combination of votes as Narutowicz. But the right-wing newspapers, and even the antisemitic Rozwój, remained calm. No one called Wojciechowski a "Jewish President," and no demonstrations against him took place in the streets. From this fact, many historians draw the conclusion that the murder of Narutowicz had been a defeat for the National Democrats, who were ultimately forced to scale-down their rhetoric and modify their demands.[22]

But such a reading of history is far too superficial. As we have seen in the last chapter, the right did not significantly scale-down its demands. Further, the logic behind Rataj's actions illustrates that the murder and the riots of December 11 had a powerful impact on the political thinking of centrist Polish politicians. In Rataj's memoirs, one finds no indication that the marshal of the Sejm had considered the notion of a "Polish Majority" to be important to the governance of the country prior to the election of Gabriel Narutowicz. If anything, prior to the December Events, Rataj appears to have judged the legitimacy of political developments primarily in terms of their conformity with the constitution, rather than with the extraconstitutional principle of ethnicity. But in the face of the forceful and violent opposition to the participation of the Jews in Narutowicz's election, Rataj appears to have become convinced that only a Polish majority, as it was understood by the National Democrats, was capable of ruling the country.

This decision does not appear to have been motivated by fear for his personal safety. Rataj had reasons to fear for his life on a number of occasions, and there is no indication that this changed his political thinking in a significant way.[23] Rather, his newly found dedication to the principle of the Polish majority appears to have been underpinned by a sophisticated political calculation: That this was the only way to guarantee political stability in Poland without embarking on a socially radical program of land reform. But however pragmatic or moderate the marshal's stance may have seemed, it was highly questionable from the vantage point of *his own* moral convictions. In his memoirs, Rataj lamented that despite being sentenced to death, Niewiadomski "had not been morally annihilated" at his trial.[24] Yet, a part of the responsibility for this state of affairs surely rests with Rataj himself who, for the sake of calm and stability, chose to make peace with many elements of Niewiadomski's credo.

Rataj was unusually lucid in articulating his bargain with the purveyors of ethnic hatred, but he was far from unique. Sikorski, who as premier wielded real political power in the country, appeared to have adopted the same logic. In his first speech before the Sejm, on January 19, 1923, the new premier was presented with the perfect opportunity to condemn the principles in the name of which Niewiadomski had acted. Indeed, he told the Sejm that he believed that "the evil had to be destroyed at its very root."[25] Yet, in his speech he did not mention this "root" at all. He spoke elliptically about "December Events," "partisan squabbles," "the lack of parallelism" between the actions of the left and the right, and the "rendering of the authority of the President and the state laughable."[26] But he said absolutely nothing about the principles that animated both the rioters and Niewiadomski—hatred toward the national minorities, especially the Jews, and the idea that only ethnic Poles could legitimately participate in politics.

The section of his speech dealing with the national minorities was also deeply problematic, considering the events that had just transpired. Sikorski promised that Poland would "always and unconditionally" guarantee "its citizens, without regard for any differences, not only safety, peace and equality before the law, but also the freedom for full cultural development, including the safeguarding of linguistic and religious separateness."[27] However, the premier immediately qualified his own "unconditional" promise by stating that it will "naturally" apply only to those citizens who "sincerely and loyally stand on the ground of unquestionable Polish civic identity [państwowość]."[28] While Sikorski never explained how the "unquestionableness" of the latter could be measured or evaluated, he did have some praise for the Ukrainians and Belarusians.[29] But rather than reaffirming the right of the Jews to participate in the political process, which the "December Events" had so obviously raised into question, he went on to undermine it further. The sole mention of the Jews in his speech was more of a threat than anything else: "On the basis of the above, the Jewish minority will certainly understand that the rights willingly given to it by Poland will be respected by [my] government. However, a voice of caution is necessary. On the Jewish side, the justified defense of rights has too often been turned into a battle for privileges. Some organs of the international press, which judge us too harshly, have called the equality reigning in Poland "oppression." There are no rights without duties. The last years of Polish independence illustrate that not all Polish citizens have adequately understood this sentiment."[30]

A legitimate argument could be made that the Zionist leadership, which represented the Jewish Circle in the Sejm, had overreached in its demands on a number of issues, and especially in its foolish advocacy of the 1919 Minorities Treaty.[31] But this was hardly the appropriate time to enter such a discussion—at least if one *really* wanted to "destroy the evil" inherent in Niewiadomski's act "at its very root." There is absolutely no indication that Sikorski was an antisemite or that he believed in the existence of a Jewish "threat" to Poland. The real reason for his strange "warning" to the Jews was tactical. The logic behind his harsh words is simple. According to Bernard Singer, Sikorski considered tacit Jewish support for his government to be a political liability and source of embarrassment.[32] And, like Rataj, he lacked the political courage to live up to his own moral sentiments and "destroy the evil at its root" or even call it by its name.

I have spent some time discussing the political bargain conceptualized by Rataj, as well as the rhetoric of Sikorski, only because they offer particularly clear examples of a trend that appears to have affected most Piast deputies and many other influential politicians in what was generally described as the "center" of the political spectrum. The new president, Stanisław Wojciechowski, also favored a government formed by a majority of Polish parties.[33] Despite the rhetorical violence targeted at Piast and its leader Witos by the Endeks, talks to form a "Government of the Polish Majority" began almost immediately after the murder of Narutowicz.[34] These negotiations proceeded along two separate tracks but were, in both cases, sponsored by centrist political figures. On the one hand, Witos and Piast were in intermittent negotiations with the three right-wing parties to form a coalition center-right government. On the other hand, General Sikorski attempted to gain support for his minority government from the Christian Democrats (or even from the Christian Nationalists) and thus create a broad Polish coalition stretching from the PPS to "moderate" elements on the right.[35] Rataj actively participated in both these concurrent efforts.

Ultimately, Sikorski was unable to detach the Christian Democrats from their alliance with the NDs. But it may be important to note that the catalyst for the fall of his government was another entirely contingent event that, again, involved the "Jewish Question." On April 1, 1923, a Polish Catholic priest, Father Konstanty Budkiewicz, was executed for treason in the Soviet Union, on entirely spurious charges. The execution was condemned by all Polish parties and political groups, but it particularly galvanized the National Democrats, who, on April 4, organized a massive rally on Teatralny Square in Warsaw. With a number of National Democratic speakers, among them the Rozwój activist Konrad Ilski, delivering diatribes aimed at "communists and Jews" (though the latter had nothing to do with Budkiewicz's execution), it should not be surprising that Warsaw erupted into on orgy of anti-Jewish violence reminiscent of the one that took place following the election of Narutowicz, though on a somewhat smaller scale.[36]

As the *Kurjer Poranny* announced, "the demonstration, which initially impressed us with its serious character, eventually ended with a series of excesses."[37] In an eerie echo of December 11, "groups numbering from a few to a dozen individuals" stopped trams, pulled out and beat up (presumed) Jews, vandalized cinemas, and broke the windows in Jewish stores. "Down with the Jews!" "Beat the Jews!" and "Ten rabbis for one bishop!" were the choice slogans of the demonstrators.[38] Again, any individuals presumed to be Jews were attacked. Among them, as *Kurjer Polski* reported with outrage, was a certain "Count W.," whose carriage was attacked by a mob wielding sticks in the vicinity of the Wiedeński

Railway Station.[39] A Jewish high school student surrounded and beaten by a hostile mob was saved only by the personal intervention of National Populist Union deputy Father Nowakowski.[40] Army units had to help police control the situation, though the latter showed more resolve and determination than it had in December. In the end, some 40 people were admitted to emergency and 200 arrested.[41]

There is little doubt that Sikorski's inability to stave off the execution of Budkiewicz was a serious blow that precipitated the downfall of his government.[42] And there is even less doubt that, in the aftermath of this bout of antisemitic violence, Piast redoubled its efforts to create a Government of the Polish Majority. A story of Piast's attempt to create such a government was run by *Robotnik* on the day following the riots under the telling title "Illusions."[43] A mere two weeks later, however, Piast was engaged in serious open talks with the National Democrats, and the downfall of Sikorski's government was universally perceived as being but a matter of time.[44]

The negotiations, now carried on openly, took another four weeks, with the key stumbling block being Piast's demand for the new government to commit itself to (moderate) land reform, which was fiercely opposed by the Christian National Party, the junior partner in the National Democratic coalition. In the end, the Government of the Polish Majority was not achieved without some sacrifices on both sides. A group of sixteen left-wing Piast deputies, led by veteran leader Jan Dąbski, formally left the party.[45] The Christian Nationalists declined to formally join the new government, though they promised to support it. Still, less than six months after the assassination of Gabriel Narutowicz, the Doctrine of the Polish Majority, in the name of which he had been murdered, was formally accepted by Piast, the party that had played the most decisive role in electing him to the presidency.

The very first point of "The Rules of Cooperation between the Parties of the Polish Parliamentary Majority in the Sejm," as the agreement was formally called, stated the following:

> The Polish national character must be maintained in the regime and administration of the state. To this end: (1) The basis of the parliamentary majority should be a Polish majority and the government should be made up exclusively of Poles. (2) The Polish language will be declared as the state and administrative language . . . on the entire territory of the Republic. . . . (3) Polish youth will have the right to study in secondary, post-secondary, and vocational schools in accordance with its share of the population in the state [i.e., numerus clausus] . . . (5) In internal colonization,

special attention shall be paid to areas important from a military and national point of view, especially those where a Polish majority can be created. (6) In all government concessions and contracts, as well as in government jobs, the correct percentage of the Polish population will be adhered to.[46]

Another point promised to increase the privileges of the Catholic Church and ratify the Concordat. The ninth point of the agreement promised to "support Polish industry, crafts, and commerce and the nationalization of cities."[47] As Singer put it, in "every article of the Agreement, the Piast deputies, with Witos at their head, murdered Narutowicz all over again."[48] The very last point (number eleven) offered Piast the promise of watered down land reform.[49]

While the creation of the Government of the Polish Majority was significant, the discursive change that it signaled was actually more important than its immediate political impact.[50] Indeed, the coalition fell apart a mere six months after being formed, amidst protests by another group of renegade Piast deputies over the National Democrats' mismanagement of the economy. It was replaced by a minority cabinet led by the technocrat Władysław Grabski. But discursive changes that took place in the immediate aftermath of election of Narutowicz would prove lasting. Following the murder, not only Piast, but other unaffiliated "moderate" politicians close to the party, such as Sikorski and Wojciechowski, accepted the notion that only a "Polish Majority," as it was defined by the National Democrats, could successfully rule Poland. This doctrine would remain a definitive, if unspoken, component of Piast's political practice and would never be seriously challenged within the party.

This commitment to the Doctrine of the Polish Majority informed Piast's attitude toward the commemoration of Narutowicz's death. Plans for the commemoration, initiated by Thugutt and Emancipation, initially included a statue or a community center to honor the deceased president. However, due to lack of support among parliamentarians, Emancipation eventually had to settle for a commemorative plaque in the Sejm.[51] But even those plans were put in jeopardy, when a sizeable group of Piast deputies led by Witos refused to vote for the allocation of funds necessary for the plaque.[52]

At the eventual unveiling of the plaque, which took place on June 16, 1923, parliamentary leaders from across the political spectrum were present. In lieu of a wreath, the PPS made a charitable donation of one million Polish marks for a "philanthropic cause," which left only two lonely wreaths standing next to the plaque. One, not surprisingly, was from Emancipation. The second was provided by the breakaway renegade faction of sixteen Piast deputies who, under Jan

Dąbski's leadership, left the party when the latter entered the Government of the Polish Majority.[53] The absence of wreaths from the three right-wing parties was probably not a surprise to anyone. But the lack of a wreath from Piast, which had unanimously voted for Narutowicz and thus set him on the path that led to his death, spoke volumes about just how far the party was willing to go in order to distance itself from its shameful, even if inadvertent, cooperation with "the Jews."

The Left and the Politics of Amnesia

The Government of the Polish Majority, inaugurated with so much fanfare six months after Eligiusz Niewiadomski murdered President Narutowicz in the name of the eponymous Doctrine of the Polish Majority, lasted less than half a year. It fell in December 1923 when the secession of a small group of Piast deputies, disillusioned by its mismanagement of the economy, ultimately deprived the "Polish Majority" of its majority in the Sejm.[54] Witos's government was replaced by a technocratic minority cabinet headed by the nonpartisan and universally respected Władysław Grabski, which teetered on more or less successfully until 1925. Following its collapse (and the much quicker demise of its short-lived

The second Government of the Polish Majority in 1926. Wincenty Witos, the premier, is in the middle. (Narodowe Archiwum Cyfrowe)

successor), the National Democrats were able to once again reach a coalition agreement with smaller parties. To make up for the defections from Piast, which scuttled the last coalition, the NDs were finally able to entice the National Labor Party into joining a new Government of the Polish Majority. The new coalition government of the NDs, the rump Piast, and National Labor was announced on May 10, 1926.

But this second Government of the Polish Majority would collapse much quicker than the first. Two days after its inauguration, Eligiusz Niewiadomski's curious prophecy was fulfilled almost to the letter. Just as the murderer of Narutowicz had predicted, Piłsudski took a stand "at the head of street thugs, paramilitaries, and regular army units in the fight against the nationalist camp."[55] At the cost of more than 300 dead and the risk of all-out civil war, the marshal brought down the government of his despised enemies and seized power for himself. Five days after taking power, Witos's government formally resigned. So did Piłsudski's old friend, President Wojciechowski, who refused to recognize the legitimacy of the coup. After four years in the political wilderness, the Piłsudskiites were presented with the opportunity to create the Poland they long dreamed of. They certainly had ample time to bring their plans into reality, as they would continue to rule the Second Republic for the remainder of its existence. The National Democrats would never again mount a serious bid for power.

Not surprisingly, the dramatic "May Events" of 1926 and the successful regime change that took place upon their conclusion, have acted as a magnet for historians.[56] Since the Piłsudskiites defeated their rivals so decisively in 1926, it may appear that the murder of Narutowicz ultimately had little impact on the outcome of the political struggle in interwar Poland. Indeed, unlike Piast and likeminded centrists, the Polish left did not openly accept the Doctrine of the Polish Majority in the aftermath of Narutowicz's murder. Especially among the rank and file, there was a lot of anger about the parliamentary leadership's refusal to engage in armed retaliation against the spiritual authors of the murder.[57]

Piłsudski himself was particularly shaken by the assassination of Narutowicz. Even before the murder, during the riots, he was so disturbed as to appear "sick and barely in control of himself."[58] He resigned his position as chief of staff as soon as the Government of the Polish Majority came into existence. As a regular citizen, he felt free to publicly announce the reasons for his antipathy toward the latter. At a banquet held in his honor at the Bristol Hotel shortly after the resignation, he delivered the following speech to his supporters: "Our President was murdered by . . . the very same people who also heaped so much dirt, and so much monstrous, base hatred [upon me]. These people committed a crime.

They committed murder, punishable by law. Gentlemen, I am a soldier. When I thought that I might, as a soldier, have to defend these people, my conscience wavered. ... And once it wavered, I realized that I can no longer be a soldier. These, gentlemen, are the reasons and motivations for my departure from military service."[59] According to those who knew him well, for Piłsudski the murder was "a personal tragedy, which he was never able to shake."[60] He became more bitter and quick to anger. And, no doubt, he was sorely disappointed by the nation he had helped lead to independence. The extreme and crude language, which would become one of his hallmarks in his later years, was for the first time fully in evidence in his speech at the Bristol.[61]

But underneath the anger, a subtle though critically important discursive shift could be observed among the Piłsudskiites, socialists, and Emancipation radicals. An analysis of the manner in which the memory of Narutowicz's election and murder, and the role of the Jews therein, was discussed by left-wing politicians and journalists can shed light on this very subtle but important transformation. To be sure, Narutowicz himself was never forgotten. Anniversaries of the president's murder were duly celebrated by Piłsudski's Sanacja regime, and his name went on to grace streets, schools, and community centers. All Varsovians know the Narutowicz Square, located near the center of the city in the *Ochota* neighborhood. And, at least initially, some writers were willing to openly discuss the causes of the president's murder. An unusually vivid example is offered by Jan Tarnowski's article in the December 19 edition of *Kurjer Poranny*: "What in fact did [the right] have against Narutowicz? The fact that he was chosen by a majority of votes, among which were not only purely Polish votes, but also those of the representatives of other peoples that make up the Polish nation. And the fact that a Pole of great knowledge whose name was recognized abroad was elected to the highest office of the Republic with not only Polish votes was seen, in certain political circles, as a slander to the Polish name and an insult to the entire country."[62] This, indeed, summarized in a few words the true cause of Narutowicz's murder and of the riots that shook Warsaw in December 1922. Yet, Tarnowski's article is notable primarily for how exceptional it was in its frank discussion of the issue.

It may not be surprising that Rataj patently failed to mention the causes of the murder in his commemorative speech about Narutowicz to the Sejm, or that Father Antoni Szlagowski failed to discuss (or even mention) the Jews and the question of antisemitism in his homily at the president's funeral.[63] But it should give us some pause to note that left-wing politicians' and writers' attempts to honor Narutowicz's memory were also increasingly becoming subject to this troubling collective amnesia. Even the Piłsudskiite National Civic Union, so outspoken in its defense of minorities before the elections, did not mention minorities in its official response to the murder of Narutowicz.[64] It was not that the Polish left became more sympathetic toward the National Democrats—if anything the opposite was true. It just appeared to have become unwilling to discuss the role of Jews in the Polish political community and, more specifically, to even acknowledge the role of the "Jewish Question" in the election and murder of the Republic's first president. This trend would continue to intensify. In reading material about Narutowicz from the 1930s, one would never even begin to suspect that the national minorities, let alone Jews, had anything to do with his election or murder.[65]

As we have seen in the last chapter, the "forgetting" of Jewish involvement in the election of Narutowicz was already evident at the trial of Niewiadomski. For example, even as Prosecutor Rudnicki and Civil Attorney Paschalski sought to "showcase" the "moral dimension" of the murder, they could not bring themselves to challenge, or even acknowledge, Niewiadomski's rabid antisemitism.[66] Rudnicki did not mention Jews once during the trial and allowed all of Niewiadomski's (truly outlandish) antisemitic claims to go unanswered.[67] Paschalski, for his part, raised the question of the national minorities just once, and did so indirectly. In an attempt to refute the murderer's claim that Narutowicz had made a mistake by accepting the nomination from the hands of the minorities, Paschalski countered that "this was no mistake." Rather, he claimed, the president bore witness to the tradition of "respect for diversity which permeated all of Polish history, and to that noble Poland which held out its hand to Lithuania and Ukraine, and which took in the Jews."[68] This was the only answer the two attorneys were able to offer to Niewiadomski's litany of antisemitic accusations over the entire course of the trial.

With very few exceptions, such as Tarnowski's article, the left-wing press went out of its way to avoid discussing the causes of Narutowicz's murder. When it was forced to address them, for example during official commemorations of his death, the results could be bizarre. At the six-month anniversary of the murder, the *Kurjer Poranny* ran a front-page story discussing the president's life. What followed was a scathing attack on the National Democrats, who were accused of everything from loyalty to the Tsar during the Partitions to treason during the Polish-Bolshevik war. But when it came time to discuss the causes of the president's death, the article offered a new explanation: "What was this quiet, non-partisan man, who was far removed from any social radicalism and raised in aristocratic society . . . guilty of? The official answer was this: he took power from the hands of the Jews, Germans, and Ukrainians. But this was a lie, as the election of the second president by the very same coalition proved."[69] What, then, was the president *really* guilty of? According to *Kurjer Poranny*, the real cause of the right's hatred was the fact that Narutowicz "acted in the spirit of the same faith that animated Piłsudski," whereas Wojciechowski was acceptable to the National Democrats because he had cooperated with them during World War I.[70]

The claims of the *Kurjer Poranny* were patently untrue on a number of counts. In the first place, as we have seen, Piłsudski himself championed the candidacy of Wojciechowski over that of Narutowicz. Secondly, Wojciechowski's election raised little opposition from the right because of the violence that had just transpired, and because Warsaw was under a state of emergency. The real cause of the right's hatred for Narutowicz was, of course, the one pointed out by Jan Tarnowski immediately after Narutowicz's death in the very same *Kurjer Poranny*. But the fact that one of Poland's most liberal newspapers would attempt to redefine the causes of the murder, and present them as having had nothing to with the minorities, is most instructive.

The same determination to collectively forget particular aspects of the "December Events," affected Poland's political class. We will recall that on December 12, 1922, all parties drafted resolutions demanding an inquiry into the riots of the previous day. These were wrapped into a single motion and dispatched to the Sejm's Administrative Commission for further investigation. The Commission took until June 1923 to deliver its findings, which were presented to the Sejm by none other than Stanisław Thugutt, the man who was almost singlehandedly responsible for persuading Narutowicz to accept candidacy for the presidency.

But if anyone expected Thugutt to openly discuss the causes of the violence and murder, they would be sorely disappointed. Indeed, even Thugutt's summary of the events of December 11 virtually ignored the question of the national minorities or the fact that a good part of the violence was directed against Warsaw's Jewish community. According to Thugutt, the "excesses" consisted of "stopping and insulting deputies, preventing them from fulfilling their obligations in the National Assembly, harassing the representatives of foreign states, and in this manner not only trampling upon the rule of law in Poland but making Poland into an object of embarrassment in the entire civilized world."[71]

Thugutt claimed that the actual "physical perpetrators" of these events, that is the students from the right-wing militias, were "the least guilty," due to their age and "level of intellectual development."[72] Who, then, bore responsibility for what happened? According to Thugutt, the primary culprit for the events of December 11 was not a political group, party, or organization but "a certain legal-political theory."[73] Such a framing of the issue was bound to please the National Democratic deputies gathered in the Sejm. And, indeed, Thugutt's entire speech was not even once interrupted by heckles from the right—which was highly unusual in the normally raucous Parliament. The "theory" that Thugutt had in mind was expressed in conciliatory and legalistic language that effectively stripped his speech of any moral power. According to Thugutt, the key culprit of the violence was the notion that "every Pole-citizen (*Polak-obywatel*) has the sacred right to act over and above the Constitution."[74]

This formulation was deeply problematic even if we accept Thugutt's premise that "theories" could be moral agents and thus be "guilty." As anyone who read the right-wing press in December 1922 was bound to know, the *real* culprit (again, if theories could be culprits) was not the vague and general notion that citizens had moral responsibilities beyond the Constitution (which Thugutt himself would probably have to accept, if he had thought it through more deeply) but the *highly specific* claim that ethnically non-Polish citizens of Poland had no right to participate in the political process. This was, in other words, the Doctrine of the Polish Majority, which had been formulated by the National Democrats in the run-up to the presidential election and which had so recently been embodied in the Government of the Polish Majority. By choosing deliberately obscure and legalistic terms, Thugutt was able to skirt around the most controversial issues and win the support of the entire Sejm for his report. But this victory, if it can be called that, came at the cost of purposefully distorting the real causes of the violence and the president's murder.

The same thing can be said with regard to the second "culprit" identified by Thugutt—"a certain portion of the Warsaw press." No newspapers, let alone writers, were identified in Thugutt's exposé. And his admonitions to the press were almost comically vague: journalists were accused of "leading a certain portion of the population onto a false path with the help of imprecise logic."[75] In the end, Thugutt expressed the hope that in the future the press "would be mindful of its great power and not use it for evil ends."[76] And while the Emancipation leader was highly critical of the police, he argued against any calls for additional investigations into the riots or their causes.[77]

In his memoirs, Thugutt acknowledged that not everyone was happy with his speech and evidently felt the need to excuse himself for his weak and conciliatory stance. "For the price of being able to tell the right certain sad facts necessary for the improvement of the political climate," he wrote, "I renounced the ability to say, in the name of the left, everything I could have said if I had rejected compromise."[78] If he had said everything he wanted to say, Thugutt went to argue, he could not have spoken in the name of the entire Administrative Commission.[79] However, there were two "stronger accents" in Thugutt's speech. The first, it must be admitted, was his harsh denunciation of the "glorification" of the murderer in churches and right-wing newspapers.[80] The second "stronger accent" of Thugutt's speech referred to Jews—though not quite in the way one may have expected.

In all likelihood, Thugutt would have preferred to ignore the Jewish question entirely, just as he was able to ignore it in discussing the violence of December 11. However, among the motions brought forth on December 12 was one from the Jewish Circle, which demanded the creation of a special parliamentary commission to investigate the role played by Rozwój in "anti-Jewish pogroms and excesses which have taken place on the lands of the Republic over the past four years."[81] The resolution could admittedly be construed as being needlessly provocative and offensive to the sensibilities of all Poles, including the left. It leveled charges that the police, the Prosecutor's Office, as well as the Ministry of Internal Affairs, and thus effectively the Polish state, openly "tolerated even and supported" antisemitic pogroms "in which hundreds had been killed."[82] In a final gratuitously provocative gesture, it demanded criminal charges to be brought against the minister of internal affairs, police officials, and prosecutors who were "guilty in the anti-Jewish excesses and pogroms of the last four years."[83]

The Jewish Circle's motion was tabled in the immediate aftermath of the December 11 riots, which can perhaps explain its highly emotional tone and unrealistic, needlessly provocative demands. Thugutt's reply, on the other hand, was made a full six months later in an atmosphere of relative political calm. Yet, reading the text of Thugutt's speech, one gets the distinct impression that he was tougher in dealing with the Jewish Circle than with the National Democrats. Indeed, while Thugutt claims that he "wanted to avoid mentioning the names of any parties or individuals," there was one party that he addressed very directly— the Jewish Circle. After making the perfunctory claim that Emancipation would always stand in defense of Jews when they were attacked, Thugutt went on to address the Jewish deputies directly:

> I have already had the unpleasant duty of warning you a number of times about the passions which you bring to political life in Poland. ... I do not know anything about numerous pogroms[84] which resulted in hundreds of dead. But I remember very well when I was in Paris in 1919, how a great wave of calumnies and hatreds [sponsored by Jewish politicians] was eroding the foundations of the Polish state. The constant barrage of lies and baseless accusations which fell on Poland in 1919

doubtlessly could not have created good relations between Poland and the Jews. I do not want to argue with you . . . but I have to let you know that the extraordinary passion with which you approach this subject, as well as the lack of any regard with which you throw your accusations not just against one class or one party but against all of Polish society, will not allow even the Polish left to support your motion.[85]

This is not the place to debate the substance of Thugutt's accusations against Poland's Jewish parliamentarians or the activities and lobbying efforts of particular Jewish leaders in 1919. What is significant is that Thugutt's rebuke of the Jewish Circle was more forceful than his timid and conciliatory critique of the National Democrats' role in the events of December 11. And while it may be true that the motion tabled by the Jewish Circle was gratuitously provocative, surely there was truth in the words of the Circle's deputy, Ignacy Schiper, who attempted to defend his party's resolution:

> We thought it necessary to underline the fact . . . that the President of Poland was murdered as a Jewish President. . . . [National Democratic] demagoguery reduced the question of the first President of the Republic of Poland to the Jewish denominator. We hope to help usher in a new political consciousness among Polish society, the consciousness that the state cannot be built on the foundation of constant warfare against citizens who fulfill their obligations and who demand their rights. . . . The same hand that was unpunished after it was raised against the life or health of a Jewish Polish citizen . . . was raised against the President of the Republic. . . . Antisemitism is a danger for the development of the state, a mask under which it is easy to prepare various coups against the rule of law. This is what we want to point out. We want to take a stand against antisemitism and we would like the Sejm to support our resolution.[86]

There is no doubt that Schiper was fundamentally correct. If one really wanted to find an impersonal culprit responsible for the riots of December 11 and the murder of the president, that culprit was antisemitism, which motivated, at the deepest levels, both Niewiadomski and the student demonstrators from Three Crosses Square. Thus, if one wanted to present an honest assessment of the events that took place between December 9 and December 16, to "eradicate the evil at its very roots" (Sikorski) or to "morally annihilate Niewiadomski" (Rataj), the question of antisemitism *had* to be addressed. And if there was ever a time to take a stand against antisemitism in Polish political life, surely the discussion of the December Events was that time.

Yet, aside from Thugutt's rebuke of the Jewish Circle, no Polish parliamentarian even mentioned Jews in the discussion of these events. Nocznicki, another Emancipation deputy who spoke after Thugutt, bemoaned the "atmosphere of hatred towards the lawful order in the state."[87] The PPS deputy Pragier blamed the right for "preparing the demonstrations, which prepared the death blow delivered against the President."[88] Anusz, a deputy of the breakaway Piast faction that refused to join the Government of the Polish Majority, complained that the right "failed to find a single word of disapproval for the murder and has instead undertaken a relentless and systematic effort to glorify it."[89] But none of them discussed the *causes* of the extraordinary hatred that manifested itself against the president. And none of them even uttered the words "Jews" or "antisemitism."

The apparent desire to forget the role of Jews in the election and the murder of Narutowicz was related to a more significant though more subtle discursive shift that occurred in the Polish press in the aftermath of December 16. As we will recall from chapter 4, prior to the presidential elections, left-wing papers and journals, such as *Głos Prawdy*, *Robotnik*, *Kurjer Poranny*, and *Kurjer Polski*, offered a spirited and sophisticated defense of the national minorities' right to participate in the political process. To be sure, the Polish left-wing press never backtracked on these claims—it just stopped airing them. After December 16, the very few articles that explicitly defended this position inevitably began with declarations reaffirming the nature of Poland as *primarily* a state for the Poles.[90] The Piłsudskiites seemed to realize that they were fighting an uphill battle. Writing in *Droga*, an author who used the penname "Old Fellow," perhaps to show the anachronism of his views, fully acknowledged that "the demagogical doctrine ... which states that the representatives of national minorities cannot take part in the government" had now become "popular even beyond reactionary circles."[91]

The "Jewish Question" Revisited

But if serious discussions of the "Minorities Question" in Polish parliamentary politics seemed to have all but disappeared from the pages of the left-wing press in the aftermath of the Narutowicz murder, the "Jewish Question" continued to make an appearance in a somewhat different and more disturbing context. While the strategy of using the "Jewish Question" in order to embarrass the right was not entirely new, it certainly accelerated after the murder of Narutowicz. In fact, following the murder, the Jews became a staple of the left's rhetorical arsenal and were routinely used to embarrass and discredit the National Democrats. For example, almost immediately after the murder of Narutowicz, *Głos Prawdy* published a list of business transactions carried out between the antisemitic Rozwój society and Jewish merchants.[92] Spurious speculations about the National Democrats seeking Jewish support for the Government of the Polish Majority were printed in left-wing newspapers.[93] Attacks on individual National Democratic politicians were made easier by the fact that many of them, including some of the most outspoken Polish antisemites like Adolf Nowaczyński or Stanisław Stroński, really did have recent and well-documented Jewish ancestry.[94] Reminding Sejm deputies of Stroński's Jewish roots became a staple strategy of Jewish Circle deputies themselves.[95] Such attacks were often extremely effective. As Singer writes: "There was no lack of reminding Stroński of his Jewish roots. This was one of the most effective ways of combating an outstanding antisemitic activist. Stroński answered all attacks directed against him quickly and wittily. Only the epithet "Jew" was always left hanging in the air without an answer."[96]

The results of such tactics could often be bizarre. While the left rarely explicitly attacked the principle that only a Polish majority could legitimately constitute the country's government, it quickly turned out that one of the most effective ways to attack the Government of the Polish Majority was to highlight the latter's (very tenuous) Jewish connection.[97] The matter was helped by the fact that one of the negotiators on the Piast side was Senator Ludwik Hammerling, a rich businessman and landowner, who was a first generation Jewish convert to Catholicism. Some of the preliminary discussions between Piast and the National Democrats took place on his estate near the village of Lanckorona. Even though the final agreement was signed in Warsaw, the awkwardly named "Rules of Cooperation between the Parties of the Polish Parliamentary Majority in the Sejm" almost immediately became known as the *Pakt Lanckoroński* or Lanckorona Pact. The label was a sore spot for both the right and Piast, and Hammerling's involvement in the negotiations was subsequently minimized by politicians such as Witos.[98]

The source of embarrassment was twofold. First, the Lanckorona appellation, with its connotation of rural great estates, was embarrassing for a peasant party like Piast. A bigger source of embarrassment, however, was Ludwik Hammerling's Jewish ancestry, which was immediately exploited by the left. *Głos Prawdy*, which rarely contained any illustrations, ran a photo of Hammerling's father, an orthodox Jew, on its cover. The caption under the photo stated that Senator Hammerling had evidently forgotten "where and from whom he was born" and that *Głos Prawdy* would like to remind him by printing a picture of his father.

Attacks such as the ones described previously were not intended to be antisemitic (though today we would judge them as such). Rather, their goal was to mock antisemites and to expose "the dubious morality of the antisemitic enterprise."[99] Nonetheless, they certainly led down a slippery slope and in certain

Rok II.

Cena 1000 Mk.

№ 68

GŁOS

TYGODNIK POLITYCZNO-SPOŁECZNY

WARSZAWA, DNIA 16 CZERWCA 1923 ROKU.

A. HAMMERLING.

Pan Senator z P. S. L. „Piast" Ludwik Hammerling, twórca i leader obecnej większości sejmowej zapomniał gdzie, kiedy i z kogo się urodził.

„Nowy Świat" wyręcza p. Senatora przez podanie powyższej fotografji jego ojca A. Hammerlinga. Powinna ona przyczynić się znakomicie do utrwalenia sławy bloku zawiązanego w gościnnych salonach p. L. Hammerlinga.

The left-wing pro-Piłsudski publication *Głos Prawdy* reminds Ludwik Hammerling, a Piast senator and one of the architects of the Government of the Polish Majority, "where and from whom he was born." Cover of *Glos Prawdy* from June 16, 1923.

cases could become very problematic. For example, shortly after the murder of Narutowicz, the Emancipation backbencher Józef Sanocja published a somewhat rambling book entitled *Those Guilty of the Crime*, which mounted a scathing attack on the National Democrats. In the book, Sanocja debunked many of the charges leveled by the Endeks against the deceased president, including the claim that he had been "elected by the Jews." Presumably to bolster the left's "Polish credentials," Sanocja posed the following question: "[The National Democrats] have a thousand times insulted the entire workers' and peasants' movement as being Jewish. But what's the real story with the Jews? Who brought the Jews to Poland? Who made Poland into a protector of Jews from around the world?"[100] His answer was that the Jews were brought to Poland by the nobility, whose class interests were now represented by the National Democrats.[101] Thus, the right was "guilty" of bringing Jews to Poland. Clearly, even though Sanocja was attempting to attack the right, he was operating within its discursive universe and was enthralled by the Doctrine of the Polish Majority. The problem for him was not antisemitism but, just as for the National Democrats, "the Jews."

But even if we disregard Sanocja's case, which was not representative of the Polish left, the rhetorical usage of the "Jewish Question" as a *weapon* against the right illustrates the left's tacit acquiescence to the Doctrine of the Polish Majority, and the extraordinary power that the latter had achieved in a relatively short time. Most importantly, the usage of the "Jewish Question" to embarrass the right, even when done in a tongue-in-cheek manner and with the best intentions (which was not always the case), and even if engaged in by Jewish politicians themselves, validated a central thesis of National Democratic discourse—that "the Jews" were a problem. Such arguments were especially problematic given that, following the murder of Narutowicz, the left had drastically limited its advocacy for the participation of the minorities in the political process. By desisting from publicly challenging the Doctrine of the Polish Majority and by using the "Jewish Question" as something to be deployed against one's political opponents in order to embarrass them, the left was effectively allowing the National Democratic brand of nationalist and antisemitic discourse to become the dominant, if not yet hegemonic, mode of speaking publicly about the nation.

The most troubling implications of this development were still in the future, but they were foreshadowed by one of the most interesting and controversial articles ever published by *Droga*, the Piłsudskiites' theoretical organ.[102] The short article in question was prefixed by a special and highly unusual editorial note that stated that while the editors "disagreed with many of the views expressed by the author," they were compelled to "admit that he framed a number of issues correctly and valued the freshness and sincerity of his thought." In sum, they decided to print the article, without endorsing its contents, as a "valuable material for discussion." The article, entitled "Of the Left, Right, and So-Called Fascists," was signed only with the initials A. N-A., which leads to the intriguing possibility that the author was no other than the right-wing journalist Adolf Nowaczyński, who had been briefly thrown in jail for his portrayal of Niewiadomski as a hero and a martyr.[103]

The article was remarkable for its insightful and succinct discussion of the internal contradictions of Piłsudskiite thought and political practice.[104] For example A. N-A. wrote:

Every day, your "liberalism" is contradicted by your calls for repressions against speculators and "Endeks." Your pacifism is contradicted by your "great power politics" (especially directed against Russia), which is mentioned so frequently by activists from the Polish Military Organization and the PPS. Your "republicanism" contradicts your often blind devotion to Piłsudski, who is doubtlessly an exceptional man but who has also committed many errors. Your "civic instinct" is in some strange way reconciled with calls for subversive political strikes. Your "democratism" is full of contradictions.[105]

Indeed the author brilliantly highlighted many of the deep cleavages that could be easily reconciled while the followers of Piłsudski were in opposition, but that would lead to serious schisms within the movement after it seized power in 1926. The article's central thesis, however, was that the radicals among the Polish left and right were, despite superficial impressions to the contrary, converging on many points. Most Poles, he argued, were tired of the partisanship of established political parties on both the right and the left and wanted a (presumably non-democratic) "government of real patriots."[106] The deep division of Poland into two camps was an "illusion." Only a few issues stood in the way of the left and the right coming together. For example, according to A. N-A., the left had to stop "holding on to the constitution in a doctrinaire manner" and give up its "cult of the eight hour workday, which lowers productivity."[107]

In other words, A. N-A suggested, the Polish left and right were converging on a basically fascist platform. But the two biggest issues still dividing the two groups and preventing them from coming together were historical animosities and the "Jewish Question." History, the author thought, would eventually be forgotten. But on the Jewish Question, the Piłsudskiites were clearly losing the battle. Most Poles, A. N-A. argued, wanted to show that "we" rather than "enemy elements" were in charge. Fortunately, he claimed, the left was now "turning against the Jews." "Even radical socialist workers," he went on, were "now anti-Semites in private" and it was high time for the left to "stop defending" the principle of "equal rights for the Jews."[108] If that could be achieved, then radical left-wing organizations like the Polish Military Organization or the paramilitary Piłsudskiite group Strzelec (Marksman) would not appear all that different from the right-wing student groups that made up the most militant core of the nationalist movement.

The author admitted that the latter groups had, from the perspective of the left, committed the "original sin" of "creating the setting for the mad and unfortunate act of Niewiadomski."[109] He also acknowledged that many right-wing leaders had been shamefully slavish during the Partitions. But he promised that the youth would no longer allow themselves to be manipulated and used for partisan purposes by the parliamentary representatives of the right. Deep down, their desires "for action for the entire nation ... and for building the Polish state ... through the work of the Poles alone" were pure and justified. In service of this goal, the right-wing youth groups would be willing to "stand with a clear sense of discipline, duty, and solidarity."[110]

The article ended with a half-exhortation and half-threat to the Piłsudskiites. According to A. N-A, the right now had the hearts of the majority of Polish youth, just as the left had them before World War I. "He who believes in the healthy instinct of the Polish race," the author concluded somewhat ominously, "will draw his conclusions from this fact."[111] If the author was indeed Nowaczyński, then his proposal to the left was exactly the same, albeit delivered in a very different tone, as the one expressed in his infamous article "Testament," which had landed him in jail. In that article, published by the ultranationalist *Myśl Narodowa*, Nowaczyński had expressed the hope that Niewiadomski's last "noble" words would convert Marshal Piłsudski to the gospel of antisemitism.[112] What he was advocating, therefore, was an alliance of the radical elements among both the left and the right built around an essentially fascist platform of antisemitism, authoritarian politics, and an activist (though evolutionary rather than revolutionary) commitment of the state to social and economic reform. To bring about national unity and broaden their base of support, the author intimated, the Piłsudskiites had to get over the death of Narutowicz and embrace antisemitism.

The rapprochement between the followers of Piłsudski and antisemitic nationalism—so eagerly anticipated by Eligiusz Niewiadomski in his final "letter to the nation," Adolf Nowaczyński in the Endek *Myśl Narodowa*, and the mysterious A. N-A. in Piłsudskiite *Droga*—could never take place as long as Piłsudski was alive. But following the latter's death in 1935, the faction of Marshal Edward

Rydz-Śmigły outmaneuvered his anointed successor, Colonel Walery Sławek, and won power in the internal struggle within the post-Piłsudskiite Sanacja regime. To bolster their flagging popularity and mobilize supporters, Rydz-Śmigły's followers attempted to create a mass-based party organization. The result of these attempts was the Camp of National Unity, which embraced economic and political antisemitism in an explicit effort to reach out to a number of National Democratic splinter groups.[113]

The organization's "Ideological-Political Declaration," unveiled with much fanfare on February 20, 1937, by Colonel Adam Koc, who according to some sources was blamed by Piłsudski for failing to engineer a coup in the wake of Narutowicz's murder, eschewed violent solutions to the "Jewish Question" but endorsed "Polish society's understandable instinct of self-defence" against the Jews in the cultural and economic realms. The Camp of National Unity's exclusion of Jews from its membership, despite its eponymous rhetoric of "national unity" and inclusiveness toward "all those willing to participate in the common effort," aptly represented the new conception of the Polish nation embraced by Piłsudski's heirs.

While it is obviously impossible to draw a simple causal relationship between the December Events and some Piłsudskiites' eventual adoption of political antisemitism, there is no doubt that the retreat from civic nationalism, and even flirtation with elements among the radical right, could first be observed in the aftermath of the Narutowicz murder. Essentially, the murder of President Narutowicz presented the Polish left with two options: Either to seize power and deal violently with the right or to continue the contest for the Poles' hearts and minds in the sphere of democratic politics. Having chosen (or perhaps in some cases having been forced to follow) the latter course, many leftists and Piłsudskiites appear to have concluded that "the Jews" were a liability in this struggle. And since the minorities were never really seen as Poles in the full sense of that word, the temptation to sacrifice the minorities in the service of political expediency was inherently embedded in Piłsudskiite political calculus.[114] The contingent events surrounding the election and the murder of Narutowicz created a situation in which such a bargain appeared evermore tempting. These considerations may help explain why the Piłsudskiites were willing to tone down, and eventually abandon, their defense of the civic conception of the Polish nation.

Droga's publication of A. N-A.'s article during the period in which the left was for the first time showing an unspoken acquiescence in the Doctrine of the Polish Majority, was the first flirtation of the Piłsudskiite movement with the antisemitic nationalism to which a large part of it would succumb after the marshal's death.

As we have seen, it was the reflection of a wider trend that seized Polish politics in the aftermath of the Narutowicz assassination, and that expressed itself in the left's silent withdrawal from its hitherto vigorous public stance supporting the right of the minorities to participate in the Polish polity as full-fledged members. In this sense, even the obvious military victory of the May Coup could not undo the more subtle discursive defeat that the idea of Polish civic nationhood suffered in the aftermath of the December Events.

Conclusion

At first glance, the murder of President Gabriel Narutowicz by Eligiusz Niewiadomski can appear to be an "accident of history." The murderer acted alone, and on the surface level, the shots he fired into the president's back at the Zachęta Art Gallery appear to tell us little about Polish history or radical-right politics in interwar Europe. Yet, when interpreted in a slightly broader historical context, the "December Events" emerge not only as a window into the world of radical-right politics but also as an important, perhaps pivotal, event in the transformation of the discourse of the nation in Poland.

The long-term causes of the murder can be adduced to the culture of hatred cultivated by the National Democrats (NDs) and their allies in early-twentieth-century Poland. A closer look at right-wing rhetoric, both in the pre-election period and during the riots, forces us to reconsider the periodization of Polish nationalism and antisemitism in the interwar period. While Polish historians have traditionally portrayed National Democratic antisemitism in the 1920s as "moderate," a glance beyond official party programs not only shows the virulence of the NDs' hatred of the Jews but also points to interesting parallels between National Democratic and fascist politics. In particular, an analysis of National Democratic electoral literature yields a Manichean vision of the world, in which good "Poles" (the National Democrats themselves) were locked in battle for survival with the evil "Jews" and their "stooges" (all nonnationalists). This palingenetic myth of national rebirth through struggle with "the Jews" lies at the heart of the National Democrats' mobilizing cultural and political vision. In fact, the NDs had almost nothing else to offer their supporters. It also bears repeating that while Polish historians usually write about anger against the "national minorities," in reality the Ukrainians and Belarusians, and even the Germans, were scarcely mentioned during the December Events and in their aftermath. The anger and hatred were focused almost exclusively against Jews and their (supposed) Polish lackeys. But this does not mean that antisemitism had "triumphed in Polish society." In the run-up to the election, the left, and the followers of Marshal Piłsudski, offered a powerful counternarrative of the nation, which emphasized an inclusive and civic patriotism.

But these deep divisions in Polish society did not inevitably lead to violence between the National Democrats and their enemies. Nor did antisemitic rhetoric inevitably lead to mass violence against Jews. Rather, the violent confrontation between the partisans of these two visions of the national community, and the closely related violence against Warsaw's Jewish community, was provoked by a series of contingent events, which triggered the latent reservoir of hatred created by the National Democrats' rhetoric.

The emergence of the Doctrine of the Polish Majority, which effectively excluded all non-Poles from politics, can only be understood in the context of the particular and highly contingent outcome of the parliamentary elections of 1922. The situation in which the national minorities appeared to be the kingmakers in the presidential election resulted from the electoral system adopted in the March Constitution, the split in the left-wing vote, the formation of a cohesive minorities' bloc, and the president being elected by the National Assembly rather than by popular vote. This situation was simply tailor made to be exploited by advocates of antisemitism eager to convince Poles that "the Jews" were plotting to take over their country. Most importantly, it allowed the right to present what had previously been a vague and mysterious scepter of "Jewish dominion" over Poland as a concrete and specific danger, embodied by the nation's first president being beholden to Jewish political parties.

The election of Gabriel Narutowicz to the presidency was also the result of highly contingent factors, such as Piłsudski's refusal to run, Stanisław Thugutt's insistence on Narutowicz's candidacy even in the face of opposition from Piłsudski, the left's inability to agree upon a single candidate prior to the vote, the National Democrats' foolish selection of Count Zamoyski as their candidate, and the national minorities' refusal to vote for Piast candidate Stanisław Wojciechowski. This unique interplay of events led to the election of a president who was seen by many as an "overseas devil" or "elder of Zion," and who was perhaps uniquely well-suited to be depicted as a "Jewish stooge." In all likelihood the election of the charismatic Piłsudski, or even the well-known Wojciechowski, would not have galvanized Varsovians to quite the same extent as that of the Swiss-educated, cosmopolitan, and virtually unknown Narutowicz.

The transgression of the newly formulated Doctrine of the Polish Majority by the election of Narutowicz with the aid of the national minorities brought forth genuine popular anger. It was interpreted by right-wing journalists, and student demonstrators who followed their lead, as a call to battle for the creation of a new Poland and the liberation of the nation from supposed Jewish control. The flames of hatred were stoked by journalists, politicians, and student organizations dedicated to antisemitism, but there was no Mussolini or Hitler pulling the strings behind the curtains and waiting to be invited into the corridors of power. In this sense, the December Events were almost the polar opposite of Piłsudski's seizure of power in 1926, which was a conventional military coup. Nor did anyone in the National Democratic movement appear to have a plan of action beyond forcing the president, whose post was largely ceremonial anyway, to resign. This explains the National Democrats' spectacular failure to capitalize on the mobilization of their supporters during the December Events. While the loyalty of the Polish army to Piłsudski must have been an implicit factor in the NDs' political calculus, the lack of effective leadership was probably even more important. Dmowski's absence from Warsaw, and the fact that the National Democratic leadership, at this point in the hands of "old school" Galician parliamentarians, was genuinely committed to parliamentary politics, ensured that there would be no "March on Warsaw." The top National Democrats' inspiration was France, not Italy, and they appeared to be mired in an earlier era of right-wing politics and out of step with the radical impulses of their own younger followers.

The sense of spiritual kinship to Fascism displayed by the students during the riots of December 10 and 11 illustrates an interesting dynamic about the National Democratic movement and, perhaps, the east European radical right more generally. On the surface, the NDs and the Fascists had little in common: The former were dedicated almost exclusively to antisemitism and were still formally committed to democracy, while the latter were not antisemitic and saw democracy itself as their main enemy. In this sense, the National Democrats' closest parallels are protofascist movements in Hungary and Romania. In the latter two countries, in the early 1920s the radical right had not yet articulated a comprehensive political vision or totalitarian program (such as would come later with the development of the Iron Guard and the Arrow Cross) but, like in Poland, was violent, focused on "internal enemies" of the nation, and obsessed with the "Jewish Question." At the radical right's cultural core was the palingenetic myth of the nation's regenerative struggle with its enemies. And in Poland, unlike in Italy, though similar to Hungary, Romania, and Germany, at the very heart of this myth was antisemitism.

It was "the Jews" who were the primary enemy and who stood in the way of the nation's success. The hatred embedded in this myth ultimately motivated Niewiadomski to kill President Narutowicz and explains why his action was applauded by so many Poles.

The murder of Narutowicz created a second, often forgotten, revolutionary moment. Indeed, a word needs to be said about the reluctance (or failure) of the left to carry out a coup immediately after the assassination—a coup that in all likelihood would have brought Piłsudski to power four years earlier and rendered the "May Events" of 1926 unnecessary. It appears that two separate factors can help explain the survival of democracy in Poland. On the one hand, one can certainly commend Maciej Rataj and Władysław Sikorski, who charted an independent course between the right and the left and were able to quickly and effectively carry out a transfer of power in full accordance with the constitution. While a coup carried out in the immediate aftermath of the murder would most likely have been accepted by Polish society as necessary, that situation changed as soon as Rataj's assumption of the powers of head of state under the constitution was publicly announced. Prompt and decisive action by democratic elites can certainly have an impact on the preservation of democratic regimes in moments of crisis.

However, an even more important factor was the reluctance of the left itself to carry out a coup. The parliamentary leaders of the left, Igancy Daszyński and Stanisław Thugutt, were committed to the constitution and parliamentary rule. They did all they could to dampen the revolutionary fervor of their more radical followers, and in this respect they bear a surprising similarity to their National Democratic counterparts. A more complicated question concerns Piłsudski's reluctance to act. As we have seen, according to some of his followers, the marshal expected them to arrange a coup, in which he would have emerged as a power broker and arbiter between the left and the right. If that were true, then Piłsudski miscalculated gravely. His plans failed due to the indecisiveness of his followers and their failure to win the backing of the socialists, compounded by Rataj's extraordinarily quick resolution of the looming constitutional crisis. However, we should remain cognizant of the fact that such explanations were delivered with full knowledge of what transpired in May of 1926. Was Piłsudski ready to assume dictatorial powers in December 1922? Despite his obvious disappointment with democracy, and with the Polish nation, the marshal may simply not have been ready to destroy the democratic regime that he had actively helped create. While we will never know the precise nature of Piłsudski's plans, one thing is almost certain—the survival of Polish democracy in 1922 owed more to the indecisiveness of its (potential) enemies than to its own strength.

The long-term effects of the assassination of Narutowicz are most surprising. Contrary to what historians have argued, the December Events should ultimately be seen as a victory for the National Democrats. To be sure, antisemitism had been a staple of the ND's political rhetoric since at least 1905. However, the formulation of the Doctrine of the Polish Majority provided the proponents of antisemitism with a new focus and lent their credo a new coherence. Further, in the aftermath of the election of Narutowicz, all Poles witnessed the extraordinary power of antisemitic nationalism to mobilize its adherents. Most important, the hateful sentiments and rhetoric that led to the murder of the president were never repudiated by the National Democratic elite. Even the murderer was quickly accepted as a nationalist hero and martyr. His trial and execution, as covered by the major right-wing newspapers, actually provided the right with the opportunity to reaffirm the legitimacy of the principles in the name of which President Narutowicz was murdered. Thus, even if the murder was a short-term political setback for the right, there is no doubt that it was a long-term discursive victory.

The most profound impact of the December Events, however, was not on the National Democrats but on the center and the left of the political spectrum. The violence directed against Narutowicz appears to have convinced many Polish politicians that it was more expedient to appease the antisemites than to challenge them. This was the political choice very rationally and explicitly made by Maciej Rataj, the marshal of the Sejm. The acceptance of the Doctrine of the Polish Majority also underpinned the political strategy and rhetoric of centrist politicians such as Wincenty Witos, Władysław Sikorski, and Stanisław Wojciechowski. It bears repeating that none of these figures accepted political antisemitism. But they clearly decided that defending the political rights of the Jews and other minorities was not a battle worth fighting. The centrist politicians from Piast seemed eager to adopt the Doctrine of the Polish Majority not so much because of the numbers commanded by the advocates of exclusive nationalism and antisemitism, which in all likelihood did not change all that much following the December Events, but because of their intensity, intransigence, and willingness to resort to violence.

But while the fear of violence and anarchy can certainly help explain the capitulation of Piast and other centrist politicians to the "Polish Majority," it by no means rendered this capitulation inevitable. Indeed, this story is about agency as much as it is about contingency. As Maciej Rataj's decision to embrace the Doctrine of the Polish Majority illustrates, Piast deputies had a very clear alternative to an alliance with the National Democrats. According to Rataj, a shrewd and intelligent political leader, most Poles would have opted for land reform even in alliance with "the Jews" (or the minorities to be more precise). Yet, it was Piast *leadership*, rather than grassroots members, who effectively made the decision to opt for an alliance with antisemites in order to deflect more radical calls for land reform. In the case of Rataj, this decision was certainly the result of pragmatic calculations rather than visceral fears.

The impact of the December Events on the left and on the Piłsudskiites was more subtle but perhaps equally profound. Following the murder of Narutowicz, two partly contradictory trends emerged on the left side of the political spectrum. Most obvious was the unquestionable anger felt by Piłsudski himself, and many of his followers, toward the National Democrats. The seeds of the May Coup of 1926 were sown in December 1922. Less visible, but equally important, were the first steps of the left's silent acquiescence in the Doctrine of the Polish Majority. Immediately after the murder, the left had certainly had the opportunity to employ violence against the right and/or forcefully challenge the antisemitic discourse responsible for inciting Niewiadomski. For a variety of reasons, neither option was taken, and the role of antisemitism in the president's murder was never openly addressed or discussed. Quite the opposite, the mass mobilization witnessed during the December Events appears to have convinced many left-leaning Poles that there was little to gain, and much to lose, from overtly championing the right of Jews to participate in Polish national life as full-fledged members. In this manner, the December Events helped to ensure that the Doctrine of the Polish Majority would not be seriously challenged again in the Second Republic.

Still, the alliance between the Piłsudskiites and antisemites advocated by the mysterious A. N-A., by Adolf Nowaczyński, and by Eligiusz Niewiadomski was absolutely unthinkable as long as Piłsudski remained in charge of his followers. Until the end of his life, the marshal forcefully resisted ever-increasing calls by the right for the implementation of antisemitic legislation. But his followers muted their defense of the civic conception of the Polish nation. And a mere two years after Piłsudski's death, a group of his successors centered around Poland's de facto ruler Marshal Edward Rydz-Śmigły openly endorsed political antisemitism and attempted to reach out to elements among the nationalist right in order to bring them into the (post-)Piłsudski camp.

The adoption of political antisemitism by the post-Piłsudski Sanacja regime was the culmination of a long and complicated process, and it is obviously impossible to trace a simple line or postulate a direct causal relationship between the December Events and the antisemitism of the Camp of National Unity. However, the beginning of the Piłsudskiites' gradual retreat from the forceful and public defense of civic nationhood, which ultimately made the latter possible, can be traced back to the tragic events of December 1922. This fundamentally important legacy of the December Events aptly illustrates the power of violent action to transform discursive structures.

By the time Piłsudski's successors officially adopted the antisemitic ideology of their enemies, the memory of what the election and murder of Gabriel Narutowicz represented had become a liability for virtually everyone in Poland. According to the long-time Sejm correspondent Bernard Singer, when the first Government of the Polish Majority was in power, a legend circulated among the Sejm janitorial staff about a ghost haunting the parliamentary chambers.[1] The janitors claimed that at night they could hear strange noises in the back rooms and the sound of slow, heavy footsteps on the floor, walking between the offices of Piast and those of the National People's Union. But by the 1930s, Singer writes, this legend was forgotten—just like the true significance of President Narutowicz's election and the causes of his death.

Notes

Introduction

1. "The assassination of a head of state," especially in a poorly consolidated and internally divided society such as interwar Poland, generally leads "to an increase in the extent of political unrest." Zaryab Iqbal and Christopher Zorn, "The Political Consequences of Assassination," *Journal of Conflict Resolution* 52, no. 3 (June 2008): 388.

2. Norman Davies, *God's Playground: A History of Poland* (Oxford: Oxford University Press, 2005), 2:315. It is a tribute to the obscurity of this event in the English-speaking world that it is absent even from the *Encyclopedia of Assassinations*, which claims to catalog important political assassinations from antiquity into the modern era. Carl Sifakis, *Encyclopedia of Assassinations* (New York: Facts on File, 2001).

3. For example, see Mikołaj Stanisław Kunicki, *Between the Brown and the Red: Nationalism, Catholicism, and Communism in Twentieth-Century Poland—The Politics of Bolesław Piasecki* (Athens: Ohio University Press, 2012); Eva Plach, *The Clash of Moral Nations: Cultural Politics in Piłsudski's Poland, 1926–1935* (Athens: Ohio University Press, 2006); Antony Polonsky, *Politics in Independent Poland 1921–1939: The Crisis of Constitutional Government* (Oxford: Clarendon Press, 1972). Traditional Polish accounts, which pay little attention to the cultural impact of political events, tend to portray the murder of Narutowicz as the work of a fanatic or madman, greatly underestimate the role of antisemitism in creating the crisis, and ignore the assassination's long-term effects. For examples of this literature, see Jan M. Ciechanowski, *O genezie i upadku II Rzeczypospolitej* (London: Odnowa, 1981); Antoni Czubiński, *Spory o II Rzeczpospolitą: Ewolucja poglądów publicystyki i historiografii polskiej na temat przyczyn odbudowy i znaczenia niepodległego państwa dla narodu polskiego* (Poznań: Krajowa Agencja Wydawnicza, 1983); Marian Marek Drozdowski, *Społeczeństwo, państwo, politycy II Rzeczypospolitej: Szkice i polemiki* (Cracow: Wydawnictwo Literackie, 1972); Marian Eckert, *Historia Polski, 1914–1939* (Warsaw: Wydawnictwa Szkolne i Pedagogiczne, 1990); Andrzej Garlicki, *Pierwsze lata Drugiej Rzeczypospolitej* (Warsaw: Krajowa Agencja Wydawnicza, 1989); Aleksandra Nowak, Maria Kuczyńska, and Witold Stankiewicz, *Druga Rzeczpospolita 1918–1939* (Warsaw: Biblioteka Narodowa, 1978).

4. Daria Nałęcz and Tomasz Nałęcz, "Gabriel Narutowicz, prezydent Rzeczypospolitej 14XIII-16XIII 1922," in *Prezydenci i premierzy Drugiej Rzeczypospolitej*, ed. Andrzej Chojnowski and Piotr Wróbel (Wrocław: Zakład Narodowy im. Ossolińskich, 1992), 48.

5. Chojnowski and Wróbel's contention that Narutowicz's days in office are among the most underresearched episodes of interwar Polish history still rings true today. Andrzej Chojnowski and Piotr Wróbel, eds., *Prezydenci i premierzy drugiej Rzeczypospolitej* (Wrocław: Zakład Narodowy im. Ossolińskich, 1992), 6. Some popular biographies of Narutowicz have been published in Polish, but these do not provide an analytical inquiry into the political context and implications of the murder. Danuta Pacyńska-Drzewińska, *Śmierć Prezydenta* (Warsaw: Wydawnictwo Ministerstwa Obrony Narodowej, 1965); Marek Ruszczyc, *Strzały W "Zachęcie"* (Katowice: Śląsk, 1987); Marek Ruszczyc, *Pierwszy Prezydent Gabriel Narutowicz* (Warsaw: Książka i Wiedza, 1967). A recent popular biography of Eligiusz Niewiadomski deals with the assassination but is journalistic rather than scholarly and concerns itself primarily with a pseudopsychological study of Niewiadomski. See Patryk Pleskot, *Niewiadomski—zabić prezydenta* (Warsaw: Demart, 2012). The best and most recent biography is Janusz Pajewski, *Gabriel Narutowicz: Pierwszy Prezydent Rzeczypospolitej* (Warsaw: Książka i Wiedza, 1993). The most detailed study of the Narutowicz assassination remains Władysław Pobóg-Malinowski, *Najnowsza historia polityczna Polski, 1864–1945* (London: Świderski, 1983).

6. Juan J. Linz and Alfred C. Stepan, *The Breakdown of Democratic Regimes* (Baltimore: Johns Hopkins University Press, 1978), 3.

7. The idea of a seemingly random event leading to long-term cultural changes may not be intuitive. For centuries, of course, events had been at the very center of history—as Blaise Pascal famously remarked, if Cleopatra's nose had "been different the whole face of the world would have changed." And while the "Crux of Cleopatra's Nose" view of history has come under attack from philosophers ranging from Montesquieu to Marx, in the twentieth century it has come under sustained critique from professional historians. Skepticism regarding the role played by events in understanding historical change characterized the great French "Annales" school as well as the "new social history" in American academia. In both schools, historical change was seen as being determined by deeper (usually socioeconomic) structures, in the face of which contingency, as well as agency, appeared to be nothing more than illusory epiphenomena. More recently, however, events have made a comeback in historical scholarship. William H. Sewell believes that the concept of a "historical event" is essential to understanding the process of structural change. More specifically, he argues that historical change occurs in spurts rather than linearly and that contingent events "transform social relations in ways that could not be fully predicted from the gradual changes that may have made them possible." In Sewell's model, discursive structures and cultural schema, such as Polish nationalist discourse(s), generally tend to be reproduced over time and are transformed only in the face of ruptures in social relations. A historical event is defined as such on the basis of whether or not it produces a rupture and a transformation in existing structures. It is my argument that the murder of Narutowicz is a historical event in this sense. William H. Sewell, "Historical Events as Transformations of Structures: Inventing Revolution at the Bastille," *Theory and Society* 25, no. 6 (December 1996): 841–81.

8. Scott Ury, *Barricades and Banners: The Revolution of 1905 and the Transformation of Warsaw Jewry* (Stanford, CA: Stanford University Press, 2012), 215–16.

9. Ron Eyerman writes that "like natural disasters, political assassinations provide an opportunity for collectivities to reflect on themselves." Ron Eyerman, *The Cultural Sociology of Political Assassination: From MLK and RFK to Fortuyn and Van Gogh* (New York: Palgrave Macmillan, 2011), 210.

10. *Nationalism* can be defined as "a political principle, which holds that the political and the national unit should be congruent." Ernest Gellner, *Nations and Nationalism* (Ithaca, NY: Cornell University Press, 1983), 1. For another famous definition, which is not incompatible with Gellner's, see Benedict R. Anderson, *Imagined Communities: Reflections on the Origin and Spread of Nationalism* (London: Verso, 1983), 6. In the discourse of civic nationalism, as the latter is traditionally defined, "the nation constitutes a common political space, defined around a set of institutions, values, and political projects, a free-will union based on the adherence to the principles of the social contract." *Civic nationalism* is, at least in theory, inclusive and open to all those who wish to join the national community. This is in stark opposition to *ethnic nationalism*, in which the nation is defined by ethnicity or blood, and which is exclusive and closed to outsiders. In this book I employ the terms "civic" and "ethnic" not as descriptors of an empirical reality, but as ideal-types, in the Weberian sense, used to analyze and deconstruct actual historical manifestations of nationalism. Geneviève Zubrzycki, "The Classical Opposition between Civic and Ethnic Models of Nationhood: Ideology, Empirical Reality and Social Scientific Analysis," *Polish Sociological Review* 3 (2002): 275–95.

11. See Andrzej Walicki, *Philosophy and Romantic Nationalism: The Case of Poland* (Oxford: Clarendon Press; New York: Oxford University Press, 1982).

12. *Endejca*'s ideological evolution is traced in Brian Porter-Szűcs, *When Nationalism Began to Hate: Imagining Modern Politics in Nineteenth-Century Poland* (New York: Oxford University Press, 2000). For the intellectual development of Dmowski, see Grzegorz Krzywiec, *Szowinizm po polsku: Przypadek Romana Dmowskiego, 1886–1905* (Warsaw: Neriton, 2009).

13. For an analysis of this process, see Porter-Szűcs, *When Nationalism Began to Hate.*

14. For a detailed analysis, see Joseph Marcus, *Social and Political History of the Jews in Poland, 1919–1939* (Berlin: Mouton Publishers, 1983).

15. Ibid., 233. Robert Blobaum, "Introduction," in *Antisemitism and Its Opponents in Modern Poland*, ed. Robert Blobaum (Ithaca, NY: Cornell University Press, 2005), 4–6.

16. The radically irrational and visceral nature of antisemitism is perhaps best summarized by Norman Cohn, a historian commissioned by the British Army to study Nazi literature. While reading the Nazi materials, Cohn writes, "I began to suspect that the deadliest form of antisemitism has little to do with real conflicts of interest between living people, or even with racial prejudice as such. What I kept coming across was, rather, a conviction that Jews—all Jews everywhere in the world—form a conspiratorial body set on ruining and then dominating the rest of mankind." Quoted in David Norman Smith, "The Social Construction of Enemies: Jews and the Representation of Evil," *Sociological Theory* 14, no. 3 (November 1996): 210.

17. See Joshua D. Zimmerman, *Poles, Jews, and the Politics of Nationality: The Bund and the Polish Socialist Party in Late Tsarist Russia, 1892–1914* (Madison: University of Wisconsin Press, 2004).

18. Waldemar Potkański, *Odrodzenie czynu niepodległościowego przez PPS w okresie rewolucji 1905 roku* (Warsaw: Wydawnictwo DiG, 2008), 251.

19. For a more thorough discussion of this question, see my article: Paul Brykczynski, "Reconsidering 'Piłsudskiite Nationalism,'" *Nationalities Papers* 42, no. 5 (September 3, 2014): 771–90.

20. The literal translation of Lewica Niepodległościowa would be Independence or Pro-Independence Left. The term *niepodległościowa* (pro-independence) was meant to distinguish leftist patriots from Communists and internationalist socialists, who did not believe that the independence of Poland was an important objective. I have taken the liberty to use the term "Patriotic Left" because it is much less awkward in English than the literal translation but still fully captures the latter's spirit.

21. As late as 1989, the great émigré journalist Jerzy Giedroyc offered this well-known and illustrative quip: that even after the fall of Communism, Poland continued to be ruled by two coffins—those of Dmowski and Piłsudski. Jerzy Giedroyc, "Droga na wschód," *Więź* 10 (1989). Similarly, the conservative Stanisław Mackiewicz wrote, "The history I am writing might as well be entitled 'Dmowski and Piłsudski.' The history of my generation is defined by the struggle between these two men." Stanisław Mackiewicz, *Historja Polski od 11 listopada 1918 r. do 17 września 1939 r.* (London: M. I. Kolin, 1941), 34.

22. The question of struggles *within* particular nationalist traditions or discourses has resulted in some of the most interesting work in the field. Prasenjit Duara follows the sociologist Pierre Bourdieu in characterizing nationalism not as a monolithic ideology but as a polyphonic field in which competing visions, articulations, and discourses of the nation coexist and battle for hegemony. As Duara puts it, "the multiplicity of nation-views and the idea that political identity is not fixed but shifts between different loci introduces the idea that nationalism is best seen as a relational identity." Prasenjit Duara, *Rescuing History from the Nation: Questioning Narratives of Modern China* (Chicago: University of Chicago Press, 1995), 15.

23. The critic Konstanty A. Jeleński writes that the "chasm" that divided the National Democrats from their enemies transcended "the plane of politics" and involved the realm of "emotions." Konstanty A. Jeleński, *"Kultura": Polska na wygnaniu* (Warsaw: Instytut Dokumentacji i Studiów nad Literaturą Polską, 2005), 17.

24. According to the PPS activist Michał Sokolnicki, "fratricidal battles [between the PPS and the NDs], which initially began as assassinations of leaders or individuals, turned into regular shootouts in factories and streets and into random murder." Michał Sokolnicki, *Czternaście lat* (Warsaw: Instytut Badania Najnowszej Historji Polski, 1936), 285. In the industrial city of Łódź alone, some four hundred people were killed in fratricidal fighting between rival organizations ostensibly dedicated to the Polish national cause.

25. See Robert Blobaum, "The Politics of Antisemitism in Fin-de-Siècle Warsaw," *Journal of Modern History* 73, no. 2 (June 2001): 275–306.

26. For more on this question, see Jan Molenda, *Piłsudczycy a Narodowi Demokraci 1908–1918* (Warsaw: Książka i Wiedza, 1980).

27. See Mieczysław Pruszyński, "Rozmowa historyczna ze St. Grabskim," *Zeszyty Historyczne* 36 (1976): 38–49; Mieczysław Pruszyński, "Jak straciliśmy Mińsk i federację z Białą Rusią," *Zeszyty Historyczne* 36 (1976): 50–59.

28. Henry Morgenthau, *All in a Life-Time* (Garden City, NY: Doubleday, 1922), 358.

29. This definition has been suggested by Jacob Katz, *From Prejudice to Destruction: Anti-Semitism, 1700–1933* (Cambridge, MA: Harvard University Press, 1980), 4.

30. For example, Shmuel Almog writes, in one of the most extreme renditions of this view, that antisemitism in interwar Poland "tended to be nearly total." Shmuel Almog, *Nationalism and Antisemitism in Modern Europe, 1815–1945* (New York: Pergamon, 1990), 107. As Scott Ury writes when analyzing this position, "for many it is almost a truism to assert that Poles and Jews are mortal enemies and that the forces of separatism that divide these groups are as old as time itself." Ury, *Barricades and Banners*, 217. Similarly, according to Ezra Mendelsohn, many traditional works on Polish-Jewish relations assume that Poland was "an extremely, perhaps even uniquely, antisemitic country." Ezra Mendelsohn, "Jewish Historiography on Polish Jewry," in *Jews in Independent Poland, 1918–1939*, ed. Antony Polonsky, Ezra Mendelsohn, and Jerzy Tomaszewski (London: Institute for Polish-Jewish Studies, 1994), 6–7. The classic example of this narrative is Celia Stopnicka Heller, *On the Edge of Destruction: Jews of Poland between the Two World Wars* (New York: Columbia University Press, 1977). For further discussion, see Mendelsohn, "Jewish Historiography on Polish Jewry." One could also see this view as the specific case of the more general tendency, still common in Western Europe and North America, to "depict Poland as a land of backward peasants" prone to "violent xenophobia." Brian Porter-Szűcs, *Poland in the Modern World: Beyond Martyrdom* (New York: John Wiley & Sons, 2014), 3. For an in-depth discussion of orientalist portrayals of Eastern Europe, see Larry Wolff, *Inventing Eastern Europe: The Map of Civilization on the Mind of the Enlightenment* (Stanford, CA: Stanford University Press, 1994).

31. Ury, *Barricades and Banners*; Theodore R. Weeks, *From Assimilation to Antisemitism: The "Jewish Question" in Poland, 1850–1914* (DeKalb: Northern Illinois University Press, 2006); Zimmerman, *Poles, Jews, and the Politics of Nationality*; Blobaum, "The Politics of Antisemitism"; Stephen D. Corrsin, "Polish-Jewish Relations before the First World War: The Case of the State Duma Elections in Warsaw," *Gal-Ed: On the History of the Jews in Poland* 11 (1989).

32. Historians traditionally contrast the supposedly moderate antisemitism of the 1920s with its more radical Nazi-inspired manifestations in the 1930s. For example, Andrzej Chojnowski writes: "On the Jewish Question, the utterances of key National Democratic journalists [in the 1920s] were far removed from later extremism. They mostly pointed out the economic consequences of the occupational structure of the Jewish population, as well as the national character of this group and its international ties." Andrzej Chojnowski, *Koncepcje polityki narodowościowej rządów polskich w latach 1921–1939* (Wrocław: Zakład Narodowy im. Ossolińskich, 1979), 19. Similar arguments are advanced in Małgorzata Domagalska, *Antysemityzm dla inteligencji? Kwestia Żydowska w publicystyce Adolfa Nowaczyńskiego na łamach "Myśli narodowej" i "Prosto z mostu" na tle porównawczym* (Warsaw: Żydowski Instytut Historyczny, 2004), 44; Roman Wapiński, *Świadomość polityczna w Drugiej Rzeczypospolitej* (Łódź: Wydawnictwo Łódzkie, 1989), 424.

33. Mark Mazower, *Dark Continent: Europe's Twentieth Century* (New York: Vintage, 2000), 27.

34. Quoted in ibid., 4.

35. In Spain, of course, democratic institutions were briefly reestablished and then followed by civil war and the reimposition of dictatorship. For more on the breakdown of democracy in interwar Europe, see K. Newman, *European Democracy between the Wars* (London: Allen & Unwin, 1971); Joseph Rothschild, *East Central Europe between the Two World Wars* (Seattle: University of Washington Press, 1974); Hugh Seton-Watson, *Eastern Europe between the Wars, 1918–1941* (Cambridge: Cambridge University Press, 1945).

36. To this day, the best study of the Piłsudski coup remains Joseph Rothschild's *Piłsudski's Coup D'etat* (New York: Columbia University Press, 1966).

37. For a comparative of the role of fascism in this breakdown and the emergence of authoritarianism, see Stanley G. Payne, *A History of Fascism, 1914–1945* (Madison: University of Wisconsin Press, 1995), esp. 129–46.

38. Ibid., 321. Piotr S. Wandycz writes: "Polish fascism, operating on the margins of Poland's political life, was in many instances an artificial and imported product. . . . Polish fascism went against the long traditions of Polish ideals of freedom, individualism, and moderation." Piotr S. Wandycz, "Fascism in Poland," in *Native Fascism in the Successor States, 1918–1945*, ed. Peter F. Sugar (Santa Barbara, CA: ABC-Clio, 1971), 97.

39. See Antony Polonsky, "Roman Dmowski and Italian Fascism," in *Ideas into Politics: Aspects of European History, 1880 to 1950*, ed. R. J. Bullen, Hartmut Pogge von Strandmann, and A. B. Polonsky (London: Croom Helm, 1984).

40. For an example of the studies focusing on the National Democrats' ideology, see Bogumił Grott, *Nacjonalizm chrześcijański: Myśl społeczno-państwowa formacji narodowo-katolickiej w Drugiej Rzeczypospolitej* (Cracow: Universitas, 1991); Jerzy Jedlicki, *Jakiej cywilizacji Polacy potrzebują: Studia z dziejów idei i wyobraźni XIX wieku* (Warsaw: Państwowe Wydawnictwo Naukowe, 1988); Ewa Maj, *Związek Ludowo-Narodowy 1919–1928: Studium z dziejów myśli politycznej* (Lublin: Wydawnictwo Uniwersytetu Marii Curie-Skłodowskiej, 2000); Włodzimierz Mich, *Obcy w polskim domu: Nacjonalistyczne koncepcje rozwiązania problemu mniejszości narodowych, 1918–1939* (Lublin: Wydawnictwo Uniwersytetu Marii Curie-Skłodowskiej, 1994); Ronald Modras, "The Interwar Polish Catholic Press on the Jewish Question," *Annals of the American Academy of Political and Social Science* 548, no. 1 (1996): 169–90; Mieczysław Sobczak, *Narodowa Demokracja wobec kwestii żydowskiej na ziemiach polskich przed I Wojną Światową* (Wrocław: Wydawnictwo Akademii Ekonomicznej im. Oskara Langego, 2007); Roman Wapiński, *Narodowa Demokracja, 1893–1939: Ze studiów nad dziejami myśli nacjonalistycznej* (Wrocław: Zakład Narodowy im. Ossolińskich, 1980); Roman Wapiński, *Świadomość polityczna w Drugiej Rzeczypospolitej* (Łódź: Wydawnictwo Łódzkie, 1989); Adam Wątor, *Działalność Związku Ludowo-Narodowego w latach 1919–1922* (Szczecin: Uniwersytet Szczeciński, 1992).

41. One of the most influential (and most complicated) typological descriptions of fascism is provided by Payne, *A History of Fascism, 1914–1945*, 7.

42. See Mazower, *Dark Continent*, 468.

43. Roger Griffin, *The Nature of Fascism* (London: Psychology Press, 1991), 26–38. Griffin famously defines fascism as "a genus of political ideology whose mythic core in its

various permutations is a palingenetic form of populist ultra-nationalism." "At the heart of the palingenetic political myth," he continues, "lies the belief that contemporaries are living through or about to live through a 'sea-change', a 'water-shed' or 'turning-point' in the historical process."

44. Franklin L. Ford, *Political Murder: From Tyrannicide to Terrorism* (Cambridge, MA: Harvard University Press, 1985), 256.

45. Paul A. Hanebrink, *In Defense of Christian Hungary: Religion, Nationalism, and Antisemitism, 1890–1944* (Ithaca, NY: Cornell University Press, 2006), 88.

46. Ford, *Political Murder*, 265.

47. Giovanni Capoccia, *Defending Democracy: Reactions to Extremism in Interwar Europe* (Baltimore: Johns Hopkins University Press, 2005), 229.

48. Radio was, of course, available in interwar Poland, but was used primarily for entertainment. Daria Nałęcz, *Nie szablą, lecz piórem: Batalie publicystyczne II Rzeczypospolitej* (Warsaw: Wydawnictwo IBL, 1993), 6. For a more extensive discussion of the role of the press in the political life of interwar Poland, see Andrzej Paczkowski, *Prasa drugiej Rzeczypospolitej, 1918–1939* (Warsaw: Państwowy Instytut Wydawniczy, 1971).

49. Porter-Szűcs, *When Nationalism Began to Hate*, 6.

50. About 90 percent of the ministry's collection was destroyed during the war.

51. The Polish press of the interwar period was fiercely partisan. Newspapers were unabashedly tied to particular ideological positions and did not necessarily strive for apolitical "objectivity." See Paczkowski, *Prasa drugiej Rzeczypospolitej*.

Chapter 1. "Down with the Jews!"

1. After each round of voting, the candidate with the fewest votes would be eliminated.

2. Although the Christian Democrats would later go on to chart an independent course, in the early 1920s, they were universally regarded as being under the tutelage of their National Democratic cousins. For a discussion of the differences between the three parties, see chapter 3.

3. Stanislaw Thugutt, "Przyczynek do historii pierwszego Zgromadzenia Narodowego," in *Gabriel Narutowicz we wspomnieniach współczesnych polityków*, ed. Kazimierz Stembrowicz (Warsaw: Wydawnictwo Sejmowe, 1992), 54.

4. For example, Stanisław Car, "Fragmenty," in *Gabrjel Narutowicz pierwszy Prezydent Rzeczypospolitej: Księga pamiątkowa* (Warsaw: Komitet Uczczenia Pierwszego Prezydenta Rzeczypospolitej śp. Gabrjela Narutowicza, 1925), 236–39; Józef Piłsudski, "Wspomnienia o Gabrielu Narutowiczu," in *Pisma zbiorowe*, ed. Kazimierz Świtalski (Warsaw: Instytut Józefa Piłsudskiego, 1937), 6:42.

5. Janusz Pajewski, *Gabriel Narutowicz: Pierwszy Prezydent Rzeczypospolitej* (Warsaw: Książka i Wiedza, 1993), 141–42.

6. "Manifestacje z powodu wyborów," *Gazeta Warszawska*, December 10, 1922.

7. This reputation was universal, and even Haller in his memoirs admits that Jews were particularly scared of his soldiers, even as he tries to refute the charges of complicity in pogroms leveled against his units. Józef Haller, *Pamiętniki: Z wyborem dokumentów i zdjęć* (London: Veritas, 1964), 209–10.

8. The right was poorly represented at the highest levels of the Polish military, which, it must be remembered, was largely the handiwork of Piłsudski. Moreover, since the National Democrats were opposed to the armed struggle for independence, none of their leaders had any military experience. Besides Haller, the only high-profile, right-wing general was Dowbor-Muśnicki. However, he had lost much political capital when he refused to take an important command post during the Polish-Soviet War and remained alienated from both the army and politics until his death.

9. "Manifestacje z powodu wyborów," *Gazeta Warszawska*.

10. "Manifestacje z powodu wyborów," *Gazeta Warszawska*.

11. "Manifestacje z powodu rezultatu wyborów," *Gazeta Poranna*, December 10, 1922.

12. Sadzewicz specifically referred to the 1912 Duma elections, in which Jewish electors were able to push through a socialist Polish candidate, Eugeniusz Jagiełło, despite opposition from the National Democrats, who won the majority of the non-Jewish vote in Warsaw. "In 1912 the Jews imposed Jagiełło upon Poland as a deputy to the Duma," Sadzewicz thundered, "and now Narutowicz as president." "Manifestacje z powodu wyborów," *Gazeta Warszawska*.

13. "Manifestacje z powodu wyborów," *Gazeta Warszawska*.

14. Piłsudski, "Wspomnienia o Gabrielu Narutowiczu," 56.

15. Komisariat Rządu na Miasto Stołeczne Warszawę (KRMSW) 297/IV, t. 4/547.

16. Stanisław Stroński, "Ich Prezydent," *Rzeczpospolita*, December 10, 1922.

17. Ibid.

18. "Złowróżbne zwycięstwo," *Kurjer Warszawski*, December 10, 1922.

19. "Wybór Prezydenta Rzeczypospolitej," *Gazeta Warszawska*, December 10, 1922.

20. "Gabryel Narutowicz," *Gazeta Warszawska*, December 10, 1922.

21. "Zamoyski-Narutowicz," *Gazeta Poranna*, December 10, 1922.

22. "Zwycięstwo nad Polską," *Gazeta Poranna*, December 10, 1922.

23. "Wielki wiec," *Gazeta Poranna*, December 10, 1922.

24. "Rodacy," *Gazeta Poranna*, December 10, 1922.

25. See Roger Griffin, *The Nature of Fascism* (Routledge: London and New York, 1991), 35.

26. "Oświadczenie Chrz. Zw. Jedn. Nar," *Gazeta Warszawska*, December 10, 1922.

27. Ewa Maj, *Związek Ludowo-Narodowy, 1919–1928: Studium z dziejów myśli politycznej* (Lublin: Wydawnictwo Uniwersytetu Marii Curie-Skłodowskiej, 2000), 52.

28. For a detailed discussion, see Szymon Rudnicki, "Towarzystwo Rozwoju Handlu Przemysłu i Rzemiosła," in *Gospodarka, ludzie, władza: Studia historyczne*, ed. Antoni Mączak and Michal Kopczyski (Warsaw: Krupski i S-ka, 1998), 316–33.

29. "Demonstracje uliczne Chjeny," *Kurjer Poranny*, December 11, 1922.

30. "Warszawa po wyborze prezydenta," *Gazeta Poranna*, December 11, 1922.

31. Ibid. In his memoirs, Haller claims that he had nothing to do with the demonstrations and that he was falsely accused of making an antisemitic speech. However, his version of events is supported neither by the left-wing nor by the right-wing press. See Haller, *Pamiętniki*, 234.

32. The Polish terms were "Hańba!" and "Precz!"

33. "Warszawa po wyborze prezydenta," *Gazeta Poranna*. The president-elect had moved out of his apartment at the hotel and was staying in a villa near the Łazienki Park.

34. Most states did not yet have embassies in Poland.

35. "Migawki sejmowe," *Kurjer Poznański*, December 13, 1922.

36. "Winowajcy," *Głos Prawdy*, December 16, 1922, 761.

37. Władysław Pobóg-Malinowski, *Najnowsza historia polityczna Polski, 1864–1945* (London: Świderski, 1983), 600.

38. "Winowajcy," *Głos Prawdy*, 761.

39. "Wiec w Rozwoju," in *Gabrjel Narutowicz pierwszy Prezydent Rzeczypospolitej: Księga pamiątkowa* (Warsaw: Komitet Uczczenia Pierwszego Prezydenta Rzeczypospolitej śp. Gabrjela Narutowicza, 1925), 302.

40. "Demonstracje uliczne Chjeny," *Kurjer Poranny*.

41. Ibid.

42. Ibid.

43. Bernard Singer, "Blok mniejszości narodowych," *Nasz Przegląd*, December 17, 1922, quoted in Bernard Singer, *Od Witosa do Sławka* (Warsaw: Verum, 1990), 113.

44. "Zajścia na ulicy," *Kurjer Polski*, December 11, 1922.

45. Maciej Rataj, *Pamiętniki 1918–1927* (Warsaw: Ludowa Spółdzielnia Wydawnicza, 1965), 124.

46. "Zajścia na ulicach," *Kurjer Polski*, December 11, 1922.

47. Rataj, *Pamiętniki*, 123.

48. "Przebieg dnia wczorajszego," *Kurjer Warszawski*, December 11, 1922. This version of events finds no corroboration in Rataj's memoirs. Nevertheless, it is not impossible that Rataj would have suggested such a solution, given the panic that seized many Piast deputies.

49. Wincenty Witos, *Moje wspomnienia* (Paris: Instytut Literacki, 1965), 31.

50. Ibid.

51. "Rezolucja PSL," *Kurjer Poranny*, December 11, 1922.

52. Indeed, as Tadeusz Hołówko observed, "in any normal state with a higher level of culture . . . the fact that the minorities voted for Narutowicz would have been utilized in foreign relations to show that the minorities want to play a constructive role in the life of the Polish state and share the responsibility for its fate." Tadeusz Hołówko, *Prezydent Gabrjel Narutowicz: Życie i działalność* (Warsaw: E. Wende, 1924), 153.

53. Witos, *Moje wspomnienia*, 32.

54. "Po wyborze prezydenta," *Gazeta Warszawska*, December 11, 1922.

55. "Po wyborze prezydenta," *Gazeta Warszawska*.

56. "Migawki Sejmowe," *Kurjer Poznański*, December 12, 1922.

57. Rataj, *Pamiętniki*, 123.

58. Witos, *Moje wspomnienia*, 31. Witos claims that he "knew" Narutowicz was supported in his categorical refusal to resign by "other powers," against which Witos himself was "powerless." What were these "other powers"? It seems there are two possibilities. On the one hand, Witos could have been referring to the Piłsudskiites and the mafialike secret

networks of former Legionnaires and Polish Military Organization members. However, the cryptic and conspiratorial tone of Witos's utterance is strikingly similar to many National Democratic claims about the Jews, who were often referred to as a "secret" or "anonymous" power. Therefore, Witos may have also been referring to the Jews, and their supposed control of Poland's political life. It would be a supreme irony if Witos—who had, in fact, been the ultimate kingmaker in the contest between Narutowicz and Zamoyski—attributed the former's victory to some mysterious Jewish conspiracy rather than to the actions of his own party. I suspect that Witos was too intelligent a politician to believe such nonsense. But it is also possible that he may have mentioned the "other powers" in order to justify his own cooperation with the minorities against the candidate of the "Polish majority." Clearly, the charge of having been a traitor to the "Polish majority" still stung even decades after the event itself.

59. Piłsudski, "Wspomnienia o Gabrielu Narutowiczu," 55.

60. According to *Kurjer Polski*, this debate pitted the "conservative" against the "nationalist" wings of the coalition, which corresponded roughly, though not exactly, to the Christian National Party and National Populist Union. It was the latter that carried the day. "Wczorajsze obrady klubów," *Kurjer Polski*, December 11, 1922.

61. "Manifest Rozwoju," in *Gabrjel Narutowicz pierwszy Prezydent Rzeczypospolitej: Księga pamiątkowa* (Warsaw: Komitet Uczczenia Pierwszego Prezydenta Rzeczypospolitej śp. Gabrjela Narutowicza, 1925), 302–3.

62. "Zajścia na ulicach," *Kurjer Polski*.

63. "Agitacja Chjeny wśród publiczności," *Kurjer Poranny*, December 11, 1922.

64. Piłsudski, "Wspomnienia o Gabrielu Narutowiczu," 55. While Piłsudski does not indicate what these were, it would appear that he was preparing himself for an exit from public life and was not happy about the direction Poland was headed. Certainly more energetic action on his part would have made the events of December 11 impossible, and his uncharacteristic failure to act must be seen as yet another contingent factor that contributed to making the crisis more severe than it would otherwise have been.

65. "Marszałek Sejmu i kluby wobec demonstracji," *Kurjer Poranny*, December 11, 1922.

66. "Komunikat PSL 'Wyzwolenie,'" *Kurjer Polski*, December 11, 1922.

67. "Zamach na praworządność I konstytucje," *Robotnik*, December 11, 1922.

68. Kazimierz Lutosławski, "Po wyborze," *Gazeta Poranna*, December 11, 1922.

69. The exact route went through the Saxon Garden and the Jewish quarter; to the Kierbedź Bridge, Powiśle Street, and Książęca Street or Czerniakowska Street; and down to Wiejska Street and the Sejm. "Przebieg zajść wczorajszych," *Kurjer Poranny*, December 12, 1922.

70. Piłsudski, "Wspomnienia o Gabrielu Narutowiczu," 55.

71. "Uwolnienie towarzyszy Limanowskiego i Daszyńskiego," *Robotnik*, December 12, 1922.

72. Stenogramy Sejmu Rzeczpospolitej Polskiej 2-ej Kadencji (SSRP), no. 48 (June 19, 1923): 6.

73. "Dzień wczorajszy w świetle faktów," *Kurjer Warszawski*, December 12, 1922.

74. "Zbiórka band faszystowskich," *Robotnik*, December 12, 1922; Stanisław Thugutt, *Autobiografia* (Warsaw: Ludowa Spółdzielnia Wydawnicza, 1984), 86.

75. Bernard Singer, "Gwardia Republikańska na ulicach Warszawy," *Nasz Przegląd*, December 18, 1922, quoted in Singer, *Od Witosa do Sławka*, 118.

76. "Echa chijeńskiego zamachu," *Robotnik*, December 13, 1922.

77. "Ex-komendant policji Sikorski przed sądem," *Robotnik*, April 17, 1923.

78. There is no indication for why it was the Japanese envoy who was attacked, but old-fashioned racism seems like the most likely culprit. "Burzliwy dzień w stolicy," *Kurjer Polski*, December 12, 1922.

79. "Ex-komendant policji Sikorski przed sądem," *Robotnik*.

80. "Zbiórka band faszystowskich," *Robotnik*.

81. The exact address was 10 Plac Trzech Krzyży.

82. "Zbiórka band faszystowskich," *Robotnik*. This relationship is confirmed by the right-wing papers.

83. The Polish word is *szczeniak*, which literally translates as "pup." Its meaning, however, is closer to the English "brat," but much more insulting.

84. "Przebieg zajść wczorajszych," *Kurjer Poranny*.

85. "Zbiórka band faszystowskich," *Robotnik*.

86. Tadeusz Caspaeri-Chraszczewski, "Wspomnienia," Biblioteka Narodowa, sygn. 15537 II, 80.

87. "Dzień swawoli ulicznej i tryumfu praw państwa," *Kurjer Poranny*, December 12, 1922.

88. Apparently, without identifying herself, Piłsudska attempted to explain that she knew the Narutowicz family well and that none of them had Jewish roots, but this had no discernible effects on anyone in the crowd. Aleksandra Piłsudska, *Wspomnienia* (London: Gryf, 1960), 262–63.

89. "Pożyczony cylinder," *Głos Prawdy*, December 16, 1922, 729.

90. Zofia Kodisówna, "Wspomnienie," in *Gabrjel Narutowicz pierwszy Prezydent Rzeczypospolitej: Księga pamiątkowa* (Warsaw: Komitet Uczczenia Pierwszego Prezydenta Rzeczypospolitej śp. Gabrjela Narutowicza, 1925), 230.

91. Pajewski, *Gabriel Narutowicz*, 154.

92. "Ex-komendant policji Sikorski przed sądem," *Robotnik*.

93. "Przejazd prezydenta Narutowicza," *Robotnik*, December 12, 1922.

94. "Dzień swawoli ulicznej i tryumfu praw państwa," *Kurjer Poranny*.

95. Kodisówna, "Wspomnienie," 230.

96. "Dzień swawoli ulicznej i tryumfu praw państwa," *Kurjer Poranny*.

97. Hołówko, *Prezydent Gabrjel Narutowicz*, 171.

98. Singer, "Gwardia republikańska na ulicach Warszawy."

99. Rataj, *Pamiętniki*, 125.

100. "Zaprzysiężenie prezydenta," *Kurjer Warszawski*, December 11, 1922; Thugutt, *Autobiografia*, 86.

101. Adam Pragier, *Czas przeszły dokonany* (London: B. Świderski, 1966), 238; Kodisówna, "Wspomnienie," 230.

102. Thugutt, "Przyczynek do historii pierwszego Zgromadzenia Narodowego," 86.

103. "Dzień swawoli ulicznej i tryumfu praw państwa," *Kurjer Poranny*, December 12, 1922.

104. "Zaprzysiężenie prezydenta," *Gazeta Poranna*, December 12, 1922.

105. Predictably, the two sides blamed each other for firing first, and it is impossible to ascertain which account is true. However, in other respects, the accounts provided by right- and left-wing papers are virtually identical. "Dzień wczorajszy w świetle faktów," *Kurjer Warszawski*; "Uwolnienie towarzyszy Limanowskiego i Daszyńskiego," *Robotnik*, December 12, 1922.

106. "Dzień wczorajszy w świetle faktów," *Kurjer Warszawski*; "Uwolnienie towarzyszy Limanowskiego i Daszyńskiego," *Robotnik*.

107. "Dzień wczorajszy w świetle faktów," *Kurjer Warszawski*; "Uwolnienie towarzyszy Limanowskiego i Daszyńskiego," *Robotnik*.

108. "Echa chijeńskiego zamachu," *Robotnik*, December 15, 1922.

109. "Uwolnienie towarzyszy Limanowskiego i Daszyńskiego," *Robotnik*.

110. "Wczorajsze zajścia," *Gazeta Poranna*, December 12, 1922.

111. "Przebieg zajść wczorajszych," *Kurjer Poranny*.

112. "Wczorajsze zajścia," *Gazeta Poranna*; Jan Jacyna, *W wolnej Polsce: Przeżycia, 1918–1923* (Warsaw: Wolnicki, 1927), 141.

113. "Burzliwy dzień w stolicy," *Kurjer Polski*.

114. Ibid.

115. "Żywiołowa manifestacja robotników," *Robotnik*, December 12, 1922.

116. Singer, "Gwardia republikańska na ulicach Warszawy."

Chapter 2. From Protest to Assassination

1. "Nieudany strajk," *Gazeta Warszawska*, December 12, 1922.

2. "Przebieg dnia wczorajszego," *Kurjer Poranny*, December 13, 1922.

3. Maciej Rataj, *Pamiętniki 1918–1927* (Warsaw: Ludowa Spółdzielnia Wydawnicza, 1965), 126.

4. Juan J. Linz and Alfred C. Stepan, *The Breakdown of Democratic Regimes* (Baltimore: Johns Hopkins University Press, 1978), 57–58.

5. Adrian Lyttelton, *The Seizure of Power: Fascism in Italy, 1919–1929*, rev. ed. (New York: Routledge, 2009), 92–93.

6. "Przebieg zajść wczorajszych," *Kurjer Poranny*, December 12, 1922.

7. Rataj, *Pamiętniki*, 126.

8. Józef Haller, *Pamiętniki: Z wyborem dokumentów i zdjęć* (London: Veritas, 1964), 235.

9. Ewa Maj, "Roman Dmowski i Związek Ludowo-Narodowy (1919–1928)," *Kwartalnik Historyczny* 2 (1993): 43.

10. Stanisław Grabski, *Pamiętniki* (Warsaw: Czytelnik, 1989), 132; Stanisław Kozicki, *Pamiętnik, 1876–1939* (Słupsk: Akademia Pomorska w Słupsku, 2009), 470.

11. Roman Wapiński, *Roman Dmowski* (Lublin: Wydawnictwo Lubelskie, 1988), 282–83. Mariusz Kułakowski, ed., *Roman Dmowski w świetle listów i wspomnień* (London: Gryf Publications, 1968), 2:148.

12. Grabski, *Pamiętniki*, 132; Kozicki, *Pamiętnik*, 470.

13. According to Antony Polonsky, Dmowski's acceptance of fascism and the formal rejection of democracy was made manifest in the aftermath of Piłsudski's 1926 coup. See Antony Polonsky, "Roman Dmowski and Italian Fascism," in *Ideas into Politics: Aspects of European History, 1880 to 1950*, ed. R. J. Bullen, Hartmut Pogge von Strandmann, and A. B. Polonsky (London: Croom Helm, 1984).

14. Roger Griffin, "Fascism: General Introduction," in *Comparative Fascist Studies: New Perspectives*, ed. Constantin Iordachi (London; New York: Routledge, 2009), 117–18.

15. For example, see "Ktokolwiek nim będzie," *Gazeta Warszawska*, November 15, 1922.

16. Rataj, *Pamiętniki*, 126.

17. "Odezwa Chrz. Związku Jedności Narodowej," *Gazeta Poranna*, December 12, 1922.

18. "Odezwa Chrześćjańskiej demokracji," *Gazeta Poranna*, December 12, 1922.

19. "Spokoju!" *Kurjer Warszawski*, December 12, 1922.

20. "Jezus Marja!" *Kurjer Warszawski*, December 12, 1922.

21. "Co dalej?" *Gazeta Warszawska*, December 12, 1922.

22. "Dzień wczorajszy w świetle faktów," *Kurjer Warszawski*, December 12, 1922.

23. "Bezczynność policji wobec zamachu na Zgromadzenie Narodowe," *Kurjer Polski*, April 19, 1923.

24. Stenogramy Sejmu Rzeczpospolitej Polskiej 2-ej Kadencji (SSRP), no. 48 (June 19, 1923): 11.

25. "Bezczynność policji wobec zamachu na Zgromadzenie Narodowe," *Kurjer Polski*.

26. Ibid.

27. "Ex-komendant policji Sikorski przed sądem," *Robotnik*, April 17, 1923.

28. Little is known about the *Pogotowie*, since all copies of the report about this secret organization commissioned by a special parliamentary commission appear to have been destroyed during World War II.

29. Adam Pragier, *Czas przeszły dokonany* (London: B. Świderski, 1966), 238.

30. "Smutny bilans," *Gazeta Warszawska*, December 13, 1922.

31. Stanisław Stroński, "Zawada," *Rzeczpospolita*, December 14, 1922.

32. "Zapora," *Gazeta Warszawska*, December 15, 1922.

33. Stanisław Car, "Fragmenty," in *Gabrjel Narutowicz pierwszy Prezydent Rzeczypospolitej: Księga pamiątkowa* (Warsaw: Komitet Uczczenia Pierwszego Prezydenta Rzeczypospolitej śp. Gabrjela Narutowicza, 1925), 241; Tytus Zbyszewski, "Z ostatnich dni śp Prezydenta Gabriela Narutowicz," in *Gabrjel Narutowicz pierwszy Prezydent Rzeczypospolitej: Księga pamiątkowa* (Warsaw: Komitet Uczczenia Pierwszego Prezydenta Rzeczypospolitej śp. Gabrjela Narutowicza, 1925), 231.

34. Józef Piłsudski, "Wspomnienia o Gabrielu Narutowiczu," in *Pisma zbiorowe*, ed. Kazimierz Świtalski (Warsaw: Instytut Józefa Piłsudskiego, 1937), 6:56.

35. Ibid.

36. The famed First Brigade was the military unit organized by Piłsudski on the eve of World War I to fight the Russians in a somewhat quixotic plan to win Polish independence by force of arms. Politically, most of its members had leftist or socialist leanings and

virtually all were devoted to Piłsudski. They were also highly unusual soldiers—some had called them "the most intelligent army in the world." A sample of 1,215 officers from February 1917 contained the following professions: 3 university professors, 9 teaching assistants, 100 teachers, 106 engineers and architects, 59 medical doctors, 76 civil servants, 27 artists, 29 lawyers and law students, 10 journalists, and 11 poets/writers. Most of Marshal Piłsudski's closest collaborators got their start in the First Brigade and former Legionaries, as they were known, constituted an informal but extremely influential network whose members were embedded in various political parties, and which could be activated by Piłsudski when it suited his needs. Former members of the First Brigade would play a paramount role in Polish politics through the entire interwar period. It is noteworthy that the National Democrats, who did not believe that independence could be won by force of arms, had no comparable elite formation to draw upon as a resource in their bid for power. See Bohdan Urbankowski, *Józef Piłsudski: Marzyciel i strateg* (Warszawa: ALFA, 1997), 230–33.

37. Rataj, *Pamiętniki*, 128–29. For Narutowicz's attempts to reach out to the right, see Daria Nałęcz and Tomasz Nałęcz, "Gabriel Narutowicz, prezydent Rzeczypospolitej 14XIII-16XIII 1922," in *Prezydenci i premierzy Drugiej Rzeczypospolitej*, ed. Andrzej Chojnowski and Piotr Wróbel (Wrocław: Zakład Narodowy im. Ossolińskich, 1992), 46–47.

38. Tadeusz Hołówko, *Prezydent Gabrjel Narutowicz: Życie i działalność* (Warsaw: E. Wende, 1924), 107. Narutowicz's political ideas will be discussed more closely in chapters 3 and 4.

39. See chapter 4.

40. "Ostatni wywiad z prezydentem Narutowiczem," *Kurjer Polski*, December 17, 1922.

41. The president had two children, Stanisław Józef (born in 1902) and Anna (born in 1907). His wife, Ewa (neé Krzyżanowska), died of cancer in 1920 shortly before Narutowicz moved back to Poland from Switzerland.

42. "Ostatni akt państwowy prezydenta," *Kurjer Polski*, December 17, 1922.

43. Jan Skotnicki, *Przy sztalugach i przy biurku: Wspomnienia* (Warsaw: Państwowy Instytut Wydawniczy, 1957), 210.

44. Ibid.

45. Kazimiera Iłłakiewiczówna, *Ścieżka obok drogi* (Warsaw: Rój, 1939), 77; Skotnicki, *Przy sztalugach*, 210.

46. Skotnicki, *Przy sztalugach*, 209–14.

47. Akta Władysława Grabskiego, 10, "List o zabójstwie prezydenta Narutowicza"; Iłłakiewiczówna, *Ścieżka obok drogi*, 77.

48. Kazimierz Lasocki, "Pamiętniki," vol. 2, Biblioteka Narodowa microfilm 6484, 540; Skotnicki, *Przy sztalugach*, 210–12. While the shots were fired, a funeral for Jan Kałuszewski, the PPS worker killed on December 11, was taking place, and it was generally assumed that if news of murder reached the march, retaliatory violence against the right would be impossible to stop.

49. Lasocki, "Pamiętniki," 540.

50. Ibid.; Skotnicki, *Przy sztalugach*, 213.

51. These were so serious that the new premier, General Sikorski, had to call a special conference to dispel them. The figures mentioned by Sikorski as having been supposedly assassinated included himself, Marshal Rataj, General Haller, and the National Democratic deputy Father Godlewski. "Prezes ministrów gen. Sikorski do przedstawicieli prasy," *Kurjer Poranny*, December 19, 1922.

52. Letter from Bogusław Miedziński to Władysław Pobóg-Malinowski, April 12, 1955. Cited in Władysław Pobóg-Malinowski, *Najnowsza historia polityczna Polski, 1864–1945* (London: Świderski, 1983), 605–6.

53. Janusz Pajewski, *Gabriel Narutowicz: Pierwszy Prezydent Rzeczypospolitej* (Warsaw: Książka i Wiedza, 1993), 175.

54. Pragier, *Czas przeszły*, 240.

55. Ibid., 187–91.

56. Pobóg-Malinowski, *Najnowsza historia polityczna Polski*, 605–6.

57. Stanisław Thugutt, *Autobiografia* (Warsaw: Ludowa Spółdzielnia Wydawnicza, 1984), 88.

58. Bernard Singer, "Mordowanie po śmierci," *Nasz Przegląd*, December 20, 1932, quoted in Bernard Singer, *Od Witosa do Sławka* (Warsaw: Verum, 1990), 121.

59. Tadeusz Caspaeri-Chraszczewski, "Wspomnienia," Biblioteka Narodowa, sygn. 15537 II, 88.

60. Ibid., 94.

61. Thugutt, *Autobiografia*, 88.

62. This view not only is expressed by the Piłsudskiite historian Pobóg-Malinowski, admittedly not an unbiased observer, but also finds confirmation in sources close to General Władysław Sikorski. Specifically, in January 1923, Captain Tadeusz Dzieduszycki advised Sikorski that Polish public opinion "among diverse social classes" awaited "the salvation" of a "strong government" capable of curbing "demagoguery and partisanship." Akta Władysława Sikorskiego, Archiwum Akt Nowych, sygn, 17, 47. Pobóg-Malinowski, *Najnowsza historia polityczna Polski*, 606.

63. Andrzej Garlicki, *Józef Piłsudski, 1867–1935* (Warsaw: Czytelnik, 1990), 252.

64. This was General Władysław Sikorski's assessment of Piłsudski's intentions. Rataj, *Pamiętniki*, 131; Haller, *Pamiętniki*, 237.

65. Pragier, *Czas przeszły*, 240.

66. Bogusław Miedziński, "Relacja Bogusława Miedzińskiego," in *Przewrót majowy 1926 r.*, ed. Arkadiusz Adamczyk (London: NWP, 2003), 111–12.

67. Stanisław Skwarczński, "Przełom maja 1926 r.," in *Przewrót majowy 1926 r.*, ed. Arkadiusz Adamczyk (London: NWP, 2003), 220.

68. Prezydium Rady Ministrów (PRM), December 16, 1922, 679.

69. PRM, December 16, 1922, 680.

70. Rataj, *Pamiętniki*, 130–31; Pajewski, *Gabriel Narutowicz*, 172–73.

71. According to Pobóg-Malinowski, it was Piłsudski who suggested the choice of Sikorski to Rataj. However, the sources do not support this. Rataj claims to have explicitly rejected Piłsudski's suggestion that Darowski remain premier, and then presented the marshal with the choice of Sikorski despite Piłsudski's indication that he would like to

assume this position himself. Still, according to Rataj, Piłsudski readily assented to Sikorski's premiership because he saw the latter as capable of instilling order and respect for the law. Haller claims Sikorski told him that Piłsudski was fully prepared to seize power immediately after Narutowicz's death, and that it was only Rataj's speedy appointment of Sikorski as premier that derailed this plan. Pobóg-Malinowski, *Najnowsza historia polityczna Polski*, 606; Rataj, *Pamiętniki*, 131; and Haller, *Pamiętniki*, 237. The relationship between Piłsudski and Sikorski is a fascinating one and deserves more careful study. While it is clear that Piłsudski immensely respected Sikorski's military abilities, he distrusted his political judgment and personal loyalty. There were many superficial reasons for this distrust, but it ultimately boiled down to a clash of egos. More specifically, Piłsudski was unwilling to share power within his "camp," and Sikorski was unwilling, or unable, to play second fiddle to Piłsudski. After 1926, this personal rivalry led to Sikorski's exile from both politics and the army. For an excellent discussion of the relationship between Piłsudski and Sikorski, see the chapter on Sikorski in Wacław A. Zbyszewski, *Gawędy o ludziach i czasach przedwojennych* (Warsaw: Czytelnik, 2000).

72. PRM, December 16, 1922, 681–82; "Echa Zamachu w Sejmie," *Gazeta Warszawska*, December 16, 1922.

73. The Piłusdskiites were still in charge of the military, with General Kazimierz Sosnkowski as minister of defense and Piłsudski himself as chief of staff.

74. "Odezwa rządu," PRM, 687.

75. Pajewski, *Gabriel Narutowicz*, 176.

76. "Eksportacja zwłok ś.p. Prezydenta Gabrjela Narutowicza z Belwederu do zamku królewskiego," *Polska Zbrojna*, December 20, 1922.

77. Kazimierz Rudnicki, *Wspomnienia prokuratora* (Warsaw: Czytelnik, 1957), 166.

78. Thugutt, *Autobiografia*, 88.

Chapter 3. Hatred and Electoral Politics

1. For a discussion of Polish folk beliefs about Jews, see Alina Cała, *The Image of the Jew in Polish Folk Culture* (Jerusalem: Magnes Press, Hebrew University, 1995). For the role of the "Jewish question" in the nineteenth-century Polish national movement, see Brian Porter-Szűcs, *When Nationalism Began to Hate: Imagining Modern Politics in Nineteenth-Century Poland* (New York: Oxford University Press, 2000).

2. See Magdalena Opalski and Israel Bartal, *Poles and Jews: A Failed Brotherhood* (Hanover, NH: University Press of New England, 1992).

3. See Brian Porter-Szűcs, "Making a Space for Antisemitism: The Catholic Hierarchy and the Jews in the Early Twentieth Century," *Polin* 16 (2003): 415–29; Brian Porter-Szűcs, *Faith and Fatherland: Catholicism, Modernity, and Poland* (New York: Oxford University Press, 2011).

4. The specific reasons for National Democrats' turn toward antisemitism are complex and cannot be treated here at length. For the intellectual foundations of political antisemitism in Poland, see Porter-Szűcs, *When Nationalism Began to Hate*. See also Grzegorz Krzywiec, *Szowinizm po polsku: Przypadek Romana Dmowskiego, 1886–1905* (Warsaw: Neriton, 2009); Mieczysław Sobczak, *Narodowa Demokracja wobec kwestii żydowskiej na*

ziemiach polskich przed I Wojną Światową (Wrocław: Wydawnictwo Akademii Ekonomicznej im. Oskara Langego, 2007); Roman Wapiński, *Narodowa Demokracja, 1893–1939: Ze studiów nad dziejami myśli nacjonalistycznej* (Wrocław: Zakład Narodowy im. Ossolińskich, 1980).

5. For the impact of the 1905 revolution on Polish-Jewish relations, see Scott Ury, *Barricades and Banners: The Revolution of 1905 and the Transformation of Warsaw Jewry* (Stanford, CA: Stanford University Press, 2012), 214–72. For a comprehensive history of the Revolution, see Robert Blobaum, *Rewolucja: Russian Poland, 1904–1907* (Ithaca, NY: Cornell University Press, 1995). For the evolution of the National Democratic position on the "Jewish Question," see Mieczysław Sobczak, *Narodowa Demokracja wobec kwestii żydowskiej na ziemiach polskich przed I Wojną Światową* (Wrocław: Wydawnictwo Akademii Ekonomicznej im. Oskara Langego, 2007).

6. On the whole, World War I had a very negative impact on Polish-Jewish relations, with many Poles accusing Jews of siding with the Germans. Konrad Zieliński, *Stosunki polsko-żydowskie na ziemiach Królestwa Polskiego w czasie pierwszej wojny światowej* (Lublin: Wydawnictwo Uniwersytetu Marii Curie-Skłodowskiej, 2005), 277, 385.

7. Grzegorz Krzywiec, "Komitet Narodowy Polski wobec kolektywnej przemocy antysemickiej. Przyczynek do dziejów antysemityzmu nacjonalistycznego na ziemiach polskich (1917–1919)" (forthcoming).

8. Alexander V. Prusin, *The Lands Between: Conflict in the East European Borderlands, 1870–1992* (New York: Oxford University Press, 2010), 94.

9. See Alexander V. Prusin, *Nationalizing a Borderland: War, Ethnicity, and Anti-Jewish Violence in East Galicia, 1914–1920* (Tuscaloosa: University Alabama Press, 2005), 141–59.

10. The stories of anti-Jewish pogroms, which rocked many hitherto peaceful communities between 1918 and 1920, are fairly well-known, but it is often forgotten that similar episodes of violence and robbery were perpetrated by Polish Christians against other Polish Christians. According to Maciej Rataj, military jails were "full of young officers accused of theft, robbery, or stealing army property . . . brave officers, caught robbing peaceful citizens." Rataj also recounts a personal story in which he ran into his former acquaintance awaiting a military tribunal. The man, a journalist and writer of historical fiction, was caught along with his school-aged son plundering a noble estate outside of L'viv. Such incidents were commonplace. Maciej Rataj, *Pamiętniki 1918–1927* (Warsaw: Ludowa Spółdzielnia Wydawnicza, 1965), 44–48. See also Piotr Wróbel, "The Seeds of Violence: The Brutalization of an East European Region, 1917–1921," *Journal of Modern European History* 1, no. 1 (2003): 125–49. The question of the impact of the Polish-Soviet War on the solidification of the "Judeo-Communism" myth has not hitherto been examined in detail. For an interesting discussion, see Marcin Zaremba, *Wielka Trwoga: 1944–1947* (Warsaw: Znak, 2012), 53–85.

11. Komisariat Rządu na Miasto Stołeczne Warszawę (KRMSW) 297 IV, t. 4/474, 485, 501. In particular, the police reported fights between Zionists and Bundists, Zionists and Folkists, as well as between Bundists and (Jewish) Communists.

12. According to Maciej Rataj, an Emancipation and later a Piast deputy, peasants in the Congress kingdom, who had no experience with democracy whatsoever, often cast

their votes based on rather dubious considerations. According to Rataj, the victory of the radical left-wing Emancipation in his own district was greatly facilitated by a series of posters produced by the local National Democrats. The posters depicted a devil, marked with the number 2 (the number of the Emancipation voting list), attacking the Virgin Mary with a pitchfork. It then exhorted the voters to elect the National Democratic candidate in order to protect religious values. However, according to Rataj, the peasants in his district interpreted the poster as saying that the National Democratic candidate was in league with the devil and refused to vote for him, which greatly contributed to Rataj's own victory. In general, the peasants voted more on the basis of "personal trust" in an individual candidate than on party programs. "The only issue which animated rural voters," he wrote, "was the question of land reform." Constitutional questions played almost no role in the election. Rataj, *Pamiętniki*, 30.

13. Andrzej Ajnenkiel, *Historia Sejmu Polskiego* (Warsaw: PWN, 1989), 2:15–19.

14. Ibid., 2:24.

15. Adam Pragier, *Czas przeszły dokonany* (London: B. Świderski, 1966), 230.

16. Janusz Faryś, *Piłsudski i Piłsudczycy: Z dziejów koncepcji polityczno ustrojowej* (Szczecin: Uniwersytet Szczeciński, 1991), 32–33. Ajnenkiel, *Historia Sejmu Polskiego*, 2:55.

17. Szymon Rudnicki, *Żydzi w parlamencie II Rzeczypospolitej* (Warsaw: Wydawnictwo Sejmowe, 2004), 126.

18. See paragraph 113 of the Constitution. Both the left and the right believed that they would augment their power in the forthcoming elections. Thus, the intention of both parties was to leave the interpretation deliberately open ended, and for subsequent governments to have greater freedom of maneuver.

19. The D'Hondt system is used in Poland, as well as in a number of other states, today.

20. Ajnenkiel, *Historia Sejmu Polskiego*, 2:71.

21. The term literally translates to "state list."

22. Ajnenkiel, *Historia Sejmu Polskiego*, 2:80.

23. Rudnicki, *Żydzi w parlamencie II Rzeczypospolitej*, 128–29.

24. Among Ukrainians, East Galicians boycotted the elections, while the relatively pro-Polish Small Agrarians' Party, popularly known as Chliboroby, contested the elections independently and introduced five deputies into the Sejm. Among Jews, the Bund, Folkists, and Left-Zionists contested the elections independently, almost entirely without success, the sole exception being the election of a Folkist deputy from Warsaw.

25. Pragier, *Czas przeszły*, 228.

26. Ajnenkiel, *Historia Sejmu Polskiego*, 2:71.

27. Porter-Szűcs, *When Nationalism Began to Hate*, 191.

28. As he wrote in his masterpiece, *Thoughts of a Modern Pole*: "Even though we see throughout human history that the space taken up by particular peoples is in a constant flux . . . and that national territory nowhere possesses steady borders delineated by Providence, but rather depends on the dynamism of the nation and its ability to expand, and that based on this ability some nations grow, while others shrink and even die, we [the Poles] imagine some stable boundaries between nations which no one should be allowed

to cross either through [conquest or assimilation] and we base our plans for the future on the fact that these boundaries will one day be recognized as being sacred." Roman Dmowski, *Myśli nowoczesnego Polaka* (London: Nakładem Koła Młodych Stronnictwa Narodowego, 1953), 32.

29. Hence, standing outside the imagined national community were not only those who didn't want to, or weren't invited to, assimilate, but also those who denied the need for national solidarity at all costs and invited the "others" into the nation.

30. I would like to thank Brian Porter-Szűcs for suggesting this formulation.

31. For example, Andrzej Chojnowski writes: "On the Jewish Question, the utterances of key National Democratic journalists [in the 1920s] were far removed from later extremism. They mostly pointed out the economic consequences of the occupational structure of the Jewish population, as well as the national character of this group and its international ties." Andrzej Chojnowski, *Koncepcje polityki narodowościowej rządów polskich w latach 1921–1939* (Wrocław: Zakład Narodowy im. Ossolińskich, 1979), 19. Similar arguments are advanced in Małgorzata Domagalska, *Antysemityzm dla inteligencji? Kwestia Żydowska w publicystyce Adolfa Nowaczyńskiego na łamach "Myśli narodowej" i "Prosto z mostu" na tle porównawczym* (Warsaw: Żydowski Instytut Historyczny, 2004), 44; Roman Wapiński, *Świadomość polityczna w Drugiej Rzeczypospolitej* (Łódź: Wydawnictwo Łódzkie, 1989), 424.

32. For a history of the National People's Union as a political party, see Ewa Maj, *Związek Ludowo-Narodowy 1919–1928: Studium z dziejów myśli politycznej* (Lublin: Wydawnictwo Uniwersytetu Marii Curie-Skłodowskiej, 2000).

33. Ibid., 30–31. The change of brand was not entirely to the liking of many orthodox National Democrats, including Dmowski himself. Stanisław Kozicki, *Pamiętnik 1876–1939* (Słupsk: Akademia Pomorska w Słupsku, 2009), 489.

34. Antony Polonsky, *Politics in Independent Poland 1921–1939: The Crisis of Constitutional Government* (Oxford: Clarendon Press, 1972), 67.

35. Ibid., 83.

36. A literal translation would be the Christian Union of National Unity.

37. Ajnenkiel, *Historia Sejmu Polskiego*, 2:84.

38. The flyers, which are available at the Archiwum Akt Nowych, constitute a valuable and underutilized source for understanding Endek strategy and discourse. Zbiór Druków Ulotnych (ZDU), t. 127.

39. For an analysis of this trope in the 1905 revolution see Ury, *Barricades and Banners*, 235–41.

40. ZDU 127/9.

41. ZDU 127/14; emphasis in the original. Perl, a universally respected PPS leader, handily won his seat and represented the PPS in the Sejm until his death. He had also been a very close personal friend of Piłsudski (the latter left his testament with Perl during his riskiest military adventure). Lejb (or Leib as it would be transliterated into English) was the Yiddish diminutive of Trotsky's first name, while Sobelson was the real family name of the Polish-Jewish Communist activist Karol Radek.

42. Herman Diamand, like Perl, was an acculturated Jewish Pole who occupied a prominent position in the PPS through the 1920s. ZDU 127/7.

43. ZDU 127/38.

44. ZDU 127/38.

45. ZDU 127/8.

46. ZDU 127/6. For a similar example see 127/22.

47. Even when the Jews were not mentioned directly, it was implied that they would be the ones benefitting from the "Polish" vote being split. ZDU 127/12, 15, 51.

48. ZDU 127/56.

49. This strategy would be embraced by the left following the election and murder of Narutowicz. See chapter 6.

50. "Mniejszości narodowe a wybory," *Gazeta Warszawska* October 30, 1922.

51. KRMSW 297 IV, t. 1/185. In reality, of course, interwar Poland was inhabited by just over three million Jews.

52. KRMSW 297 IV, t. 1/185.

53. KRMSW 297 IV, t. 3/268, 288; KRMSW 297 IV, t. 4/458, 464. *Zażydzanie* was used as a verb or adjective (*zażydzony*) and could be roughly translated as to "to be made Jewish" or "to be overrun by Jews." This particularly nasty term was a staple of National Democratic speeches, newspapers, and electoral literature.

54. KRMSW 297 IV, t. 4/468, 501.

55. Outside of the electoral context, there were times when the National Democrats' obsession with the Jews temporarily subsided—usually when a pressing political exigency interfered. In July 1922, an important constitutional struggle broke out over the question of whether it was the Sejm or the Head of State (i.e., Piłsudski) who had the prerogative to appoint the premier. During this crisis, National Democratic rallies expressed clear and concrete political demands—that the Christian Democrat leader Wojciech Korfanty be made premier and that the constitutional prerogatives of the Head of State be curtailed. With such concrete goals occupying their minds, the NDs presumably had no need to resort to diatribes about Jewish conspiracies. Yet, this is the exception which proves the rule that on the street level, the National Democrats had little more than hatred to offer their supporters.

56. For example, in a generally nuanced work, Theodore R. Weeks writes that as early as 1910, National Democratic antisemitism "reflected an almost universal attitude in Polish society." Theodore R. Weeks, *From Assimilation to Antisemitism: The "Jewish Question" in Poland, 1850–1914* (DeKalb: Northern Illinois University Press, 2006), 161.

57. Lewica Niepodległościowa. The literal translation is Independence Left or Pro-Independence Left. The term originated during the Partitions and was used to distinguish the patriotic revolutionary forces from the internationalists who cared little for Polish independence.

58. Later, of course, the PPS and the Piłsudskiites would go on to chart separate political desinties.

59. "O co idzie?" *Piast*, September 17, 1922. Władysław Pobóg-Malinowski, *Najnowsza historia polityczna Polski, 1864–1945* (London: Świderski, 1983), 606 note 40a.

60. See Brykczynski, "Reconsidering 'Piłsudskiite Nationalism.'" The English word "tolerance" does not quite capture the essence of the Polish *tolerancja*. While the former

implies merely a minimum of acceptance, the latter is much more expansive and is more correctly translated as respect. See Porter-Szűcs, *Faith and Fatherland*, 5.

61. Tadeusz Hołówko, *Kwestia narodowościowa* (Warsaw: Druk. "Robotnika," 1922), 51.

62. "Niech przyjeżdża," *Gazeta Polska*, July 18, 1919; "Wybrki endeckie," *Głos Prawdy*, March 4, 1921, 218–19; Stanisław Bukowiecki, *Polityka Polski niepodległej: szkic programu* (Warsaw: Wende, 1922), 171.

63. Józef Lewandowski, "Unia Narodowo-Państwowa," in *Z dziejów wojny i polityki: Księga pamiątkowa ku uczczeniu 70-ej rocznicy urodzin Prof. Dra. Janusza Wolińskiego* (Warsaw: WAP, 1964), 40.

64. Ibid., 41.

65. Ibid., 40.

66. "Unja Narodowo-Państowa," *Głos Prawdy*, April 15, 1922, 310.

67. To quote *Głos Prawdy*, the party's goal was to "bring together all those elements, especially among the intelligentsia, which are capable of building the state and treating all events from the perspective of state, rather than partisan, interests. Under this banner, we find many different ideological elements. The radical democrat stands next to the enlightened conservative. . . . Maybe these people will end up going in different directions once the state is consolidated. But today they must walk together since the state is in need." "O centrum państwowe," *Głos Prawdy*, September 23, 1922, 546.

68. Lewandowski, "Unia Narodowo-Państwowa," 43.

69. "Wiec Unji NP," *Kurjer Polski*, November 3, 1922.

70. "Sprostowanie fałszów," *Kurjer Polski*, October 31, 1922.

71. This was the same Kucharzewski who opposed Dmowski in the 1912 Duma elections.

72. "Przemówienie Jana Kucharzewskiego na wiecu Unji Narodowo-Państwowej w dniu 2 listopada 1922 r," *Kurjrer Polski*, November 5, 1922.

73. KRMSW 297 IV, t. 4/501. "Przemówienie St. Bukowieckiego na wiecu Unji Narodowo-Państwowej w dniu 2 listopada 1922 r."

74. Just like the Polish advocates of the "civic" nation, the Zionists were obviously inconsistent in their rhetoric. For example, the Zionist leader Yitzhak Grünbaum claimed that the word *Polish* should always be used only in a civic (*państwowy*) sense rather than in an ethnic sense, and therefore, Jews were to be treated as Poles. But this did not stop him from using the word *Jewish* in an explicitly ethnic sense. Thus, while he denied Poles the right to see themselves as an ethnic nation, he actively encouraged the Jews to think of themselves as one. Stenogramy Sejmu Ustawodawczego (SSSU), no. 267 (December 2, 1921): 50–51.

75. Druki Życia Społeczego (DŻS), "Władza Ustawodawcza 1922," sygn. Iac6.

76. Wróbel, "The Seeds of Violence: The Brutalization of an East European Region, 1917–1921."

77. The National Civic Union received 38,159 votes and the Civic Union of the Borderlands 48,442 votes. Tadeusz Rzepecki, *Sejm i Senat 1922–1927: Podręcznik dla wyborców zawierający wyniki wyborów w powiatach, okręgach, województwach* (Poznań: Wielkopolska Księgarnia Nakł. K. Rzepeckiego, 1923), 514, 518.

78. Tadeusz Hołówko, *Prezydent Gabrjel Narutowicz: Życie i działalność* (Warsaw: E. Wende, 1924), 139.

79. T. Zagórski, "Przed oddaniem głosu," *Głos Prawdy*, November 4, 1922, 629.

80. Ibid., 630.

81. KRMSW 297 IV, t. 4/501. "Przemówienie St. Bukowieckiego na wiecu Unji Narodowo-Państwowej w dniu 2 listopada 1922 r."

82. DŻS, "Władza Ustawodawcza 1922," sygn. Iac6.

83. Lewandowski, "Unia Narodowo-Państwowa," 45.

84. The role of anger in Polish politics will be discussed in more depth in chapter 6.

Chapter 4. "The Jewish President"

1. This number is arrived at by adding up the votes cast for all non-minority parties on the broadly defined center-left.

2. "Olbrzymia większość narodu za Piłsudskim," *Głos Prawdy*, November 25, 1922, 677.

3. "Przed wyborem prezydjum sejmu i senatu," *Kurjer Warszawski*, December 1, 1922.

4. Wincenty Witos, *Moje wspomnienia* (Paris: Instytut Literacki, 1965), 11–12.

5. Władysław Pobóg-Malinowski, *Najnowsza historia polityczna Polski, 1864–1945* (London: Świderski, 1983), 596, 606n40a.

6. "My i oni," *Gazeta Poranna*, November 17, 1922.

7. "Wielka ofensywa żydowska," *Gazeta Poranna*, November 19, 1922.

8. "Żydzi a Polska," *Gazeta Poranna*, November 21, 1922.

9. Kazimierz Lutosławski, "Obróciło się koło historji," *Myśl Narodowa*, November 18, 1922, 2.

10. Lutosławski, "Obróciło się koło historji."

11. Komisariat Rządu na Miasto Stołeczne Warszawę (KRMSW) 297 IV, t. 4/524.

12. "Walka o polskość wyższych uczelni w Polsce," *Gazeta Poranna*, November 24, 1922.

13. KRMSW 297 IV, t. 4/531.

14. KRMSW 297 IV, t. 4/533.

15. KRMSW 297 IV, t. 4/543.

16. "Zdrowy odruch wśrod młodzierzy," *Gazeta Warszwska*, November 5, 1922.

17. "Walka o polskość wyższych uczelni w Polsce," *Gazeta Poranna*.

18. Stenogramy Sejmu Rzeczpospolitej Polskiej 2-ej Kadencji (SSRP), no. 2 (December 2, 1922): 15–16.

19. Kazimierz Lutosławski, "Ostatnia walka o niepoległość," *Myśl Narodowa*, December 2, 1922, 1.

20. Lutosławski, "Ostatnia walka o niepoległość," 3.

21. Ibid., 4.

22. "Dzień wczorajszy w sejmie," *Gazeta Poranna*, November 24, 1922.

23. "Żydzi są gotowi do rządów," *Gazeta Warszawska*, December 1, 1922.

24. "Ktokolwiek nim będzie," *Gazeta Warszawska*, November 15, 1922.

25. "Nieporozumienie," *Gazeta Warszawska*, November 16, 1922. See also Witos, *Moje wspomnienia*, 30.

26. "Nieporozumienie," *Gazeta Warszawska*.

27. Kazimierz Lutosławski, "Zmora," *Myśl Narodowa* 50 (December 9, 1922): 5–6.

28. "P. Witos na rozdrożu," *Kurjer Poznański*, December 5, 1922.

29. Ibid.

30. For example: "O Polskę w Polsce," *Gazeta Poranna*, December 3, 1922; "Przed decyzją," *Dziennik Poznański*, December 3, 1922; and "O Polskość kierowników Narodu," *Gazeta Warszawska*, November 24, 1922.

31. The devil has had a long association with the crossroads. This is no less true in central European peasant culture than in the Mississippi Delta.

32. "Kuszenie Witosa," *Gazeta Poranna*, November 21, 1922.

33. It is true that most Jews, Ukrainians, Belarusians, and Germans ended up in the Polish state against their will and that many did not aspire to becoming Poles even in the civic sense. The point, however, is that the National Democrats denied this claim a priori even to those who wanted to become loyal citizens of Poland.

34. This number is based on the breakdown of the popular vote excluding the Bloc and other explicitly ethnic parties. Of course, it is likely that many Jews, Ukrainians, Belarusians, and Germans voted for non-ethnic parties, so the actual percentage of ethnic Poles could be somewhat smaller than 61 percent.

35. However, under Yitzhak Grünbaum's impetuous leadership, the Jews chose, perhaps somewhat foolishly, to assume a highly visible position as the leaders of the Bloc.

36. "Na marginesie list kandydatów," *Głos Prawdy*, October 7, 1922, 567.

37. T. Zagórski, "Przed oddaniem głosu," *Głos Prawdy*, November 4, 1922, 629.

38. Yitzhak Grünbaum was widely considered to be utterly tactless and was detested by the entire Polish press. Indeed, many of his remarks in the Sejm could be described as gratuitously provocative. For example, when the Polish Parliament passed a law, supported by the left, declaring Sunday as a mandatory day of rest, Grünbaum exclaimed that "Now you have lost Wilno, Mińsk and Lwów!" His remark was widely assumed to mean that Grünbaum would attempt to use his influence with the Western powers in order to ensure that these cities did not go to Poland. Grünbaum himself later explained that he only meant to indicate that after having passed such a law, the Poles could not count on the support of the Jewish population of these cities. Whatever his intentions may have been, the comment won him few friends. On another occasion he referred to Jewish life in Poland as "hell." To what extent this statement was accurate may depend on one's point of view, but there is little doubt that it was not politically astute and resulted in Grünbaum being detested by even the most progressive Poles. See Stenogramy Sejmu Ustawodawczego (SSSU), no. 41 (May 23, 1919): 72; SSSU, no. 180 (October 29, 1920): 59.

39. According to Adam Pragier, the Germans were the most hostile toward Poland but also the most discreet. But it was the Jews who "foolishly decided to publicly play the role of the Bloc's organizers." Adam Pragier, *Czas przeszły dokonany* (London: B. Świderski, 1966), 228.

40. Indeed, Jewish left-wing parties, such as Poalei Zion or the Bund, were not represented in the Bloc. "P. Grünbaum, Blok Mniejszóści a demokracja," *Robotnik*, November 19, 1922.

41. "Ostatnie zabiegi," *Gazeta Warszawska*, November 21, 1922.

42. "Trudne zadanie," *Kurjer Polski*, November 9, 1922.

43. Ibid.

44. "Chjena a mniejszości narodowe," *Robotnik*, November 17, 1922.

45. Ibid.

46. Adam Płomnieńczyk, "Pod hasłem silnej wladzy," *Droga*, November 10, 1922.

47. "Bajka o zwrocie na prawo," *Robotnik*, November 18, 1922.

48. Stanisław Thugutt, "Przyczynek do historii pierwszego Zgromadzenia Narodowego," in *Gabriel Narutowicz we wspomnieniach współczesnych polityków*, ed. Kazimierz Stembrowicz (Warsaw: Wydawnictwo Sejmowe, 1992), 53.

49. Józef Piłsudski, "Przemówienie na zebraniu w Prezydium Rady Minstrów (4 grudina 1922 r.)," in *Pisma zbiorowe*, ed. Kazimierz Świtalski (Warsaw: Instytut Józefa Piłsudskiego, 1937), 5:296.

50. Stanisław Thugutt, *Autobiografia* (Warsaw: Ludowa Spółdzielnia Wydawnicza, 1984), 85.

51. Janusz Pajewski, *Gabriel Narutowicz: Pierwszy Prezydent Rzeczypospolitej* (Warsaw: Książka i Wiedza, 1993), 131.

52. "Przed wyborami prezydenta," *Kurjer Warszawski*, December 9, 1922.

53. "Czy PSL zawrze sojusz z Ch.Z.J.N: Rozmowa z prezesem zarządu głównego PSL, posłem Janem Dębskim," *Kurjer Polski*, November 26, 1922.

54. "Przed wyborami prezydenta," *Kurjer Warszawski*.

55. "Przed posiedzeniem Zgromadzenia Narodowego," *Robotnik*, December 10, 1922.

56. Bernard Singer, "Blok mniejszości narodowych," *Nasz Przegląd*, December 18, 1922, quoted in Bernard Singer, *Od Witosa do Sławka* (Warsaw: Verum, 1990), 116.

57. Thugutt, *Autobiografia*, 83.

58. Zamoyski, like many other politicians, had fallen to the charms of Piłsudski's charisma and while initially ill-disposed toward the latter, became a friend after their first meeting. Stanisław Kozicki, *Pamiętnik 1876–1939* (Słupsk: Akademia Pomorska w Słupsku, 2009), 392. The left-leaning *Kurjer Polski* thought Zamoyski to be "moderate and sympathetic." "Odruchy," *Kurjer Polski*, December 11, 1922. Ironically enough, Gabriel Narutowicz suggested Zamoyski to Piłsudski as a possible compromise candidate, capable of placating the right without antagonizing the left. Józef Piłsudski, "Wspomnienia o Gabrielu Narutowiczu," in *Pisma zbiorowe*, ed. Kazimierz Świtalski (Warsaw: Instytut Józefa Piłsudskiego, 1937), 6:52.

59. Thugutt, "Przyczynek do historii," 56.

60. Pragier, *Czas przeszły*, 233.

61. Piłsudski, "Wspomnienia o Gabrielu Narutowiczu," 49.

62. Pragier, *Czas przeszły*, 235.

63. Baudouin de Courtenay was a fascinating character, and a life-long critic of racism and antisemitism. According to Pragier: "He was at war with the mighty of this world, and

a defender of the oppressed. He didn't pull his punches for the left or the right, and attacked the National Democrats, the clergy, antisemites, freethinkers, rich Jews, tax evaders, militarists. He was a secular saint, who was so nonconformist that he was too much even for the Freemasons." Pragier, *Czas przeszły*, 232.

64. Thugutt, *Autobiografia*, 83.

65. "Przed posiedzeniem Zgromadzenia Narodowego," *Robotnik*.

66. Ibid.

67. Thugutt, *Autobiografia*, 84.

68. "Przed posiedzeniem Zgromadzenia Narodowego," *Robotnik*.

69. Ibid.

70. This was the claim made by the *Kurjer Poranny*, and it seems like the most plausible explanation of the additional votes garnered by the ChJN, which had only 216 deputies. "Pierwszy Prezydent Rzeczypolitej Polskiej," *Kurjer Poranny*, December 10, 1922.

71. *Protokół Zgromadzenia Narodowego dla wyboru Prezydenta Rzeczypospolitej Polskiej z dn. 9 grudnia 1922 r.*

72. Thugutt, *Autobiografia*, 84.

73. Pragier, *Czas przeszły*, 237.

74. "Wybór Prezydenta Rzeczpospolitej," *Gazeta Warszawska*, December 10, 1922.

75. "Na marginesie wczorajszego głosowania," *Kurjer Warszawski*, December 10, 1922; Witos, *Moje wspomnienia*, 30.

76. Witos, *Moje wspomnienia*, 30.

77. "Walka dwóch obozów," *Gazeta Warszawska*, December 10, 1922.

78. Piłsudski, "Wspomnienia o Gabrielu Narutowiczu," 36, 42.

79. For the fascinating and tragic life of Stanisław Narutowicz, see Krzysztof Buchowski, "Stanisław Narutowicz: Szkic do portretu idealisty," *Biuletyn Historii Pogranicza* 2 (2001): 41–51.

80. Narutowicz himself left no written records behind, and it is difficult to tell precisely how he thought or felt about his Polish nationness. However, his background, political affiliation, and the testimonies of those who knew him would indicate that his vision of Poland was very close to that of Piłsudski's.

81. Piłsudski, "Wspomnienia o Gabrielu Narutowiczu," 46.

82. Thugutt, "Przyczynek do historii," 53.

83. Ibid., 54.

84. Ibid., 57.

85. Ibid., 56–57. Piłsudski, "Wspomnienia o Gabrielu Narutowiczu," 53–54.

86. Thugutt, "Przyczynek do historii," 54.

87. Piłsudski, "Wspomnienia o Gabrielu Narutowiczu," 42.

88. Pragier, *Czas przeszły*, 236.

89. Ibid., 233.

Chapter 5. The Unrepentant Right

1. Daria Nałęcz and Tomasz Nałęcz, "Gabriel Narutowicz, prezydent Rzeczypospolitej 14XIII-16XIII 1922," in *Prezydenci i premierzy Drugiej Rzeczypospolitej*, ed. Andrzej

Chojnowski and Piotr Wróbel (Wrocław: Zakład Narodowy im. Ossolińskich, 1992), 48. In a recent more nuanced, though somewhat popularized, biography of Niewiadomski, Patryk Pleskot concludes that the latter was not mentally ill. However, Pleskot also believes that it is impossible to answer the question of *why* Niewiadomski killed Narutowicz. Patryk Pleskot, *Niewiadomski—zabić prezydenta* (Warsaw: Demart, 2012), 436–37. As we will see, in this chapter I take a radically different interpretation of Niewiadomski's motivations and argue that his worldview was neither inexplicable nor insane but was in reality not far beyond the mainstream of National Democratic cultural politics.

2. Quoted in Adolf Nowaczyński, "Po zamachu," *Myśl Narodowa*, December 23, 1922, 6.

3. Władysław Pobóg-Malinowski, *Najnowsza historia polityczna Polski, 1864–1945* (London: Świderski, 1983), 606.

4. Nowaczyński, "Po Zamachu," 6.

5. "Wobec zbrodniczego zamachu," *Gazeta Warszawska*, December 16, 1922.

6. For Stroński's infamous article, see Stanisław Stroński, "Ich Prezydent," *Rzeczpospolita*, December 10, 1922.

7. Stanisław Stroński, "Ciszej na ta trumną!" *Rzeczpospolita*, December 17, 1922.

8. "Wam w odpowiedzi," *Robotnik*, December 19, 1922.

9. Antoni Anusz, "Ręke karaj nie ślepy miecz!" *Kurjer Poranny*, December 18, 1922.

10. "Dokąd idziemy?" *Rzeczpospolita*, December 17, 1922.

11. "Wobec zbrodniczego zamachu," *Gazeta Warszawska*.

12. Ibid.

13. The assumption that Niewiadomski was part of a larger conspiracy was nearly universal. Kazimierz Rudnicki, *Wspomnienia prokuratora* (Warsaw: Czytelnik, 1957), 155.

14. For a popular biography of Niewiadomski, see Pleskot, *Niewiadomski—zabić prezydenta*.

15. Stanisław Kijeński, *Proces Eligjusza Niewiadomskiego o zamach na życie prezydenta Rzeczypospolitej Polskiej Gabryela Narutowicza w dniu 16 Grudnia 1922 r.* (Warsaw: Perzyński Niklewicz, 1923), 14.

16. Ibid., 23.

17. "Odezwa rządu," Prezydium Rady Ministrów (PRM), 687.

18. Admittedly, on December 17, the Prosecutor's Office issued warrants for the arrests of parliamentary deputies and "Development" activists Konrad Ilski, Tadeusz Dymowski, and Adam Wyrębowski, for their role in leading the violence of December 11. But there were no large-scale arrests of right-wing journalists or politicians. Pobóg-Malinowski, *Najnowsza historia polityczna Polski*, 607. As parliamentary deputies, the three escaped punishment. Pobóg-Malinowski mistakenly notes that Nowaczyński was also arrested on that day. In fact, his arrest took place later, after he published an article praising Niewiadomski.

19. "Tragiczyny konflikt," *Gazeta Warszawska*, December 17, 1922.

20. Ibid.

21. Compare the strikingly different tones of "Tragiczyny konflikt," *Gazeta Warszawska*, December 17, 1922, and "Wobec zbrodniczego zamachu," *Gazeta Warszawska*, December 16, 1922.

22. "Dni przełomowe," *Gazeta Warszawska*, December 16, 1922.

23. Ibid.

24. Stroński, "Ciszej na ta trumną!"

25. "Po zgonie prezydenta," *Gazeta Warszawska*, December 18, 1922.

26. "Zasada państwa narodowego," *Gazeta Warszawska*, December 21, 1922.

27. Ibid.

28. Stanisław Głąbiński, "Przemówienie programowe," *Gazeta Warszawska*, December 23, 1922.

29. It must be remembered that the National Democrats' alliance with the Roman Catholic Church was still rather fragile in the early 1920s and reflected more the sympathies of parish priests than the policy of the Church hierarchy. On the one hand, the Church hierarchy discouraged participation in politics by clergymen and viewed the National Democrats, who had only recently abandoned their atheism, with suspicion. In fact, Bishop Teodorowicz, the most militant high-ranking clergyman with Endek sympathies, who had been a deputy to the 1919 Sejm, was ordered by Rome to leave public life. On the other hand, Dmowski was still in the process of shaking off the NDs' atheistic image, in an attempt to move closer to the Church. The violence and anarchy of December 11 was unsurprisingly frowned upon by the Church hierarchy and the Vatican, and it could have led to a fracturing of the fragile alliance between the Church and the NDs. Głąbiński's prioritization of the Concordat must be seen partly in this context. For more on the relationship between the National Democrats and the Catholic Church in 1920s Poland, see Brian Porter-Szűcs, *Faith and Fatherland: Catholicism, Modernity, and Poland* (New York: Oxford University Press, 2011), esp. 175–81.

30. Głąbiński, "Przemówienie programowe."

31. Ibid.

32. "Sprawa mordercy prezydenta," *Kurjer Poranny*, December 29, 1922.

33. Rudnicki, *Wspomnienia prokuratora*, 156.

34. Ibid.

35. Ibid., 166.

36. Ibid., 167.

37. Kijeński, *Proces Eligjusza Niewiadomskiego*, 58.

38. Rudnicki, *Wspomnienia prokuratora*, 169.

39. Kijeński, *Proces Eligjusza Niewiadomskiego*, 12. It is interesting that the very same argument was put forth by the Norwegian mass murderer Anders Breivik.

40. Ibid.

41. Ibid., 13.

42. Ibid., 14.

43. Ibid., 16.

44. Ibid., 18.

45. Ibid., 20–21.

46. The latter would hardly have been surprising, since very few Poles spoke, and let alone read, Yiddish.

47. Kijeński, *Proces Eligjusza Niewiadomskiego*, 22–25.

48. Ibid.

49. Ibid.

50. Ibid., 56.

51. Ibid., 13.

52. Stanisław Kozicki, *Pamiętnik 1876–1939* (Słupsk: Akademia Pomorska w Słupsku, 2009), 496.

53. Kijeński, *Proces Eligjusza Niewiadomskiego*, 56.

54. Ibid.

55. Ibid., 87.

56. Patryk Pleskot, *Niewiadomski—zabić prezydenta* (Warsaw: Demart, 2012), 109.

57. Maurycy Urstein, *Eligiusz Niewiadomski w oświetleniu psychiatry* (Warsaw: Rola, 1923).

58. Kijeński, *Proces Eligjusza Niewiadomskiego*, 82.

59. Ibid., 84.

60. Ibid., 86–87.

61. "Sprawa E. Niewiadomskiego," *Gazeta Warszawska*, January 1, 1923. The provincial National Democratic press also printed the full text of Niewiadomski's speeches, and even that of Rudnicki, though not that of Paschalski. "Proces Eligiusza Niewiadomskiego," *Kurjer Poznański*, January 3, 1923.

62. "Sprawa E. Niewiadomskiego," *Gazeta Warszawska*, 1–3; Kazimierz Lutosławski, "Zmora," *Myśl Narodowa*, December 16, 1922, 5.

63. Although censorship in Poland was very mild, following the murder of Narutowicz, articles overtly praising Niewiadomski were confiscated. Adolf Nowaczyński was arrested and held in the Mokotów jail for his article "Testament" in *Myśl Narodowa*, January 6, 1923. According to the Polish Telegraph Agency, Nowaczyński was arrested for "obviously showing approval for the crime perpetrated upon the highest person in the state." "Aresztowanie A. Nowaczyńskiego," *Gazeta Warszawska*, January 4, 1923.

64. "Uwagi," *Gazeta Warszawska*, January 1, 1923.

65. "Prawda i dykteryjki," *Gazeta Warszawska*, January 4, 1923.

66. Władysław Rabski, "Rząd zemsty," *Myśl Narodowa*, January 13, 1923.

67. "Prawda i dykteryjki," *Gazeta Warszawska*.

68. Ibid.

69. Rabski, "Rząd Zemsty," 7.

70. Nowaczyński, "Testament."

71. Ibid.

72. Ibid.

73. However, the courts found no basis for Nowaczyński's detention, and he was released within a matter of days.

74. Stanisław Stroński, "W ostatniej chwili," *Rzeczpospolita*, January 29, 1923. Stroński complained that the trial was carried out by a panel of judges, a holdover from the Russian judicial system, rather than by a jury, as the new Polish law demanded.

75. "Stracenie E Niawiadomskiego," *Gazeta Warszawska*, January 30, 1923.

76. Ibid.

77. Ibid.

78. "Stracenie Eligjusza Niewiadomskiego," *Rzeczpospolita*, January 30, 1923.

79. Ibid.

80. Zygmunt Wasilewski, "Ś.p. Eligiusz Niewiadomski," *Gazeta Warszawska*, January 30, 1923.

81. Ibid.

82. Roger Griffin, "Fascism: General Introduction," in *Comparative Fascist Studies: New Perspectives*, ed. Constantin Iordachi (London; New York: Routledge, 2009), 118.

83. "Pogrzeb Eligjusza Niewiadomskiego," *Rzeczpospolita*, February 6, 1923; "Pogrzeb Ś.p. Eligjusza Niewiadomskiego," *Gazeta Warszawska*, February 6, 1923.

84. "Pogrzeb Ś.p. Eligjusza Niewiadomskiego," *Gazeta Warszawska*.

85. Ibid.

86. Ibid.

87. "Pogrzeb Eligjusza Niewiadomskiego," *Rzeczpospolita*.

88. "Na grobie ś.p. E. Niewiadomskiego," *Gazeta Warszawska*, February 6, 1923.

89. Pobóg-Malinowski, *Najnowsza historia polityczna Polski*, 608.

90. Wincenty Witos, *Moje wspomnienia* (Paris: Instytut Literacki, 1965), 34.

91. Initially newspapers with the open letter were confiscated, but the letter was subsequently published without further protests from censorship.

92. "Po straceniu i pogrzebie Ś.p. Eligjusza Niewiadomskiego," *Gazeta Warszawska*, February 7, 1923.

93. Maciej Rataj, *Pamiętniki 1918–1927* (Warsaw: Ludowa Spółdzielnia Wydawnicza, 1965), 138.

Chapter 6. The Defeat of the Civic Nation

1. Ron Eyerman, *The Cultural Sociology of Political Assassination: From MLK and RFK to Fortuyn and Van Gogh* (New York: Palgrave Macmillan, 2011), 210.

2. Bernard Singer, "Bohater złotego środka," *Nasz Przegląd*, July 25, 1929, quoted in Bernard Singer, *Od Witosa do Sławka* (Warsaw: Verum, 1990), 44.

3. "Zamordowanie prezydenta Rzeczypospolitej Gabrjela Narutowicza," *Kurjer Polski*, December 17, 1922.

4. Władysław Pobóg-Malinowski, *Najnowsza historia polityczna Polski, 1864–1945* (London: Świderski, 1983), 606n40a.

5. See chapter 1.

6. Singer, "Bohater złotego środka."

7. Maciej Rataj, *Pamiętniki 1918–1927* (Warsaw: Ludowa Spółdzielnia Wydawnicza, 1965), 127.

8. Ibid.

9. According to Ost, all politics is permeated and motivated by anger. Ost writes: "Politics does not become angry only when non-elites shout. Anger is built into politics through the everyday activities of political parties, which continually both stoke and mobilize anger in order to gain and maintain support. ... Anger always exists (often

latently) as a result of economic inequalities. Since so many people in all societies believe that compensation differences do not accord with their notions of justice (such as remuneration according to effort, merit, or community value), there is always a large amount of popular frustration and discontent ready to be tapped. Capturing that 'economic anger' is a key way of attracting supporters." Therefore, politics is not simply about the aggregation of interests. Rather, Ost writes, "people understand their interests only within a given narrative framework that offers an explanation of what is wrong" with their society, and how it can be made better. Politics, thereby, is about getting people to accept one's narrative of what is wrong and, equally important, who is to blame. Anger can be articulated and mobilized in very different ways, depending on whose narrative of what is wrong one accepts and chooses to act on. David Ost, "Politics as the Mobilization of Anger," *European Journal of Social Theory* 7, no. 2 (May 1, 2004): 229–44. See also David Ost, *The Defeat of Solidarity: Anger and Politics in Postcommunist Europe* (Ithaca, NY: Cornell University Press, 2005).

10. It is interesting that the Bloc had consistently and forcefully supported the Polish peasant parties in their demands for land reform. See Sławomir Mańko, *Polski ruch ludowy wobec Żydów (1895–1939)* (Warsaw: Instytut Pamięci Narodowej, 2010), 198–202.

11. Rataj, *Pamiętniki*, 132.

12. "Kluby sejmowe i dzisiejszy wybór," *Kurjer Poranny*, December 20, 1922.

13. Rataj, *Pamiętniki*, 132.

14. Ibid.

15. In all likelihood, Emancipation could have repeated its success from the first election, beating the Piast candidate with the support of the Bloc, and the National Democratic one with the support of the Bloc, PPS, and Piast. Stanisław Thugutt, *Autobiografia* (Warsaw: Ludowa Spółdzielnia Wydawnicza, 1984), 88.

16. The candidacy of Wojciechowski actually represented a concession by Piast. While it was Piast that had put forth Wojciechowski in the first election, the party shifted its support to Sikorski after Narutowicz's murder. Both men were considered politically centrist, but Wojciechowski had little support of his own and was a personal friend of Piłsudski, who had supported his candidacy. Sikorski, on the other hand, had considerable support of his own, was considered to be genuinely independent, and could be construed as a rival to Piłsudski. Therefore, Piast's preference for Sikorski over Wojciechowski is significant. It would seem to support Pobóg-Malinowski's claim and indicate that Piast was slowly withdrawing its support from Piłsudski. At any rate, it should not be surprising that the pro-Piłsudski Emancipation vetoed the choice of Sikorski. See Thugutt's discussion with Witos in Rataj, *Pamiętniki*.

17. Rataj, *Pamiętniki*, 133.

18. Bernard Singer, "Mordowanie po śmierci," *Nasz Przegląd*, December 20, 1932. Kościałkowski would assume the post of premier under Piłusdski's post-1926 dictatorship.

19. Rataj, *Pamiętniki*, 133.

20. Głąbiński, Korfanty, and Chaciński intimated to Rataj that if there was a runoff, some right-wing deputies may be willing to cast their votes for Wojciechowski. Ibid.

21. Wincenty Witos, *Moje wspomnienia* (Paris: Instytut Literacki, 1965), 33. Witos subsequently claimed that he too was ready to vote for Morawski, but this would not have been acceptable to the party's left-wing.

22. For example, Daria Nałęcz and Tomasz Nałęcz, "Gabriel Narutowicz, prezydent Rzeczypospolitej 14XIII-16XIII 1922," in *Prezydenci i premierzy Drugiej Rzeczypospolitej*, ed. Andrzej Chojnowski and Piotr Wróbel (Wrocław: Zakład Narodowy im. Ossolińskich, 1992), 48.

23. Rataj, *Pamiętniki*, 132–33.

24. Ibid., 138.

25. Stenogramy Sejmu Rzeczpospolitej Polskiej 2-ej Kadencji (SSRP), no. 7 (January 19, 1923): 6.

26. Ibid., 6–7.

27. SSRP, no. 7 (January 19, 1923): 11.

28. Ibid.

29. SSRP, no. 7 (January 19, 1923): 12.

30. Ibid.

31. The Polish Minority Treaty, forced upon Poland at Versailles, was resented by all Poles and particularly by the Polish left. The lobbying efforts of Polish Zionists for the treaty over the heads of the Polish Government were universally perceived as a sign of disloyalty.

32. Singer, "Mordowanie po śmierci."

33. Rataj, *Pamiętniki*, 134.

34. Ewa Maj, *Związek Ludowo-Narodowy 1919–1928: Studium z dziejów myśli politycznej* (Lublin: Wydawnictwo Uniwersytetu Marii Curie-Skłodowskiej, 2000), 75.

35. Indeed, Sikorski began secret meetings with moderate National Democratic leaders as early as December 19 and was open to other concessions in order to win them over for supporting his government. Rataj, *Pamiętniki*, 133–34. The hope of making an alliance with the Christian National Party may seem surprising and requires some explanation. Although the Christian Nationalists were more conservative and thus often considered more "right-wing" than the People's National Union, their conservatism was, in fact, of a more traditional kind. As a result, the Christian National Party was less radical and relatively more focused on preserving the economic status quo than on identity politics. In the aftermath of the 1926 coup, some Christian Nationalists broke their alliance with the National Populist Union and attempted to cozy up to Piłsudski's Sanacja regime, as the latter grew more conservative.

36. "Po haniebnym mordzie Sowieckim," *Kurjer Poranny*, April 6, 1923.

37. Ibid.

38. "Wczorajsze manifestacje," *Robotnik*, April 6, 1923.

39. "Wczorajsza manifestacja protestująca," *Kurjer Polski*, April 6, 1923.

40. Ibid.

41. "Po haniebnym mordzie Sowieckim," *Kurjer Poranny*.

42. According to Pobóg-Malinowski, the execution of Budkiewicz provided the ultimate impetus for the fall of Sikorski's government and for the agreement between Piast

and the National Democrats. The successful visit of France's Marshal Foch gave it a few more weeks of existence, but its fate was effectively sealed. Pobóg-Malinowski, *Najnowsza historia polityczna Polski*, 612.

43. "Złudzenia," *Robotnik*, April 6, 1922.

44. "Atmosfera przesileniowa w gmachu Sejmowym," *Kurjer Poranny*, April 21, 1923.

45. This short-lived party, named PSL-Jedność Ludowa (Polish Peasants' Party—People's Unity), would eventually join Emancipation.

46. Szymon Rudnicki and Piotr Wróbel, eds., "Zasady współpracy stronnictw polskiej większości parlamentarnej w Sejmie w roku 1923, tak zwany Pakt Lanckoroński," in *Druga Rzeczpospolita: wybór tekstów źródłowych* (Warsaw: Wydawnictwa Uniwersytetu Warszawskiego, 1990), 124.

47. Ibid., 128.

48. Singer, "Mordowanie po śmierci."

49. Rudnicki and Wróbel, "Zasady współpracy," 130.

50. The formation of the "Government of the Polish Majority" led Piłsudski to resign from his post as chief of staff and enter a self-imposed retirement. Another high-profile resignation was that of Szymon Askenazy, the Jewish Polish historian who had acted as the Republic's ambassador to the League of Nations since 1919.

51. Singer, "Mordowanie po śmierci."

52. According to Rataj, the majority of Piast deputies went along with the leader of the party's left wing, Dąbski, and defied Witos. Rataj, *Pamiętniki*, 160.

53. "Odsłonięcie tablicy pierwszego prezydenta w Sejmie," *Kurjer Poranny*, June 16, 1923. Joseph Rothschild, *Piłsudski's Coup D'etat* (New York: Columbia University Press, 1966).

54. Ironically, the chief culprit of the crisis was Dmowski's trusted protégé Kucharski.

55. Stanisław Kijeński, *Proces Eligjusza Niewiadomskiego o zamach na życie prezydenta Rzeczypospolitej Polskiej Gabryela Narutowicza w dniu 16 Grudnia 1922 r.* (Warsaw: Perzyński Niklewicz, 1923), 13.

56. Despite the voluminous body of literature on this subject, the most incisive analysis of the May Events remains the "classic" Joseph Rothschild, *Piłsudski's Coup D'etat*. For an analysis of cultural politics in the aftermath of the coup, see Eva Plach, *The Clash of Moral Nations: Cultural Politics in Piłsudski's Poland, 1926–1935* (Athens: Ohio University Press, 2006). Unfortunately, Plach does not devote much space to the question of antisemitism. Recently, however, scores of edited works dealing mostly with the narrow political and military aspects of Piłsudski's coup have appeared in Polish.

57. See chapter 2.

58. Rataj, *Pamiętniki*, 127.

59. Józef Piłsudski, "Przemówienie na bankiecie w Hotelu Bristol (3 lipca 1923 r.)," in *Pisma zbiorowe*, ed. Kazimierz Świtalski (Warsaw: Instytut Józefa Piłsudskiego, 1937), 6:24.

60. Wacław Jędrzejewicz, *Józef Piłsudski, 1867–1935: Życiorys* (London: Polska Fundacja Kulturalna, 1982), 129.

61. During the speech, Piłsudski lashed out at the "disgusting dwarves creeping out of our [Polish] swamp ... with souls full of excrement," who spat upon him and sought to

destroy or befoul anyone close to him. Piłsudski, "Przemówienie na bankiecie w Hotelu Bristol (3 lipca 1923 r.)," 32.

62. Jan Tarnowski had been Narutowicz's personal secretary. Jan Tarnowski, "Szał czy opętanie?" *Kurjer Poranny*, December 19, 1922.

63. "Mowa żałobna," *Kurjer Poranny*, December 23, 1922; SSRP, no. 5 (December 21, 1922).

64. "Odezwa Unji Nar-Pan," *Kurjer Poranny*, December 18, 1922.

65. For example, Kazimierz Foryś, ed., *Twórcy współczesnej Polski: księga encyklopedyczna żywotów, czynów i rządów: praca zbiorowa* (Warsaw: Książnica Polska, 1938), 210.

66. Rataj, *Pamiętniki*, 138.

67. See Kijeński, *Proces Eligjusza Niewiadomskiego*.

68. Ibid., 86.

69. "Hołd pamięci pierwszego Prezydenta Polski," *Kurjer Poranny*, June 16, 1923.

70. Ibid.

71. SSRP, no. 48 (June 19, 1923): 5.

72. Ibid., 6.

73. Ibid.

74. Ibid., 7.

75. Ibid., 8.

76. Ibid.

77. Ibid., 12.

78. Thugutt, *Autobiografia*, 90.

79. Ibid.

80. SSRP, no. 48 (June 19, 1923): 14–15.

81. "Wniosek nagły posłów z Koła Żydowskiego w sprawie zaburzeń ulicznych i bezczynności władzy w dniu 11 grudnia 1922 r," Druk Sejmu Rzeczpospolitej Polski 1-ej kadencji nr. 53, 2.

82. The usage of the word *pogrom* in the context of anti-Jewish disturbances in Poland was anathema to the left. According to the Russian usage, which the Polish left continued to employ, a pogrom was an anti-Jewish action fomented or abetted by the state. The Polish left uniformly claimed that even rogue organs of the Polish state never engaged in these kinds of activities. This claim was incorrect, given the well-documented participation of Polish soldiers in anti-Jewish violence between 1919 and 1920, but using such language was bound to offend the sensibilities of almost all Poles.

83. "Wniosek nagły posłów z Koła Żydowskiego w sprawie zaburzeń ulicznych i bezczynności władzy w dniu 11 grudnia 1922 r," Druk Sejmu Rzeczpospolitej Polski 1-ej kadencji nr. 53, 2. For more on the minorities treaty and pogroms in Poland, see Carole Fink, *Defending the Rights of Others: The Great Powers, the Jews, and International Minority Protection, 1878–1938* (New York: Cambridge University Press, 2004).

84. The Polish left admitted that Poland suffered from antisemitic "excess" but refused to accept the term pogrom. It defined pogroms, as that term had been used in the Russian Empire, as a state-sponsored act of violence against Jews. Thus, according to the Poles, to use the word pogrom was to accuse the state of complicity in antisemitic violence.

85. SSRP, no. 48 (June 19, 1923): 13–14.

86. Ibid., 27–28.

87. Ibid., 16.

88. Ibid., 20.

89. Ibid., 29.

90. Thus, Leon Wasilewski began his article by contrasting Poland, "a Polish nation state," with Czechoslovakia, "a state of nationalities." Stpiczyński wrote that he had no desire to defend those nationalities "which were themselves contaminated by nationalism." "Old Fellow" acknowledged that Poland was "first and foremost for the Poles," but claimed that "no good farmer can allow a third of his farm to go to waste." Leon Wasilewski, "Zadania polskiej polityki narodowościowej," *Droga*, April 1923, 24; Old Fellow, "Zadania polskiej polityki narodowościowej," *Droga*, July 1923, 27; Wojciech Stpiczyński, "Trudności pojednania," *Głos Prawdy*, December, 30, 1922, 757.

91. Old Fellow, "Zadania polskiej polityki narodowościowej," 30.

92. "Operacje handlowe Rozwoju," *Głos Prawdy*, March 2, 1923, 925–28.

93. "Większość Chjney z Żydami bez Piasta," *Kurjer Poranny*, May 17, 1923.

94. "Błazen Judei," *Głos Prawdy*, March 10, 1923. Both Stroński and Nowaczyński had Jewish mothers.

95. SSRP, no. 5 (December 14, 1922): 13.

96. Bernard Singer, "Profesor Stroński," *Nasz Przegląd*, May 25, 1929, quoted in Singer, *Od Witosa do Sławka*, 102.

97. Left-wing publications generally put the term "Polish Majority" in quotations marks. Yet, while the new government was castigated on numerous grounds, the *principle* of the Polish majority was hardly ever openly attacked. For example, Norbert Barlicki, "Rząd 'wiekszości narodowej' i parlament," *Droga*, January 1, 1924, 16–22.

98. Witos, *Moje wspomnienia*, 27, 43.

99. "Błazen Judei," *Głos Prawdy*.

100. Józef Sanocja, *Winowajcy Zbrodni* (Warsaw: S.N., 1923), 23–24.

101. Ibid.

102. A. N-A, "O lewicy, prawicy, i tzw. faszystach," *Droga*, November 1923, 30.

103. Nowaczyński was known to sign his articles A.N. or A.N.A. The appearance of his article, if that is indeed what it was, in *Droga* is not as surprising as it initially appears. Nowaczyński prided himself on his ability to rise above partisan lines and was less doctrinaire than most National Democrats. His fierce commitment to antisemitism notwithstanding, he was known to publish in the journal *Wiadomości Literackie*, which was the literary home of leftist Polish-Jewish writers like Julian Tuwim and Antoni Słonimski, and was edited by another assimilated Jewish Pole, Mieczysław Grydzewski. *Droga*, for its part, also attempted to present itself as a nonpartisan forum of ideas, rather than as the doctrinaire organ of a specific party. The content of the article was certainly in line with Nowaczyński's thought, though presented in a much more moderate manner than his rants in *Myśl Narodowa*.

104. For more on Piłsudskiite political thought in the early 1920s, see Paul Brykczynski, "Reconsidering 'Piłsudskiite Nationalism,'" *Nationalities Papers* 42, no. 5 (September 3, 2014).

105. A. N-A, "O lewicy," 31.

106. Ibid., 32.

107. Ibid.

108. Ibid.

109. Ibid., 33.

110. Ibid.

111. Ibid.

112. See chapter 5.

113. For an account of this transformation, see Waldemar Paruch, *Od konsolidacji państwowej do konsolidacji narodowej: Mniejszości narodowe w myśli politycznej obozu piłsudczykowskiego, 1926–1939* (Lublin: Wydawnictwo Uniwersytetu Marii Curie-Skłodowskiej, 1997). While Paruch admirably discusses the changing views among the Piłsudskiites, he does not discuss the underlying causes of these changes. For the short-lived and ultimately unsuccessful alliance between the post-Piłsudskiite Camp of National Unity and the openly fascist National Radical Camp (Obóz Narodowo-Radykalny), see Mikołaj Stanisław Kunicki, *Between the Brown and the Red: Nationalism, Catholicism, and Communism in Twentieth-Century Poland—The Politics of Bolesław Piasecki* (Athens: Ohio University Press, 2012), 40–46.

114. See Brykczynski, "Reconsidering 'Piłsudskiite Nationalism.'"

Conclusion

1. Bernard Singer, "Mordowanie po śmierci," *Nasz Przegląd*, December 20, 1932.

Bibliography

Archives and Library Collections

Archiwum Akt Nowych
  Akta Władysława Grabskiego
  Komisariat Rządu na Miasto Stołeczne Warszawę (KRMSW)
  Prezydium Rady Ministrów (PRM)
  Zbiór Druków Ulotnych (ZDU)
Biblioteka Narodowa
  Druki Życia Społeczego (DŻS), "Władza Ustawodawcza 1922"
  Kazimierz Lasocki, "Pamiętniki," microfilm 6484
  Tadeusz Caspaeri-Chraszczewski, "Wspomnienia," BN sygn. 15537 II
Biblioteka Sejmowa
  Druki Sejmowe
  Protokół Zgromadzenia Narodowego dla wyboru Prezydenta Rzeczypospolitej Polskiej z dn. 9 grudnia 1922 r
  Stenogramy Sejmu Rzeczypospolitej Polskiej 2-ej Kadencji (SSRP)
  Stenogramy Sejmu Ustawodawczego (SSSU)

Newspapers and Magazines

Droga
Gazeta Polska
Gazeta Poranna "Dwa Grosze"
Gazeta Warszawska
Głos Prawdy
Kurjer Polski
Kurjer Poranny
Kurjer Poznański
Kurjer Warszawski
Robotnik

Rząd i Wojsko
Rzeczpospolita

Published Primary Sources

Adamczyk, Arkadiusz, ed. *Przewrót majowy 1926 r.* London: NWP, 2003.

Bukowiecki, Stanisław. *Polityka Polski niepodległej: Szkic programu.* Warsaw: Wende, 1922.

Gabrjel Narutowicz pierwszy Prezydent Rzeczypospolitej: Księga pamiątkowa.* Warsaw: Komitet Uczczenia Pierwszego Prezydenta Rzeczypospolitej śp. Gabrjela Narutowicza, 1925.

Haller, Józef. *Pamiętniki: Z wyborem dokumentów i zdjęć.* London: Veritas, 1964.

Hołówko, Tadeusz. *Kwestia narodowościowa.* Warsaw: Druk. "Robotnika," 1922.

———. *Prezydent Gabrjel Narutowicz: Życie i działalność.* Warsaw: E. Wende, 1924.

Iłłakiewiczówna, Kazimiera. *Ścieżka obok drogi.* Warsaw: Rój, 1939.

Jacyna, Jan. *W wolnej Polsce: Przeżycia, 1918–1923.* Warsaw: Wolnicki, 1927.

Kijeński, Stanisław. *Proces Eligjusza Niewiadomskiego o zamach na życie prezydenta Rzeczypospolitej Polskiej Gabryela Narutowicza w dniu 16 Grudnia 1922 r.* Warsaw: Perzyński Niklewicz, 1923.

Kozicki, Stanisław. *Pamiętnik 1876–1939.* Słupsk: Akademia Pomorska w Słupsku, 2009.

Kułakowski, Mariusz, ed. *Roman Dmowski w świetle listów i wspomnień.* Vol. 2. London: Gryf Publications, 1968.

Morgenthau, Henry. *All in a Life-Time.* Garden City, NY: Doubleday, 1922.

Piłsudski, Józef. *Pisma zbiorowe.* Warsaw: Instytut Józefa Piłsudskiego, 1937.

Pragier, Adam. *Czas przeszły dokonany.* London: B. Świderski, 1966.

Pruszyński, Mieczysław. "Jak straciliśmy Mińsk i federację z Białą Rusią." *Zeszyty Historyczne* 36 (1976): 50–59.

———. "Rozmowa historyczna ze St. Grabskim." *Zeszyty Historyczne* 36 (1976): 38–49.

Rataj, Maciej. *Pamiętniki 1918–1927.* Warsaw: Ludowa Spółdzielnia Wydawnicza, 1965.

Rudnicki, Kazimierz. *Wspomnienia prokuratora.* Warsaw: Czytelnik, 1957.

Rzepecki, Tadeusz. *Sejm i Senat 1922–1927: Podręcznik dla wyborców zawierający wyniki wyborów w powiatach, okręgach, województwach.* Poznań: Wielkopolska Księgarnia Nakł. K. Rzepeckiego, 1923.

Sanocja, Józef. *Winowajcy Zbrodni.* Warsaw: S.N., 1923.

Singer, Bernard. *Od Witosa do Sławka.* Warsaw: Verum, 1990.

Skotnicki, Jan. *Przy sztalugach i przy biurku: Wspomnienia.* Warsaw: Państwowy Instytut Wydawniczy, 1957.

Sokolnicki, Michał. *Czternaście lat.* Warsaw: Instytut Badania Najnowszej Historji Polski, 1936.

Stembrowicz, Kazimierz, ed. *Gabriel Narutowicz we wspomnieniach współczesnych polityków.* Warsaw: Wydawnictwo Sejmowe, 1992.

Thugutt, Stanisław. *Autobiografia.* Warsaw: Ludowa Spółdzielnia Wydawnicza, 1984.

Urstein, Maurycy. *Eligiusz Niewiadomski w oświetleniu psychiatry.* Warsaw: Rola, 1923.

Witos, Wincenty. *Moje wspomnienia.* Paris: Instytut Literacki, 1965.

Zbyszewski, Wacław A. *Gawędy o ludziach i czasach przedwojennych.* Warsaw: Czytelnik, 2000.

Secondary Sources

Ajnenkiel, Andrzej. *Historia Sejmu Polskiego*. Vol. 2. Warsaw: PWN, 1989.

Almog, Shmuel. *Nationalism and Antisemitism in Modern Europe, 1815–1945*. New York: Pergamon Press, 1990.

Anderson, Benedict R. *Imagined Communities: Reflections on the Origin and Spread of Nationalism*. London: Verso, 1983.

Blobaum, Robert, ed. *Antisemitism and Its Opponents in Modern Poland*. Ithaca, NY: Cornell University Press, 2005.

———. "The Politics of Antisemitism in Fin-de-Siècle Warsaw." *Journal of Modern History* 73, no. 2 (June 2001): 275–306.

———. *Rewolucja: Russian Poland, 1904–1907*. Ithaca, NY: Cornell University Press, 1995.

Brykczynski, Paul. "Reconsidering 'Piłsudskiite Nationalism.'" *Nationalities Papers* 42, no. 5 (September 3, 2014): 771–90.

Buchowski, Krzysztof. "Stanisław Narutowicz: Szkic do portretu idealisty." *Biuletyn Historii Pogranicza* 2 (2001): 41–51.

Bullen, R. J., Hartmut Pogge von Strandmann, and A. B. Polonsky, eds. *Ideas into Politics: Aspects of European History, 1880 to 1950*. London: Croom Helm, 1984.

Cała, Alina. *The Image of the Jew in Polish Folk Culture*. Studies on Polish Jewry. Jerusalem: Magnes Press, Hebrew University, 1995.

Capoccia, Giovanni. *Defending Democracy: Reactions to Extremism in Interwar Europe*. Baltimore: Johns Hopkins University Press, 2005.

Chojnowski, Andrzej. *Koncepcje polityki narodowościowej rządów polskich w latach 1921–1939*. Wrocław: Zakład Narodowy im. Ossolińskich, 1979.

Chojnowski, Andrzej, and Piotr Wróbel, eds. *Prezydenci i premierzy drugiej Rzeczypospolitej*. Wrocław: Zakład Narodowy im. Ossolińskich, 1992.

Ciechanowski, Jan M. *O genezie i upadku II Rzeczypospolitej*. London: Odnowa, 1981.

Corrsin, Stephen D. "Polish-Jewish Relations before the First World War: The Case of the State Duma Elections in Warsaw." *Gal-Ed: On the History of the Jews in Poland* 11 (1989).

Czubiński, Antoni. *Spory o II Rzeczpospolitą: Ewolucja poglądów publicystyki i historiografii polskiej na temat przyczyn odbudowy i znaczenia niepodległego państwa dla narodu polskiego*. Poznań: Krajowa Agencja Wydawnicza, 1983.

Davies, Norman. *God's Playground: A History of Poland*. Vol. 2, *1795 to the Present*. Oxford: Oxford University Press, 2005.

Dmowski, Roman. *Myśli nowoczesnego Polaka*. London: Nakładem Koła Młodych Stronnictwa Narodowego, 1953.

Domagalska, Małgorzata. *Antysemityzm dla inteligencji? Kwestia Żydowska w publicystyce Adolfa Nowaczyńskiego na łamach "Myśli narodowej" i "Prosto z mostu" na tle porównawczym*. Warsaw: Żydowski Instytut Historyczny, 2004.

Drozdowski, Marian Marek. *Społeczeństwo, państwo, politycy II Rzeczypospolitej: Szkice i polemiki*. Cracow: Wydawnictwo Literackie, 1972.

Duara, Prasenjit. *Rescuing History from the Nation: Questioning Narratives of Modern China*. Chicago: University of Chicago Press, 1995.

Eckert, Marian. *Historia Polski, 1914–1939*. Warsaw: Wydawnictwa Szkolne i Pedagogiczne, 1990.

Eyerman, Ron. *The Cultural Sociology of Political Assassination: From MLK and RFK to Fortuyn and Van Gogh*. New York: Palgrave Macmillan, 2011.

Faryś, Janusz. *Piłsudski i Piłsudczycy: Z dziejów koncepcji polityczno ustrojowej*. Szczecin: Uniwersytet Szczeciński, 1991.

Fink, Carole. *Defending the Rights of Others: The Great Powers, the Jews, and International Minority Protection, 1878–1938*. New York: Cambridge University Press, 2004.

Ford, Franklin L. *Political Murder: From Tyrannicide to Terrorism*. Cambridge, MA: Harvard University Press, 1985.

Foryś, Kazimierz, ed. *Twórcy współczesnej Polski: Księga encyklopedyczna żywotów, czynów i rządów: Praca zbiorowa*. Warsaw: Książnica Polska, 1938.

Garlicki, Andrzej. *Józef Piłsudski, 1867–1935*. Warsaw: Czytelnik, 1990.

———. *Pierwsze lata Drugiej Rzeczypospolitej*. Warsaw: Krajowa Agencja Wydawnicza, 1989.

Gellner, Ernest. *Nations and Nationalism*. Ithaca, NY: Cornell University Press, 1983.

Giedroyc, Jerzy. "Droga na wschód." *Więź* 10 (1989).

Grabski, Stanisław. *Pamiętniki*. Warsaw: Czytelnik, 1989.

Griffin, Roger. *The Nature of Fascism*. London: Routledge, 1991.

Grott, Bogumił. *Nacjonalizm chrześcijański: Myśl społeczno-państwowa formacji narodowo-katolickiej w Drugiej Rzeczypospolitej*. Cracow: Universitas, 1991.

Hanebrink, Paul A. *In Defense of Christian Hungary: Religion, Nationalism, and Antisemitism, 1890–1944*. Ithaca, NY: Cornell University Press, 2006.

Heller, Celia Stopnicka. *On the Edge of Destruction: Jews of Poland between the Two World Wars*. New York: Columbia University Press, 1977.

Iordachi, Constantin, ed. *Comparative Fascist Studies: New Perspectives*. London; New York: Routledge, 2009.

Iqbal, Zaryab, and Christopher Zorn. "The Political Consequences of Assassination." *Journal of Conflict Resolution* 52, no. 3 (June 2008): 385–400.

Jedlicki, Jerzy. *Jakiej cywilizacji Polacy potrzebują: Studia z dziejów idei i wyobraźni XIX wieku*. Warsaw: Państwowe Wydawnictwo Naukowe, 1988.

Jędrzejewicz, Wacław. *Józef Piłsudski, 1867–1935: Życiorys*. London: Polska Fundacja Kulturalna, 1982.

Jeleński, Konstanty A. *"Kultura": Polska na wygnaniu*. Warsaw: Instytut Dokumentacji i Studiów nad Literaturą Polską, 2005.

Katz, Jacob. *From Prejudice to Destruction: Anti-Semitism, 1700–1933*. Cambridge, MA: Harvard University Press, 1980.

Krzywiec, Grzegorz. "Komitet Narodowy Polski wobec kolektywnej przemocy antysemickiej. Przyczynek do dziejów antysemityzmu nacjonalistycznego na ziemiach polskich (1917–1919)." Forthcoming.

———. *Szowinizm po polsku: Przypadek Romana Dmowskiego, 1886–1905*. Warsaw: Neriton, 2009.

Kunicki, Mikołaj Stanisław. *Between the Brown and the Red: Nationalism, Catholicism, and Communism in Twentieth-Century Poland—The Politics of Bolesław Piasecki*. Athens: Ohio University Press, 2012.

Lewandowski, Józef. "Unia Narodowo-Państwowa." In *Z dziejów wojny i polityki: Księga pamiątkowa ku uczczeniu 70-ej rocznicy urodzin Prof. Dra. Janusza Wolińskiego*. Warsaw: WAP, 1964.

Linz, Juan J., and Alfred C. Stepan. *The Breakdown of Democratic Regimes*. Baltimore: Johns Hopkins University Press, 1978.

Lyttelton, Adrian. *The Seizure of Power: Fascism in Italy, 1919–1929*. Revised edition. New York: Routledge, 2009.

Mackiewicz, Stanisław. *Historja Polski od 11 listopada 1918 r. do 17 września 1939 r.* London: M. I. Kolin, 1941.

Maj, Ewa. "Roman Dmowski i Związek Ludowo-Narodowy (1919–1928)." *Kwartalnik Historyczny* 2 (1993): 37–54.

———. *Związek Ludowo-Narodowy 1919–1928: Studium z dziejów myśli politycznej*. Lublin: Wydawnictwo Uniwersytetu Marii Curie-Skłodowskiej, 2000.

Mańko, Sławomir. *Polski ruch ludowy wobec Żydów (1895–1939)*. Warsaw: Instytut Pamięci Narodowej, 2010.

Marcus, Joseph. *Social and Political History of the Jews in Poland, 1919–1939*. Berlin: Mouton Publishers, 1983.

Mazower, Mark. *Dark Continent: Europe's Twentieth Century*. New York: Vintage, 2000.

Mendelsohn, Ezra. "Jewish Historiography on Polish Jewry." In *Jews in Independent Poland, 1918–1939*, edited by Antony Polonsky, Ezra Mendelsohn, and Jerzy Tomaszewski. Polin 8. London: Institute for Polish-Jewish Studies, 1994.

Mich, Włodzimierz. *Obcy w polskim domu: nacjonalistyczne koncepcje rozwiązania problemu mniejszości narodowych, 1918–1939*. Lublin: Wydawnictwo Uniwersytetu Marii Curie-Skłodowskiej, 1994.

Modras, Ronald. "The Interwar Polish Catholic Press on the Jewish Question." *Annals of the American Academy of Political and Social Science* 548, no. 1 (1996): 169–90.

Molenda, Jan. *Piłsudczycy a Narodowi Demokraci 1908–1918*. Warsaw: Książka i Wiedza, 1980.

Nałęcz, Daria. *Nie szablą, lecz piórem: Batalie publicystyczne II Rzeczypospolitej*. Warsaw: Wydawnictwo IBL, 1993.

Nałęcz, Daria, and Tomasz Nałęcz. "Gabriel Narutowicz, prezydent Rzeczypospolitej 14 XIII-16 XIII 1922." In *Prezydenci i premierzy Drugiej Rzeczypospolitej*, edited by Andrzej Chojnowski and Piotr Wróbel. Wrocław: Zakład Narodowy im. Ossolińskich, 1992.

Newman, Karl. *European Democracy between the Wars*. London: Allen & Unwin, 1971.

Nohlen, Dieter, and Philip Stöver, eds. *Elections in Europe: A Data Handbook*. Nomos: Baden-Baden, 2010.

Nowak, Aleksandra, Maria Kuczyńska, and Witold Stankiewicz. *Druga Rzeczpospolita 1918–1939*. Warsaw: Biblioteka Narodowa, 1978.

Opalski, Magdalena, and Israel Bartal. *Poles and Jews: A Failed Brotherhood.* Hanover, NH: University Press of New England, 1992.

Ost, David. *The Defeat of Solidarity: Anger and Politics in Postcommunist Europe.* Ithaca, NY: Cornell University Press, 2005.

———. "Politics as the Mobilization of Anger." *European Journal of Social Theory* 7, no. 2 (May 1, 2004): 229–44.

Pacyńska-Drzewińska, Danuta. *Śmierć Prezydenta.* Warsaw: Wydawnictwo Ministerstwa Obrony Narodowej, 1965.

Paczkowski, Andrzej. *Prasa drugiej Rzeczypospolitej, 1918–1939.* Warsaw: Państwowy Instytut Wydawniczy, 1971.

Pajewski, Janusz. *Gabriel Narutowicz: Pierwszy Prezydent Rzeczypospolitej.* Warsaw: Książka i Wiedza, 1993.

Paruch, Waldemar. *Od konsolidacji państwowej do konsolidacji narodowej: Mniejszości narodowe w myśli politycznej obozu piłsudczykowskiego, 1926–1939.* Lublin: Wydawnictwo Uniwersytetu Marii Curie-Skłodowskiej, 1997.

Payne, Stanley G. *A History of Fascism, 1914–1945.* Madison: University of Wisconsin Press, 1995.

Piłsudska, Aleksandra. *Wspomnienia.* London: Gryf, 1960.

Plach, Eva. *The Clash of Moral Nations: Cultural Politics in Piłsudski's Poland, 1926–1935.* Athens: Ohio University Press, 2006.

Pleskot, Patryk. *Niewiadomski—zabić prezydenta.* Warsaw: Demart, 2012.

Pobóg-Malinowski, Władysław. *Najnowsza historia polityczna Polski, 1864–1945.* London: Świderski, 1983.

Polonsky, Antony. *Politics in Independent Poland 1921–1939: The Crisis of Constitutional Government.* Oxford: Clarendon Press, 1972.

Porter-Szűcs, Brian. *Faith and Fatherland: Catholicism, Modernity, and Poland.* New York: Oxford University Press, 2011.

———. "Making a Space for Antisemitism: The Catholic Hierarchy and the Jews in the Early Twentieth Century." *Polin* 16 (2003): 415–29.

———. *Poland in the Modern World: Beyond Martyrdom.* Chichester: Wiley Blackwell, 2014.

———. *When Nationalism Began to Hate: Imagining Modern Politics in Nineteenth-Century Poland.* New York: Oxford University Press, 2000.

Potkański, Waldemar. *Odrodzenie czynu niepodległościowego przez PPS w okresie rewolucji 1905 roku.* Warsaw: Wydawnictwo DiG, 2008.

Prusin, Alexander V. *The Lands Between: Conflict in the East European Borderlands, 1870–1992.* New York: Oxford University Press, 2010.

———. *Nationalizing a Borderland: War, Ethnicity, and Anti-Jewish Violence in East Galicia, 1914–1920.* Tuscaloosa: University Alabama Press, 2005.

Rothschild, Joseph. *East Central Europe between the Two World Wars.* Seattle: University of Washington Press, 1974.

———. *Piłsudski's Coup D'etat.* New York: Columbia University Press, 1966.

Rudnicki, Szymon. "Towarzystwo Rozwoju Handlu Przemysłu i Rzemiosła." In *Gospodarka, ludzie, władza: Studia historyczne,* edited by Antoni Mączak and Michał Kopczyński, 316–33. Warsaw: Krupski i S-ka, 1998.

——. *Żydzi w parlamencie II Rzeczypospolitej.* Warsaw: Wydawnictwo Sejmowe, 2004.

Rudnicki, Szymon, and Piotr Wróbel, eds. *Druga Rzeczpospolita: Wybór tekstów źródłowych.* Warsaw: Wydawnictwa Uniwersytetu Warszawskiego, 1990.

Ruszczyc, Marek. *Pierwszy Prezydent Gabriel Narutowicz.* Warsaw: Książka i Wiedza, 1967.

——. *Strzały W "Zachęcie."* Katowice: Śląsk, 1987.

Seton-Watson, Hugh. *Eastern Europe between the Wars, 1918–1941.* Cambridge: Cambridge University Press, 1945.

Sewell, William H. "Historical Events as Transformations of Structures: Inventing Revolution at the Bastille." *Theory and Society* 25, no. 6 (December 1996): 841–81.

Sifakis, Carl. *Encyclopedia of Assassinations.* New York: Facts on File, 2001.

Skwarczyński, Stanisław. "Przełom maja 1926 r." In *Przewrót majowy 1926 r,* edited by Arkadiusz Adamczyk. London: NWP, 2003.

Smith, David Norman. "The Social Construction of Enemies: Jews and the Representation of Evil." *Sociological Theory* 14, no. 3 (November 1996): 203–40.

Sobczak, Mieczysław. *Narodowa Demokracja wobec kwestii żydowskiej na ziemiach polskich przed I Wojną Światową.* Wrocław: Wydawnictwo Akademii Ekonomicznej im. Oskara Langego, 2007.

Sugar, Peter F., ed. *Native Fascism in the Successor States, 1918–1945.* Santa Barbara, CA: ABC-Clio, 1971.

Ury, Scott. *Barricades and Banners: The Revolution of 1905 and the Transformation of Warsaw Jewry.* Stanford, CA: Stanford University Press, 2012.

Walicki, Andrzej. *Philosophy and Romantic Nationalism: The Case of Poland.* Oxford: Clarendon Press; New York: Oxford University Press, 1982.

Wapiński, Roman. *Narodowa Demokracja, 1893–1939: Ze studiów nad dziejami myśli nacjonalistycznej.* Wrocław: Zakład Narodowy im. Ossolińskich, 1980.

——. *Roman Dmowski.* Lublin: Wydawnictwo Lubelskie, 1988.

——. *Świadomość polityczna w Drugiej Rzeczypospolitej.* Łódź: Wydawnictwo Łódzkie, 1989.

Wątor, Adam. *Działalność Związku Ludowo-Narodowego w latach 1919–1922.* Szczecin: Uniwersytet Szczeciński, 1992.

Weeks, Theodore R. *From Assimilation to Antisemitism: The "Jewish Question" in Poland, 1850–1914.* DeKalb: Northern Illinois University Press, 2006.

Wolff, Larry. *Inventing Eastern Europe: The Map of Civilization on the Mind of the Enlightenment.* Stanford, CA: Stanford University Press, 1994.

Wróbel, Piotr. "The Seeds of Violence: The Brutalization of an East European Region, 1917–1921." *Journal of Modern European History* 1, no. 1 (2003): 125–49.

Zieliński, Konrad. *Stosunki polsko-żydowskie na ziemiach Królestwa Polskiego w czasie pierwszej wojny światowej.* Lublin: Wydawnictwo Uniwersytetu Marii Curie-Skłodowskiej, 2005.

Zimmerman, Joshua D. *Poles, Jews, and the Politics of Nationality: The Bund and the Polish Socialist Party in Late Tsarist Russia, 1892–1914*. Madison: University of Wisconsin Press, 2004.

Zubrzycki, Geneviève. "The Classical Opposition between Civic and Ethnic Models of Nationhood: Ideology, Empirical Reality and Social Scientific Analysis." *Polish Sociological Review*, no. 3 (2002): 275–95.

Index

Page references for illustrations are in italics.

Printed in the United States
By Bookmasters